W9-BMJ-926

A BOOK of SONGS

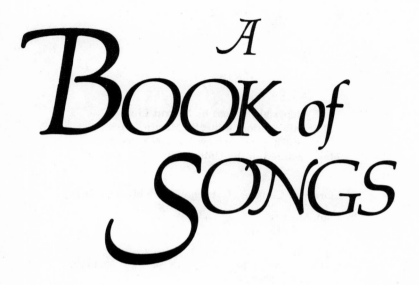

A BOOK of SONGS

A Novel By
Merritt Linn

St. Martin's Press   New York

2/1983
Am. Lit.

Library of Congress Cataloging in Publication Data

Linn, Merritt.
    A book of songs.

    I. Title.
PS3562.I544B6   1982   813'.54   82-10493
ISBN 0-312-09013-7

10 9 8 7 6 5 4 3 2

To Raoul Wallenberg

He was a Moses
to the Children of Israel
and like Moses
he was not to enter
the Promised Land.

A BOOK of SONGS

1 The window means so much to me. The soot from the stove fuses with the thin coating of ice to create an opaque haze on the glass. The frosted pane becomes a screen on which to project my memories. Even though darkness lies beyond the window, I could always conjure up scenes bathed in sunlight. My pictures were like those in a cinema; I could gaze at them only briefly, but never truly capture or hold them.

This night is so very different. On other nights the rays of the tower lights pass through the windows of the hut totally unobstructed, but on this night they meet and briefly illuminate the remains of Sheleen. His once-erect body now hangs limply from its rope. In life he had been a tense, animated man. Now, I am struck by how relaxed and uncoiled he appears. We held him above us in life, and now in death he hangs above us. He had sustained me, but now he is gone. He has been dead several hours.

I stare from Sheleen to my window and try desperately to free my mind of its blackness. No matter how hard I try, the frosted glass now offers me no peace.

I wipe the pane clean with a corner of my blanket. Looking through the glass, I realize that this place is even more devastating at night than during the day.

The tower lights make a regular grand tour of this fogshrouded world. The tour is usually very precise and highlights all that is important to the guards; the barbed-wire fences are followed on their long, straight journey around our section of the camp. As the fence turns, so does the beam of light; they are always in total harmony. Next, the light briefly scrutinizes each of the windows of the large wooden shop that stands near the main gate. To us, our shop is our temple, for without it there would be no reason to keep us alive.

All is quiet now in the hut except for the usual sounds of labored breathing and coughing that are the signs of the last stages of pneumonia. Soon others will join Sheleen in death, but for them their exit from this place will be as little noted as their arrival. Men come and go through here like silent shadows.

Above the sounds of sleep, I can hear the soft strains of the boy's violin. To hear the sweetness of his song in this place of bitterness is always a shock. The sounds of the simple melody from his violin are close by; perhaps tonight he is as near as the next compound.

Often in the dead of night, I have heard his unchanging song. It is like a bedtime lullaby, similar to one that every mother in the world has sung to every child in the world. Sheleen once said that the violin had to play the lullaby—the child had no mother to sing to him. On this night, the boy's song will be Sheleen's eulogy.

Not even Sheleen, who had once possessed all the answers, could understand why the boy was allowed to live. The lives of all the children were extinguished in less time than it took to conceive them. Still this boy roamed, seemingly at will, through the far reaches of the camp. As with Sheleen, I, too, could not comprehend how a child could inhabit this place. I longed for the day when I would finally lay my eyes on him.

Each sweep of the light briefly illuminates the inside of the hut. I see the fleeting images of my strange bedfellows with their shaven heads and emaciated faces. They sleep in their bunks, looking like gaunt, newborn chickens totally exhausted from pecking their way out of the shell. In place of feathers, they are covered by mounds of ill-fitting rags. Our many coats are the only memorials to the multitude who have passed through this place and are now gone. Their memories have faded into oblivion, but the warmth of their coats continues to protect our bodies from the cold. I fear that Sheleen's memory will also fade into nothing and without his warmth our souls will finally freeze to death.

The first rays of the sunrise begin to filter through the window and bathe Sheleen's ashen face. The meager warmth of the winter sun returns some of the human color to his features. Then the circling tower lights crash through the window and obliterate the glow of the sun. A rivulet of drool runs down from the side of his mouth. The tower lights intrude on his death as the guards' scrutinizing eyes had watched him during life.

My eyes are constantly drawn back to his body. This extraordinary man has been brought to his end by such a meaningless thing as a few feet of worn-out rope. It seems that he has always been a part of my life, even though I have known him only for a few months. I feel as if I have been here forever.

Much of the past has been blotted out of my mind. Perhaps cold and hunger are blessings, for they dull thought as well as memory. But even in my dreams, what remain in my ears are the screams of those torn from my grasp.

I was never to know why they chose to keep me alive. Others were of the same height and age, but still they were wasted. I remember few details of that final selection. I do recall that the officer asked me my occupation. Perhaps they wanted those who had led disciplined lives. We who were kept would always wonder.

I remember when I first saw Sheleen. They had herded about twenty of us onto a truck and drove us away from the main selection camp. We were all that they had harvested from a crop that once numbered in the thousands.

From the back of the departing truck, I watched the black plumes of smoke rising up into the cloudless sky. For a time the smoke blotted out the sun. Slowly the huge camp and its hovering black clouds faded into the distance.

Later, as I peered through the wooden bars, I saw lush

3

green countryside in which I had previously delighted. As we were driven through small towns, I saw people immersed in their daily lives. They would look up at us as if we didn't exist. They were well dressed; the day must have been a holiday. I wracked my mind but couldn't think of what holiday this could possibly be.

Long ago I had lost track of the days. I was no longer even certain of the month. Perhaps by now September had faded into October. Somehow I prided myself in still knowing the year.

The noise of the truck droned in my head as we made our way down the tree-lined road. The yellowed leaves of autumn fluttered through the air and fell among us. Shining above, the sun's rays did nothing to lessen the chill that raced back and forth through my body.

Throughout the journey, our guard sat impassively on the top of the truck cab. His sharply pressed uniform gave him the look of a man, but the last vestiges of his acne betrayed his youth. His expression was one of boredom rather than hate. The gleaming rifle rested limply in his lap.

We were congregated in mournful silence on the cold, damp floor. No sign of life had come from any of my companions until I noticed a hand being raised slowly into the air. Looking around, I saw the owner of the hand. He had the disheveled appearance that comes from living in the same clothes for weeks. Suddenly a jolt of the truck propelled the hand upward; it waved back and forth like that of an anxious schoolchild.

With a nod of his head, pointing the rifle, the soldier finally recognized the waving hand. The man slowly lowered his hand and in a tremulous voice asked where we were being taken. The guard did not reply and looked away as if nothing had been said. The same question was asked again, only this time louder to ensure that it would

4

be heard over the noise of the truck. From the terse words of the guard, we learned our final destination. "You're going to a work camp," he muttered.

For a moment there was silence, and then the man who had asked the question jumped to his feet and lunged for the side of the moving truck. His hands grasped the wooden rails as if he were about to climb over the top, but he made no attempt to scale the sides.

The rifle followed his every move. The rest of us crouched down and pushed against each other until we were jammed as far as possible against the back of the truck. The man, however, still did not move.

The once-indifferent guard looked suddenly bewildered. His rifle trembled as he took aim at the man's head. The two of them stared at each other without saying a word.

The man spoke again, but this time in a calm voice. "I want you to shoot," he said. "I beg of you. I want to leave this world that you've destroyed." He paused, as if waiting for the rifle to answer, but there was no response. He went on, as if talking to a child. "I can tell that you've never killed before, but it will come easy for you, just as it has for your brothers. I'm sure you believe in God; you all do. May God grant you a long life, and may every minute of that life be spent with the memory of murdering me."

There was a pause, and then the ear-piercing roar of the gun. I waited for the man to fall, but he did not. The tremulous rifle had missed. The man looked at the soldier and, nodding his head, spoke softly. "Please, try again."

With the second shot, the man's body crashed against the side of the truck and then slumped to the floor. The soldier looked away for a moment, and then his eyes fell on the face of the man he had just killed. The expression of the soldier appeared almost as contorted as that of the dead man. The man's unblinking eyes lay open to the sky; his gaping mouth seemed ready to launch more words into the air. A tide of blood spread slowly across the metal floor. Bits of debris that littered the floor now floated atop the stream of blood.

Glancing up at the soldier, I could see that his once-bored face was now covered by a sullen cast. He sat hunched over; both his military bearing and his look of youth had evaporated.

I gazed at the soldier; by chance, his eyes became fixed on my stare. We glared at each other; neither of us dropped our eyes. With the new-found look of a veteran, he motioned with his rifle for me to get up and move toward the dead man. I knew his aim would now be true.

I looked away, acknowledging his victory. I would accept their uninvited offer to work. I would continue to live, even though it would probably not be for much longer. I would warp my soul to fit the twisted contours of their mold.

As the truck continued on, I realized all that I had experienced in the past weeks. Such abominations never even course through the imaginations of men living during times of peace. Blessed are the multitude who can never know the thoughts of a drowning man or one being burned at the stake.

Unconsciously, I reached into my coat pocket to search for my watch, momentarily forgetting that they had taken everything. My hand produced only a torn stub that probably was once a theater ticket. I held the thin cardboard up to the light in a vain attempt to try to decipher the name of the play. As I rubbed the edge of the ticket across my thumb, my skin could feel its roughness. Only then did I know for certain that I existed and all of this was not a dream.

I placed the mutilated ticket between the wooden slats and watched as the wind lifted it off its tenuous perch. I lost sight of the stub as it soared skyward while the truck took us further down the road.

The green of the countryside faded away and in its place was my first sight of this camp. It had the same stark look of death about it as did the camp we had just left. The barbed-wire fences, towers at appropriate intervals, and orderly rows of buildings were what I had come to expect of their precise minds.

As our truck turned off the main road and approached the camp, I had my first glimpse of some of the inhabitants of this place. I realized that nothing in my past life had prepared me for what I now saw. Four or five of them were standing by the fence. These men looked like skeletons dressed in layers of ragged clothes now many sizes too large for them. While the truck drove slowly by the fence, I peered out through the bars of my cage at these creatures, and they in turn stared back. No glint came from their worn-out, hollow eyes. The only sign of life about them was the sunlight glistening off their shaven heads.

I turned my eyes away, wondering how long it would take before I, too, would look like them. Lying on the floor, the dead man appeared more alive than those who silently welcomed us to this place.

The truck visited each of the compounds that made up the camp. They were exactly alike: a large factorylike structure dominated each section, behind which were two long rows of dilapidated little huts. Each of these islands was isolated from the others by a barbed-wire fence. The truck would deliver one or sometimes two of my companions to each section. The gates would open, and they would be swallowed up and lost.

The truck stopped again and our guard jumped off. As I watched him trudge off toward one of the buildings, I, too, hoped that his nightmares would forever find inspiration in this day. Another soldier appeared and casually looked over those of us who still remained huddled together on the truck. His face showed no surprise at the sight of the dead man. He pointed to me. I rose quickly to my feet and walked to the back of the truck. I thought of saying good-bye to my companions but realized that I had never uttered even a word to any of them.

The guard opened the back gate and motioned for me to jump. I stumbled as I landed on the ground and found myself being helped to my feet by this soldier. There was a gentleness to his grasp that I did not expect. Unconsciously I found myself thanking him for his help, and he said, "You are welcome." I looked at this young man, hoping for some further sign of warmth, but his face showed only bored indifference.

He motioned me into the compound, and I walked through the mud until I was well within the gate. The guard climbed back onto the truck which slowly lumbered off to make the rest of its deliveries. Two soldiers pulled the gate shut behind me and then disappeared into a small building by the tower. I knew that they had seen me. I just stood there, totally alone, waiting for someone to come for me. I did not move, for I had nowhere to go.

The sunlight filtered through the timbers that supported the tower, whose dark shadows fell across me. I gazed up but could see no one, only the barrels of their machine guns pointing aimlessly upward. Still, no one came. The minutes ticked off slowly. I had only my black thoughts to keep me company.

Even after all that had happened, still I had to stand here waiting. I wondered if I were destined to stand here, sinking ever deeper into the mud, for an eternity.

The shadows lengthened around me as time continued to pass. Even the guns of the tower seemed oblivious to me. But I feared the sound of a bullet if I were to move; I feared the sound of a bullet if I remained. Looking on both sides of the field, I searched the huts for some sign of life. I knew the prisoners were in there, but no one came for me.

A lifeless tree stood beyond the huts at the far end of the compound. With its gnarled and twisted branches it, too, stood alone. I kept wishing that it might suddenly burst into flame, just as the burning bush of Moses, to signify that I had not been forgotten. It was not to be. I was invisible to everyone.

Then, out of the corner of my eye, I saw him coming toward me. From a distance he looked just like the other prisoners I had seen when we arrived, but this one walked erect and there was life to his gait. As he came closer, I could see on his face that same skeletal look I had seen before.

The man stopped about twenty paces from where I was standing. He stared at me only briefly and then riveted his eyes on the tower. I knew that he wanted to yell, but, considering the closeness of the tower, he managed only a loud whisper. Still, there was authority in his voice as he said, "You've got to get out of here! Didn't they tell you to find a hut?" I must have looked at him blankly, because then he paused and gazed toward the huts on the right side and then the left. "Go to the fourth hut," he ordered, pointing to one of the hovels in the right row. "Ask for the bunk of the teacher from Jenta. Now get out of here," he repeated, "but don't run. Now move!"

When I reached the hut, I did not knock on the door for I feared that no one would answer. Upon opening the door, I was greeted only by stench. It took my eyes a few moments to adjust to the dimness before I could make out the somber gray details of the interior. A flickering light bulb hanging from a frayed cord barely outlined a stove in the middle of the shack and the line of wooden bunks placed on either side of the narrow central aisle. A hoarse voice came from out of the shadows and yelled at me to shut the door.

I went from bunk to bunk, asking for the teacher from Jenta. Many of them seemed asleep. Others would open their eyes, silently glance up at me for an instant, and then close their eyes once again.

At the far end of the hut I noticed one of the prisoners sitting in his bunk with his back propped against the wall. I was certain that he had been watching my fruitless journey through the hut. I went over to him and asked which one was the teacher. As he looked up at me I could see that his nose had been broken. He casually pointed to the next bunk and, in a strange nasal tone, said, "That is the teacher. Go waken him."

I gently shook the blankets and coats that covered the sleeping teacher, but I could not arouse him. I looked back at the man sitting on the bunk and asked, "What's wrong with him?"

In an impatient voice he said, "That man's hard to awaken, and besides he's kind of deaf. Try shouting at him."

Kneeling beside the teacher's bunk, I began to whisper softly in his ear, but still he did not stir. I heard my voice rise gradually to a full scream as all of the pent-up misery poured out—and still this man would not hear me.

Turning around, I saw two men standing beside me. Their gaunt faces made me think my yelling had awakened the dead.

One of them spoke. "I am Sheleen." Then, motioning toward the teacher, he said, "That bunk is yours." The voice was that of the man who had come for me when I stood alone by the tower.

When I gestured toward the sleeping man, Sheleen said, "He's been dead for hours."

The man with the broken nose smirked silently.

Sheleen and the other man lifted the limp body of the teacher from the bunk. In the faint light, the dead man's weathered face reminded me of an Egyptian mummy I had once seen in a museum. They carried him over to the doorway and gently deposited him on the floor.

A few moments later, Sheleen returned. The man with the twisted nose still sat on his throne of rags, surveying the entire scene. Sheleen pointed to him and said to me, "This is the poet from Vilna." Then, perhaps speaking more to the poet than me, he went on, "The poet has found his own unique way of adapting to this place. He has developed his innate sense of sarcasm and bitter bile to heights never before seen in the history of the world." They both laughed. I was amazed to see a smile form on their skull-like faces.

The poet then made a great show of apologizing to me for having had me try to converse with the dead. "When your luggage finally arrives," he said, "I will personally carry it into the hut for you." When I told him that I came here with nothing, he said, "I know that, but my offer is still good." I was certain that it was some prisoner, rather than a guard, who had smashed this son of a bitch's nose.

When Sheleen left, I looked over my new bunk and realized that the teacher was still with me. His dying excretions had permeated the coats and blankets that covered the wooden planks of the bunk. Even though I was exhausted, I could not make myself lie in this cesspool.

I heard the poet's mocking voice telling me that sooner or later I would have to lie down. He said that only horses could sleep standing up and that I was not a horse. He seemed to reflect on this for a moment and then began to laugh. He said that if we had only been horses, we would now be living on the outside. Our captors had no interest in horses, but only in our people. Soon he gave up his soliloquy on horses and then watched me try to clean my bunk. After a while he must have become bored. He got up and went from bunk to bunk, stealing coats that covered the half-sleeping bodies. I heard no objections to his looting. He returned with an armload and threw his gifts on my bunk. I gathered up the soiled coats that had belonged to the teacher and threw them on the floor. The poet's donation was spread evenly over the wooden planks. Before I lay down, I went over to the poet's bunk and snatched one of his many coats and added it to my new collection. He looked up, rather surprised, but only laughed.

In a mocking voice he asked, "You must have many questions? You new ones always do—at least for a day or two."

I said nothing as I crawled beneath the coats and blankets.

"You thought you were secure, didn't you? You lived in a golden age, didn't you? It would all blow over, wouldn't it? Our people belonged to this country, didn't we? We helped build it. We fought for it."

He droned on and on. I covered my head with blankets, but I couldn't keep the truth from reaching my ears.

Seeing no response from me, he said, "Perhaps we should discuss our alleged sins. You know, why we are here? No? Or perhaps we could explore why a God-fearing civilized people could do this to us? No? Well, then, how about, why doesn't the rest of the world give a damn about what is happening to us?"

Then he became silent for a few moments. "You know," he said, "I think you will last here awhile. Most men live only about a month, but you look as if you might have even two months in you."

His tone then became serious. "I will give you some good advice. To survive here for any length of time, you must become mad, totally mad. Those who remain sane never live long. They can't come to grips with the fact that there is no hope of ever leaving here alive. There are no pardons or paroles here. They can't get it through their heads that becoming mad makes this life bearable."

His bony finger made a grand sweep of the desolate hut. "These fools can't give up the past. They lie in their bunks with their dead souls waiting anxiously for their bodies to catch up and finally die. An insane life is better than any death."

Pointing toward Sheleen's bunk, which was situated by the door, he added, "Sheleen has done very well here. First he buried God along with the rest of the past, and in its place he dreamed up a magnificent, insane world to live in. In fact, he has done so well that he has crowned himself the God of his new world. The man even has converts. You will probably become a disciple of his. To keep from drowning you have to grab onto something."

"Why," I asked, "have you chosen being such a bastard? You could at least have joined up with Sheleen."

"I tried," he said, "I really did, but somehow I couldn't accept Sheleen as God. After all that has happened to us, I have given up on all gods. I observe the world and reflect things as they really are. Being a bastard has sustained me. Why give up something that works? Perhaps you will be my first convert? I think you have it in you to be an apt pupil. Perhaps . . . "

I interrupted him. "All right, I do have a question. What do we do here? What do they have us make in that big building?"

"Didn't you know? We make bandages and dressings for the wounded."

The dim light went out and we were plunged into total darkness. As the beam from the tower light swept through the windows of the hut, I saw the outline of a man standing alone in the far corner. This shadowy figure swayed slowly back and forth. A few moments later another traveling beam of light poured through the window and silhouetted his outstretched arms and shaven head tilted to one side.

"That's Avron," the poet said. "His life has also flourished in madness. Look at him, he's playing a violin that doesn't even exist." The poet seemed highly amused as he related how Avron prayed twice daily to the God of old who no longer dwelled in heaven. In these prayers he begged God to preserve the life of some little boy with a

13

violin. Most amazing of all was watching Avron continue to practice on the invisible violin. The real one had been wrenched from his grasp long ago at the selection camp.

At first I thought the poet's talk of a child being in this place was just more of his sarcasm. But when I asked him, the poet said, "The child's been here longer than anyone. There's no doubt that he's one of us; he has their burned-on numbers on his chest just like we all do. This Avron has convinced himself that the last remnant of God's presence on earth lies buried within the child. If this is true," he laughed, "then God did not choose a good hiding place. The boy is nothing more than an animal. He and his god-damn violin come through here at feeding time and pry the food away from us. The violin plays some sickly sweet tune and the men give up their bread to this little bastard. He always goes after the new men. They're the easiest; they still have some human feeling."

There was bitterness in his voice as he went on. "Let me give you some more advice. If you decide you want to live, then don't give the child anything—not even a crumb—or you'll starve to death sooner than you're supposed to. You'll go the way of the teacher. He fed the boy too much and lasted less than a month. Anyone who becomes ad-dicted to the boy soon starves to death. Avron feeds him only a little, but he gets others to do most of the feeding."

The poet was silent for a moment. "We think the boy has been here most of his life. This place can only make a monster out of a child. No one should feed him, and then he would die and be free of his misery. That damn fool, Avron, will try to get you to feed him—I know he will; he always does."

I asked him if Avron was the one who broke his nose.

"Yes," he said, laughing again. "I kicked the boy out of here one day while he was trying to take the bread away from some poor wretch. Avron called upon his God to give him strength, and his fist smote my nose."

The poet rambled on, but my mind was lost in the rhythmic motions of Avron's arms. His right hand held the nonexistent bow that coursed back and forth over the void that had once held strings. His fingers darted rapidly up and down to cover the far reaches of his lost violin. The song he created must have been heard only in his memory. At times he hummed a simple tune that was difficult to hear above the constant coughing around me. The poet said that this was the same song the little boy always played.

The poet was my unasked-for guide to the horrors of this place. Perhaps he enjoyed destroying the last, minute vestiges of hope I had left. Unfortunately I knew that all that came from his tongue was to be true.

Lying there in the darkness, I knew that I had crossed over into another world. Gradually I was becoming immune to the smell of this place; I now contributed to the stench. My skin felt the first onslaught that signaled the invasion of the lice. They would always be at my side.

2 There was never a formal in-
doctrination to the camp. Even though the guards did not
bark out orders or provide us with written rules, I knew
what was expected of me. As if by instinct I knew how to
please them. Everything was so simple: As long as you
were able to work, you were allowed to live. If a man was
too sick to get out of bed, he would disappear from the face
of the earth before we returned from the shop. Only his
empty bunk was his memorial. If you were too sick to
produce, another man was ordered from the main selection camp and he was given your machine. Replacements
were plentiful—they had thousands of us in stock at the
main camp. Each day the trucks brought in new recruits
for the machines and carted away the men that this place
had consumed.

On only one occasion did they give an order, and even
this was not a command in the usual sense. That morning,
we were standing in the drenching rain for the usual
lineup. The light from the tower glistened off the slick
black raincoats of the guards. They walked listlessly back
and forth, counting the empty spaces that had once held
men in the rows in front of each hut.

Through the wire fence, I could see the inhabitants of
the other compounds marching slowly to their shops. The
entire camp always advanced as one to the rhythm of the
same silent song. Today we were not to join them. Any
change in the routine sent waves of cold tension coursing
through my body.

The door of the guard hut opened, and the commandant
of the camp appeared before us. He always wore the aris-
tocratic look of a man who had never known what it was
to bow before the feet of anyone. He carefully avoided the
puddles of water as he walked down the field between the

assembled rows of prisoners. A book was tucked as usual under his arm. Casually he warmed his hands over the fire that leaped from the oil drum positioned in the middle of the field, a perpetual haven for the guards trying to find some relief from the cold. The fire had always warmed my imagination, but never my body.

A few moments later the guards marched a prisoner over to the commandant, who still stood by the fire seemingly preoccupied only by his hands and his book. No one had ever seen this inmate before. He wore the same old clothes as the rest of us, but he was obviously not one of our men. He was much too big, well over six feet tall. Even hunched over, he still towered above the commandant and the guards.

They motioned for the prisoner to kneel in the mud, and he obeyed silently. Being careful not to drop the book, the commandant drew his pistol, and with one shot the tall man fell dead before his feet. We waited for the commandant to make some announcement befitting such a miserable occasion, but he was only to march back to the guard hut, all the while being watchful to avoid the same puddles of water.

I stood there peering at this dead man sprawled on the ground—his cold, crumpled body bathed by the warmth of the fire that continued to spout from the drum.

I had little time to ponder what I had just witnessed. The next hut was marching to the shop, and we in turn followed them.

We were never to learn the offense of the tall prisoner or even if he had committed one. To risk asking a guard was out of the question. Some thought that he must have attempted an escape, but no one could recall anyone ever trying to get through the wire. If one managed the impossible and did escape, where would he go? You have to escape to something. The writer from Esten said that perhaps the tall man had tried to sabotage one of the machines. This, too, made no sense, for the machine was the symbol of life. To work in harmony with the machine was to survive.

That night the poet gave his explanation to an unlistening audience. Perhaps he was right: "The commandant just wanted to kill someone tall."

I abandoned the black world of the poet and walked past the vacant-eyed men lying in their bunks. A group was congregated around Sheleen's bunk. Looking over at the other corner of the hut, I saw Avron deep in his prayers. His head bobbed up and down as he recited the psalm for the dead. The poet had told me that Avron said a blessing for everyone who had died. Since so many had died already, the poet thought Avron must have been at least a hundred years behind schedule in his prayers. At times Avron would stop suddenly and then stand by the window. I wondered if he was listening for the sound of the boy's violin.

I stood at the edge of the group clustered around Sheleen. Some of them had braved the night to come from the other huts. One could move around as long as the lights in the huts were on.

The conversation was about the commandant and his books. Sheleen was talking. "The man always has a book," he said. "Wherever he goes, there's a book under his arm. I know he reads them, I can see how the bookmark moves each day. They are not trash. The guards I can understand, but not this officer. I cannot fathom how this monster with such a rancid soul can read only the greatest of literature." Sheleen shook his head with a look of disbelief. "I would expect his tastes to run in some bestial vein, but no, he reads the classics. How can the words of these books register on the mind of such a man who calmly murders another man?"

Sheleen's face came alive again. "Well, my brothers," he said, "enough of the outside world. We alone have a higher form of life. We will leave them to their darkness."

Sheleen still spoke in a civilized manner. Most men soon lapsed into a permanent silence. After the long day at the machines they would find solace in their bunks by burying their heads in the blankets to shut out this world. Perhaps they, too, wished for some respite from the screams that still echoed in their ears. No one talked of this, for if they did, they would soon be ignored. Each survivor had his own tale, and everyone's story was the same.

I learned that in the outside world, Sheleen had been the professor of philosophy at Martine. Everyone had heard of him, and even I had vaguely known his name. But there were many men here who had been renowned in their past lives. When they first arrived, if they talked at all, it was only of what they had once been. Everyone learned quickly that to survive, one's former greatness—real or imagined—meant nothing. Only with Sheleen were things different. Loftier and lesser men soon blended together into the same gray landscape. Sheleen always stood out. Only he was referred to by his last name. Most of the rest of us came to be called by what we had once been and by the name of the city that had spawned us.

It was Sheleen who walked by my side that first day I entered the shop. The place was cavernous and dimly lit, and even inside, I felt the constant chill of the wind on my neck. My eyes were struck by the gleaming black machines mounted atop the wooden benches. They were laid out in exact, orderly rows across the shop. At first glance, it looked like some huge classroom. The men shuffled silently through the aisles as they went to their benches. They sat down before their machines with their expressions showing as much life as would be as seen on the faces of dead men lying in their coffins.

Sheleen, waiting until everyone was seated, then led me to an empty bench in the center of the room. "Here," he said as he pointed, "this is a good place to begin your career. The guards won't bother you here, it's too cold. Watch what the others do and you'll learn the machine."

He looked around the shop and then gestured toward an enormously fat little man in the front corner by one of the stoves. Sheleen said, "That's Verbin. He'll soon be over and record your number." He patted me on the back and was gone. I followed his every step as he walked to his bench. His machine was behind me, near a stove. In each corner of the huge room was a large coal-burning stove. Also behind me, but in the opposite corner, was the poet. Knowing what I did of his nature, it was no surprise to me that the poet would be basking in warmth.

I sat there in worried anticipation of the fat man's visit. The skin around the burned-in numbers was still red and slightly inflamed. The numbers they had engraved on my chest were all even. I smiled; I remembered that as a child I had had a fondness for even numbers.

The gross obesity of this Verbin was out of place in our world of skeletons. His walk was more of a waddle. Everyone watched him as he reached up and opened the metal box on the wall. With the pulling of the lever, the room exploded with the sound of metal striking metal. The entire world seemed to vibrate as the machines came to life.

I watched as the men around me placed pieces of scrap metal beneath the sharp jaws of the machine. A cutting blade was attached to the end of a long, upright cylinder. The cylinder rose up and down, striking the scrap. Amidst each deafening clang of steel against steel, a shiny sliver of metal was born. After creation, the spines dropped into a large canister stationed at the foot of the bench.

Each finished piece seemed identical. They were about the length of a thumb and half the thickness of a cigarette. I wondered what the hell they were making.

I soon realized that all of the machines except my own were pounding in unison. My cutting cylinder raced up and down wildly, out of control, just missing the surface of the wooden bench. As I reached for a piece of scrap metal, Verbin's puffy little hand lowered what I realized was the throttle bar. The cutting cylinder slowed and peacefully came to rest.

"Nice and easy. Remember now, nice and easy," he said in a singsong manner. As with all fat people, he breathed heavily as he spoke. There was no harshness in his voice; in fact, there was a certain warmth intermixed with his words. I remembered someone once saying that fat people are rarely cruel.

He pointed to the piece of scrap in my hand, and I gave it to him. He began to explain the intricacies of the machine. "You bring the cutter down at just the right angle. You see? Good. Now place the metal here. You see? Good. Nice and easy. The cylinder will warp if you go too fast. You see?"

He produced a few spines and then held them up for me to inspect. As he carefully rubbed his fingers along their edges, I could see that they were razor sharp. Their tips came to a perfect point.

"This is a good one," he said with satisfaction. "You see? Good."

His small features blended into his obese, round face. There was a ruddiness to his complexion even in the dimness of the shop. He reminded me of a fifty-year-old cherub. The more I gazed at him, the less I feared him.

Verbin produced an oily rag from his back pocket and cleaned the outer casing of my machine, wiping each crevice of the cylinder until the metal gleamed. As he worked, his enormous stomach brushed against the side of the machine and the grease further stained his already soiled shirt.

"This has always been a good machine to me," he said as he walked away. "Be good to it."

I tugged gently at his coat and he wheeled around with a rather surprised look. As I pointed to my chest he said,

"Ah, yes, I am sometimes forgetful." He reached into his shirt pocket and, after fumbling for a few seconds, produced a pair of old-fashioned metal-rimmed reading glasses. First he wiped the lenses on his tie; then he placed the spectacles on his nose.

After opening my collar, he carefully copied my numbers down in a black book. He recorded each number in a slow, determined manner, like one not overly schooled. When his yellow pencil finished, I knew I was officially registered in the camp's book of life.

My frozen hands tested the cold metal against the pounding cutter. I tried to pick up the clanging rhythm of the shop. It was obvious that the cutting blade required constant vigilance or a finger would be added to the canister of spines. Checking the hands of the men around me, I took some satisfaction in seeing ten fingers on each of them. Their faces looked dead, but their hands were intact.

The coughing from the man on my left became as loud as the banging of his machine. Soon the sound of his choking eclipsed the noise of his cutter. Finally the machine stopped and the man laid his head down on the bench.

Verbin came over to the man a few moments later and gently raised the cylinder so that it no longer touched the bench. "You must remember not to dull the blade," he said in a kindly tone. Only a cough indicated that the man had heard what had been said.

A few minutes later the prisoner began coughing again, and then he slumped slowly to the floor. Even with repeated attempts, he was unable to raise himself back on his chair. No one got up to aid him. I looked back, first to Sheleen and then to the poet. Both shook their heads.

I saw Verbin watching from his corner by the front stove. Several of the guards seemed to stir from their boredom and were now also looking at the fallen prisoner.

Verbin pulled himself out of his overstuffed chair and

returned to stand over the man on the floor. He seemed to listen carefully as the faint coughing finally ceased. I watched the same ritual as before. First the glasses, then the black book, and finally the yellow pencil. The lead made its mark in this book that apparently recorded our births as well as our deaths. Verbin's face never lost its look of fat good humor. He walked away and disappeared into a side room near his chair and stove.

I saw some of the guards come alive, awakened from their stupor of the morning. The man on the floor now interested them more than the warmth of the stoves. They peered over at Verbin's empty chair and then raced through the aisles and swooped down on the man. Their rifle butts ended all uncertainty as to whether he was living or dead. The remains were dragged outside. Several minutes later the soldiers returned to take up again their positions of semisleep next to the stoves.

The morning wore on and I began to feel hungry. I had not eaten in two or three days. I welcomed the hunger because I had once read that a dying man does not crave food. My machine began to produce what I knew in time would be an acceptable spine. In some perverse way, I even felt good. I now understood the rules of this place, and they were profoundly uncomplicated.

Seeing the poet loom up before my machine ended my brief period of well-being. I buried myself in making spines, hoping that he would go away. My machine ground to a halt as he reached over and depressed the throttle. I gazed first at Verbin, who was again sleeping in his chair, and then back at the poet. In a hissing voice I begged him to leave me alone.

"Come with me," he said. "You're allowed to take a break once during each shift. They haven't found a way as yet to take away our God-given right to piss. See, even I can find some reason to praise God. I'm becoming almost as pious as Avron."

I got up and followed him, not out of desire but out of necessity. As he led me to the main door of the shop, I had the feeling that all eyes were on me. I waited for a rifle butt to crash into my neck, but all I felt was the cold wind. A few paces from the shop was a small building. Even before we entered, the searing smell of ammonia began to burn my eyes and scorch my nose. Once inside, I could hardly breathe the heavy air. This had to be the coldest place on earth.

"You should take the dead man's bench," the poet said as he choked on the foul air. "Do everything you can to get near a stove. Even with the guards hanging around, it's better than the center of the shop. You'll soon freeze to death in the middle of the room. The center is the place for those who want to die sooner."

As we walked out, I asked him what the spines were meant for. "Shrapnel," he said in a voice tinged with surprise at my ignorance. "What else would you expect these masters of civilization have us create? We are renowned for making the finest shrapnel in all the world. In fact, Verbin's shop is the best producer of spines in the camp. The commandant personally thanks Verbin each day for our masterpieces."

Then the poet began mocking Verbin's singsong way of speaking. "They must be very sharp. You see? Good. When the bomb explodes, the spines must be nice and thin to tear through a man and chop him to bits. You see? Good. Perhaps if you make them sharp enough, they might even pass through one soldier and have enough energy in them to slice through another man."

I yelled at him to stop. As we walked back into the shop, the poet pointed to the vacant bench. "Take it," he said. "Start on your way to the stoves. It's only a beginning, but it's a first step."

The new machine ran smoother than my old one. There was less vibration as the cutter slammed into the metal.

Perhaps it was my imagination, but I felt warmer even though I had advanced only a few feet. Looking at the spines that dropped into the canister, I began to wish that they had assigned me to make something less lethal—like making shoes.

As the spines fell, one by one, into the canister, I thought of what piercing havoc our creations would make on some battlefield. A spine tearing through a soldier produced enough of a cry to express both his pain and our hopelessness.

I had noticed the man with the strange red cap before. At first I wasn't even certain that he was one of us. He didn't seem to belong to any particular bench but scurried around the shop, checking the machines. Usually he hovered around Verbin as if waiting for some command. The guards paid no attention to him, even when he walked out of the shop onto the dock.

Looking at him, he reminded me of being a child when I was taken to a park by my parents. I had watched an organ grinder with his little jumping monkey wearing such a red cap. Like that monkey, this prisoner had a chin strap anchoring the round hat to his head.

My smile faded as the man in the red cap came toward me. In his hand was a pair of hair clippers that could only be meant for me. I didn't want my damn head shaved. They had taken everything from me, but I still wanted my hair.

Looking at him, I saw that even his face could pass for a monkey's. He wasn't as emaciated as the others; there was a roundness to his sullen features. Instead of the usual hollow, sunken look of this place, his eyes bulged. "We'll do it on the dock," he said flatly. "Verbin doesn't like hair on the floor."

I did not move. Finally he shut the machine down. "Come on, damnit," he swore. "You'll even thank me. The lice don't like shaved heads."

As I sat on an overturned canister, I watched the wind scattering the clumps of my dark hair over the muddy ground. My head felt raw and naked. His clippers dug into my scalp. The man with the red cap scampered around me, checking to be sure he had done a good job.

I heard laughter and realized that several of the guards had been watching the show. When the monkey-faced man saw the guards, his scowl turned quickly to a smile. He laughed with them and then bowed and doffed his hat to the soldiers. A few moments later, the guards meandered back into the shop. The show was over.

I began to walk back in too, but the red cap grabbed me. "Listen, you," he snarled, "stay away from the poet." From the rough tone of his voice, I realized I was not dealing with a simple fool. "That goddamn poet is going to get us all killed. You're in hut four. Join up with Sheleen or Avron and you'll live longer. The poet's a troublemaker. Verbin's going to check him off."

I asked him what the poet was doing wrong.

"That bastard just won't fit in," he said. "He screeches his machine when the guards are sleeping. You'll soon learn that it's better to let them sleep." He went on with mounting bitterness in his voice. "I know he's letting off gas every time the commandant comes by his bench. One of these times the commandant will figure out what's going on, and then we'll all be dead. You tell that broken-nosed son of a bitch to stop all this or Verbin will check him off. What does he think he's trying to prove?" The black look on his face bore no resemblance to that of the smiling jester of a few moments ago. "I won't allow any one man to ruin this for us." With that he gave me a shove that propelled me through the door into the shop.

3 Each night by the end of the final shift, the machine had pounded every bit of strength from my body. My hands still tingled from the vibration of the cutter striking the metal. I leaned, totally exhausted, against the wall of the hut, staring blankly out of the window into the night. The roar of the cutter still banged on in my head so I could hardly savor the silence of the hut.

The night food cart had come and gone. I still had a little bread left that I would try to hoard from myself until the morning. The rest of the men lay in their bunks, nibbling slowly on the crusts to make them last as long as possible.

Peering out of the window into the darkness, I saw Avron's stooped figure silhouetted in the shadows, like a sentinel in the night. He always remained outside after the food cart had been dragged from the compound. I knew that he was hoping for some sign of the boy. He stood motionless, with his hands cupped around his ears, listening for the song of the violin. There was only the high-pitched whine of the cold wind.

I watched as Avron's face turned skyward and gazed up into the starlit night. As his arms reached upward, I was certain that he was praying to God for the return of the child. Moments later, he returned to the hut. Looking like a beaten old man, he sat for a moment on his bunk and then buried himself in his covers.

The poet was in the midst of some diatribe. Whenever I was around him, he rekindled all the pent-up rage and hate that simmered within me. I tried to lose myself in the fog that blanketed most of the men's minds, but listening to him kept me from my stupor. I screamed out at him to shut his mouth.

"I'm glad to see that you're still alive," he said. Pointing to the exhausted bodies around us, he sneered, "These others just want to sleep their miserable lives away. Why don't you go to Sheleen? He'll soothe your madness with some of his stories."

Standing up, I wanted to tear into this man whose tongue always dripped with venom. I asked him why he bothered with his crazy efforts to harass the guards and especially the commandant.

He seemed to reflect for a moment, which was not his custom, and said, "I must do something. I was never one to just sit still. I don't have the guts to flex a muscle and strike at them with a fist. All that is left in me is the power to relax the muscles in my rear end with the hope that my valiant efforts at farting will some day suffocate the commandant to death."

The poet lapsed into silence. His eyes slowly closed. I walked over and covered him with one of his coats that had fallen on the floor.

I left him and made my way to Sheleen's bunk. Each night in the midst of this filth and cold, Sheleen presided over discussions that could have befitted the most elegant of salons. Had fate not destined me to this camp, I would never have been in the company of such men. Sheleen's disciples came from every stratum of the past world. He attracted at once the highest as well as the lowliest. Anyone who still had the strength to talk, or even listen silently, was welcome to his group. Most men, however, had long ago lost their spark and chose to remain immersed in their blankets, awaiting the inevitable. Among the living, only the poet and Avron remained aloof from Sheleen's group.

We would sit around Sheleen under the flickering light bulb. The faint glow of the light would glimmer off his face that was always alive with warmth. His eyes would gleam as he spoke. "We must realize that everything has a purpose and a meaning in this world. Even the destruction of all that we held dear; even the terrors of this place.

All my life I searched for some formula that would allow men to live together in peace and harmony. This has always been the philosophers' dream."

There was now a spellbinding quality to his voice. "Here and only here have I found the answer. Look around you at the members of our group. No other men live such noble lives. Amongst us there's no strife or rancor. We live together in peace and harmony as equals.

"Always remember," he said, "as long as you live that you are living as no men before you. We are the ultimate that men can hope to achieve. The outside world has its pleasures, but it is a nightmare because of the inherent frailty of men. Here we have transcended this weakness. I beg you," he pleaded, "forget the outside world and enjoy the fruits of this noble state of man. Look around you," he would say. "There is no competition, and without competition there is no strife. The food they give us, what little there is, is doled out equally. They do not recognize excellence. We all know that they leave us alone if our machines produce the bare minimum. Without the drive to excel there is no rancor."

Sheleen's voice rose in excitement. "Look around you; there is nothing to hoard and nothing to accumulate. There is nothing to lust for and nothing to envy. We are all equals with the same future."

Sheleen's appeal was widespread throughout the compound. On many nights he would visit the other huts after the food cart had gone. In those brief, cherished minutes that our captors allowed us the freedom to visit the latrines, Sheleen would talk to the men in the other hovels. This unique man spoke even in the latrines, which were always filled with prisoners living through the misery of the ever-present dysentery.

Aside from his words, Sheleen's great attraction for us was probably very simple. Every one of us, who still harbored some semblance of life, could see that if a man of

Sheleen's inherent gifts still desired to live an exalted life, then others, too, might try. If he could find some hidden meaning to all of this, then so might lesser men. Sheleen set the pace of the heartbeat of our lives. When I was around this man, I knew I was alive. He would always congratulate us on our reaching this ultimate state of man. I know we were all somewhat dubious of our good fortune in being part of this world of his, but we hungered for a meaning to this place that the God of old could not offer. The number of Sheleen's converts grew, and they seemed to live longer than the nonbelievers. His was the only answer to this frozen world, and each of us was to know the warmth that came from being with him.

On one occasion Sheleen even spoke of the boy. A member of the group had asked him if we should feed this child if he returned to the compound. I sensed a reticence in Sheleen's voice as he spoke. "If he returns, we should each share some of our bread with him. He is one of us. But we all know why they allow him to live. He is here to remind us of what they have taken from us. I can see the commandant's devilish hand in all this. He is trying to tempt our souls with what we have lost. He is using this child to taunt us. We must forget the outside, or it will blind us to the great heights that we have reached."

The night siren would sound all too soon. This raucous noise ended our meetings. It was the signal that the light in the huts would soon be extinguished. Sheleen always offered a firm handclasp and a parting smile for each of the group. He would stand by the door and bid farewell to those men scurrying off into the night to get to their huts before the lights went out.

Even with the sudden extinguishing of the light, the time with Sheleen had served to rekindle my spirit. I always returned to my bunk walking erect like a man through the stench-filled darkness.

4 I came to know the charac-
teristics of the machines as if their gears and belts were
parts of my own body. The pounding cutter became an
extension of my hand as it ripped into the scrap to chip out
a spine.

Through the day I would turn in the direction of Sheleen's bench. Sometimes he would even look up from his
machine; his approving smile told me I was doing well. I
would listen carefully through the din of all the machines
and try to match the tempo of his cutter.

My hands were always numb from the cold. The warmth
of the corner stoves began to beckon more and more to me.
I took the poet's advice and started my journey out of the
center of the shop. My goal was to work my way over to
Sheleen and be with him. I would then survive in this
place, basking in the combined warmth of his presence
and his stove. I knew I would drown if I did not move on.

The certainty of death could always be counted on to
free up a machine. One had only to wait. In time I knew
that I would possess a machine next to Sheleen. Many of
the men never abandoned their very first bench. Perhaps
they were afraid the guards might notice the change. I was
positive, however, that the guards could not tell us apart.
Laboring in unison at the machines made us blend into
the up-and-down gyrations of the cutting cylinder. We
even cherished the thought that we were invisible to the
guards. If they could not see us, they could not strike us.

I asked the chemist from Litina why he had never
moved out of the cold to another bench. His only answer
was that it was God's will that he remain at the same
machine. The chemist was true to his faith until the very
end. One day he slumped over in a coma and was dragged
out of the shop by the guards to the "dead pile," which was

located next to the scrap pile. Each day trucks delivered fresh scrap and took away the spent men.

Most of the other permanent residents of the center section gave no explanation for remaining. Their souls were dead, but while their bodies still moved, they returned to the same frozen bench each day as if by instinct. No one ever took another's bench until death sanctioned the transaction. Perhaps this was Sheleen's influence. There were never arguments over the right of accession to a new machine. Those who chose to take over a newly vacant bench spent much time sorting out the pros and cons; it was always the same question—to be warm near a stove under the eyes of the guards or to die slowly in the serenity of the frigid center of the shop.

Sometimes a machine would remain vacant during both shifts. Finally he who vacillated the least would rise up and claim the bench. A machine would never be silent for very long; a new replacement would be ordered and arrive by the next day. Some men were indecisive, traveling back and forth from machine to machine. At times they chose paths leading to the stoves, and at other times to the center. Often in midstream a man would change course and retrace the route from whence he had come.

One could tell well in advance which machines were about to become vacant. The rhythmic song of their cutters would slowly and almost imperceptibly begin to run off-key. How one's machine sang became the barometer of the state of one's soul. Dying men usually tried to make their way back to the center of the shop, hoping that they could expire in peace without any aid from the guards. Here they would wait patiently for death to unchain them from their machines.

Another current ran through the shop that bore no relation to warmth or safety. There were many former concert musicians here. Somehow in their minds the orderly rows of benches brought back memories of the seating in an actual orchestra. They would endure the guards and the cold just to possess the same seat that in the past had taken them years of study to attain. Once they finally reached a bench that corresponded to their old symphony chair, they never moved again.

The shop was actually referred to as the "orchestra." Each region of the huge room came to represent the different sections of a grand symphony. Sheleen's area was known as the "string-bass section." The poet spent his days making spines and mocking the world in the "brass section."

The front of the shop contained the string sections, and it was actually filled with the finest of violinists and cellists. Only the best musicians had been chosen by the selection officers. As could be expected, these musicians had no idea why they had been saved from instant extinction to await a slower death.

I never met a single former machinist among us, even though hundreds of them must have passed through the selection camps. No one knew why the officers allowed men with such useful talents to die.

I remember Sheleen wincing at the poet's explanation for the overabundance of musicians. "Being a selection officer is obviously a job for only the most cultivated of men. Our captors could not pick just any ordinary man to select who should live and who should die. Any one of their idiots would know that women and children were not worth saving. But only a truly creative officer would have the brilliance to choose among all the men. Only the most cultured of their officers were fit for such a demanding task. It is all so simple," he said in his nasal voice; "cultured men love fine music, and it only follows that music lovers would save musicians." The poet concluded by imitating Verbin. "You see why they were saved? Good. It is really very simple. You see? Good."

Whatever their motives, the selection officers did seem

partial to former string players. There were so many violinists that it had become necessary for us to call them by their first names, just to distinguish between them. Through this unique custom, Avron and the other violinists were able to retain some portion of the name they were born with. Sheleen was naturally Sheleen, but the rest of us were lost in the anonymity of our former occupations and cities.

Avron's bench was in the front of the shop in the first-violin section. He occupied the premier bench of the concertmaster. To me, he paid a high price for his number-one seat in the orchestra. None of the heat from Verbin's stove reached him. The constant draft from the windows in front of the shop covered him in a blanket of cold air. Still, he kept his first chair.

As a group, the musicians were by far the finest makers of spines in the entire orchestra. They fashioned almost gemlike slivers of steel that far exceeded the unwritten specifications. The uniformity and sharpness of their creations were our standards of excellence.

I would marvel at the tranquil expressions on the faces of the musicians as they worked. The look of peace only came to Avron when he was lost in the rhythmic motions of his machine, the same serene look I had seen long ago on the faces of musicians engrossed in a concerto. How I envied these men who somehow extracted a measure of peace from the pounding machines. I was never to tire of watching them as the steady flow of shining slivers cascaded into their canisters.

As I surveyed the openings in the orchestra each day, I realized that I would freeze to death long before reaching Sheleen. So few benches became vacant in his area. Death visited his bass section, but not as often as other parts of the orchestra. To be near him was to thrive.

Disappointment was a way of life here, but knowing that I would never be with Sheleen was the bitterest of disappointments. For a few days I found myself unable to keep my machine running at the orchestra's usual rhythm. I feared that I was falling into the same stupor that constantly took the lives of those around me.

Perhaps it was the cold that saved me. I shivered as much from the temperature as from the constant vibration of the cutter. My frozen insides screamed out; I knew I had to rid myself of this center section. Slowly I began to claim benches that led into the cello section. Within a few days I advanced four spaces in the direction of the cello stove. Then I found that I could go no further. The musicians, of course, died like all the rest, but they took longer. Somehow they extracted added life from their machines.

The only stove that I could count on was that of the poet's in the brass area. Death seemed to thrive around him just as it did in the center of the orchestra. There was no sense of rhythm or peace surrounding him. I wanted no part of this man, but the path of empty benches led toward him and his stove.

Slowly I retraced my steps back through the central woodwinds and entered the outer periphery of the poet's realm. As I came ever closer to him, the poet would look up at me with his crooked smile and welcome my progress.

Many of the poorest operators had congregated around the poet. Their indifferent playing was often rewarded by the clubs of the guards. One could not maintain a decent rhythm if the surrounding machines were off-key. I thought the poet was the chief reason for the lack of harmony, and I was sure that this was by his own design. The guards would be asleep, and then a sudden screeching blast would come from his machine. Usually the poet himself received most of the guards' blows. The guards knew they could maim but not kill a prisoner who was still able to work. To smash a man across the face was tolerated, but to kill him was not legal.

After each of the poet's encounters with the guards, I

35

learned to expect the visit of the man with the red cap. Verbin's crown prince was known as the "conductor." Every orchestra has a conductor, and the monkey-faced man was ours. The red cap would threaten the poet, and then peace would reign for a time.

My travels were over. My permanent home came to be in the brass section. I remained one bench away from the poet and his stove. My journey through the shop brought back memories of the games my children had once played. They would move small wooden players on circuitous routes to the far corners of a square board. The whims of the roll of the dice determined how far a player could move. If he landed on the wrong spot, he had to return to his old position. Now, my life seemed mirrored in the games of my lost children. I had reached the final spot on the board and had left the cold behind, though I still longed to be a part of Sheleen's world.

Watching the poet, I came to know when he was about to screech his machine and infuriate the guards. That same twisted smirk would cover his face as the soldiers were blasted out of their slumber. Even while lying on the floor after a blow to the head, the poet wore his same crooked smile. The smirk seemed to madden the guards even more, and they would rain blows down on anyone in sight. My hands became a helmet to shield my head from their clubs.

Sheleen and his group always came to the rescue. Whenever a man was in trouble with the guards, the bass section would race their machines. The shrill song would reverberate through the orchestra to awaken the sleeping Verbin. One cold stare from his piercing little eyes was enough to stop the guards. The soldiers would lower their rifles and slink back to their stoves, wondering what supernatural powers lay within this simple fat man.

While we were in the shop, Verbin was our lord and master. He was actually a civilian employed by the army to run the factory. Guards came and went, and we knew our lives would eventually flicker out, but Verbin was to remain always and prosper. He was the only continuity in this world of ours.

His only concern was the well-being of his beloved machines. They were his children. Like any good father, he had no favorites; he loved them all. He knew the vagaries of each one—which of them were headstrong and apt to break down and which were gentle and sang on-key. His oily rag caressed them all with tenderness, and under his care they flourished and effortlessly produced their quotas.

It was actually the conductor who oversaw the day-to-day running of the shop. When he was not shaving heads or beards, he was commandeering prisoners to go out to the scrap pile for more food for the machines. His hands were constantly adjusting his ridiculous cap to be sure it was firmly on his head. A smash on your shoulder from his fist meant that your machine was off-key or racing too fast.

The conductor was brusque with all of us, though some measure of respect was reserved for Sheleen. The rest of us lived with the threats of "Verbin will check you off" if the red cap saw something he didn't like. The conductor's eyes were always on the poet. I realized that the poet rarely began his little riots with the guards when Verbin was awake. I could not understand this strange man who sat near me. The poet was convinced that Verbin gave the conductor extra food when they made their trips into Verbin's office. No one trusted this scowling man; next to the soldiers, we feared him the most.

One of the worst of our many fears was that our machines would break down. A man was immune from death at the hands of the guards while protected by his pounding cutter. When a machine broke down and slowly ground to a halt, the operator would be seized by an overwhelming terror. It would be the conductor who would awaken Verbin with the bad news. Ever so gently, the red cap would touch Verbin's arm and slowly restore the slumbering man to his senses. Verbin would come to life after a series of loud snorts. A few words with the conductor would send Verbin racing to the stricken machine. The conductor would follow behind, lugging the heavy toolbox. Verbin would look over the situation and make an instantaneous diagnosis that was usually correct. Verbin and the desperate operator would work side by side over the machine to bring it back to life. He alone of all our captors did not seem repelled by our filth and lice.

As they labored together, there would never be a harsh word from Verbin or a look of hate on his face. It was unthinkable that he would ever strike a prisoner. We were united with him in our deep devotion and affection for these machines, which were all we had to carry us through the desert.

Even as he slept, we knew that Verbin's closed eyes would open and ward off any evil from the guards anytime the machines cried out to him.

The guards were young and seemed proud of being soldiers. They took great pains to protect their spotless, creased uniforms from being fouled by a greasy machine or a filthy prisoner. When they beat a man it was usually with a rifle butt or a club, rather than with a clean fist or a polished boot. Much of the time the guards ignored us as if we didn't exist. When they did look us directly in the eyes, I could see a look of disgust cross their faces. I knew that they had been brought up to believe that we were guilty of all manner of sins. Yet they showed no interest in berating us for our supposed transgressions against mankind. In many ways they were like schoolboys incarcerated against their wills in a dull, never-ending classroom. They had the look of children longing to be free to play out-of-doors. Sheleen felt that most of their hatred for us stemmed from their knowing that having to guard us was the reason for their lost freedom.

In a way this was all a monumental joke. Had they not been stationed here, dying of boredom, they would have probably been at the front, dying of bullets. Had they been at the front, we would have lived longer. This camp was the first army assignment for many of the soldiers. They had gone off to war with heroic visions, only to have them dashed in the drudgery of being locked up with louse-infected prisoners.

When the newly assigned guards first arrived, they would diligently patrol the aisles of the orchestra. They soon tired of this, for we gave them no reason to be vigilant. Their scrutiny was never necessary; we labored better without them around. Soon they would abandon the cold aisles for the warmth of the stoves.

With each passing day I would look up and see more and more of them congregated before the windows. They looked out at the sights of the world that was passing them by. They fidgeted constantly. What we feared most was when they banded together in packs and looked for adventure. Stomping a prisoner to the floor would temporarily relieve their frustrations. Their bored faces would come alive as they beat us. The look of life would vanish from them as Verbin's stare returned them to their corners.

The guards hated Verbin and derided him behind his back. One of the soldiers imitated his walk, much to the amusement of the other guards. These men talked openly in front of us as if we didn't exist. Above the clamor of the machines I learned that these were good times for Verbin. His life had never amounted to anything until the war lifted him out of poverty and obscurity. One of the other guards added that Verbin had never held a real job until, through some apparent connivance, he had been granted this position. None of the soldiers could comprehend why anyone would want a job such as his. To them it was beneath the dignity of a man.

These young men who had come to fight a war could not tolerate being under the authority of a civilian. I think Verbin sensed this and tried to ingratiate himself with them. Verbin even gave them a little more free rein with us. Through trial and error, the guards learned that he would tolerate a quick jab to our ribs, just so the blow did not break the cadence of the machine. For a time Verbin even wore his old army uniform from a bygone war. He was unable to button the food-stained jacket and his stomach bulged over his belt. The guards still remained aloof, and Verbin soon abandoned the uniform.

With obvious glee, Verbin made the conductor perform for the soldiers. His red cap would be doffed and a low bow would bring momentary laughter to the soldiers. The smiling conductor continued his mechanical routine long after the soldiers tired of this same one-act play.

Verbin's weight seemed to increase in direct proportion to our progressive emaciation. Via some secret route, there was a transfer of our lost pounds to his ever expanding belly. My starving mind was always conjuring up fantasies of the varied delicacies he must have eaten to produce such a massive stomach. Unlike the guards, he never ate in front of us, but he did make frequent nourishing trips to his office. When he emerged it would often be with the smell of garlic on his breath or the sulfuric aroma of hardboiled eggs. After his lunch he usually fell asleep in the chair. From the peace of this sleep would come forth loud belches that catapulted new odors throughout the violin section.

Verbin tried fervently to interest the new guards in the beauties of his machines. He would walk up to a helpless soldier, commandeer him, and together they would make the rounds of the orchestra. Verbin spent most of his tour inspecting the canisters of the machines that sang poorly. On these excursions he carried a long wooden stick that came to be known as his baton. The baton would gently poke through the contents of the canisters, searching for defective spines. His exploration was always gentle so as not to dull the slivers of steel. He would try his best to educate his restless soldier in the various characteristics of the spines. Needless to say, we were beside ourselves on these visits.

Everyone had recurring bouts of dysentery. When we were sick, Verbin would allow the machine to remain idle for one entire shift. He would tolerate a man lying on the floor to regain his strength—or we could spend the time in the latrine. Only Verbin could tell us apart and compute how long we had neglected our machines. Even the guards knew that they could not touch a man during this period of grace.

I had spent many an hour shivering in gut-wrenching agony in the peace of the latrine. No guard would ever think of venturing in. Many a man breathed his last in its quiet serenity. For me, however, sitting in this place for an entire shift must have had some medicinal value; perhaps it was the ammonia. I would then be well enough to return to the shop and reclaim my machine and give them some more spines.

If the machine was not functioning again after Verbin's period of grace, the man was finished. I would look up and watch Verbin's steady gaze never veer from the silent machine. The same routine of the glasses, the pencil, and the black book would be repeated. The orchestra would unconsciously begin to race faster and faster as the pencil made its mark. The machines would run out of control, and not even the conductor's threats could slow the tempo. The guards beating the helpless prisoner sent the orchestra into an uproar. The banging of the machines drowned out the final screams of the dying man.

Then all would return to normal. The machines meekly followed the lead of the conductor, and the usual clanging song lulled the guards back to sleep.

There were occasions when, for some unexplainable reason, the guards were not interested in such sport. Perhaps they were satiated by these games, and the marked man would be allowed to remain in peace on the floor. The members of his hut would carry him back to his bunk at the end of the shift. Usually by the time he was brought to his bed, he would be in a coma. From the appearance of Verbin's book to the actual time of death was about four hours. The book was more accurate than any of our doctors. They ascribed great prognostic powers to this black book.

I could never understand why they didn't take better care of us. Had they provided only a little more food and warmth, we would have had the strength to reward them with a million more spines. They would then have had enough slivers of steel to rip jagged holes through all of their enemies on the far-flung battlefields. Still, they allowed experienced operators to slowly fall victim to the diseases that thrive on starvation. It took a replacement many weeks before he could even begin to master the rhythm of the machine and produce like a veteran.

Surely Verbin must have realized this, but nothing ever changed. I knew he was very aware of the quality of the scrap fed to the machines. His puffy little hands would scrutinize an irregular chunk of metal, and he would shake his head in disgust if the grade of steel was poor. Never once did I see him check the quality and amount of food fed to us.

Had I chanced to come across Verbin years ago, I would have passed him by without a second thought. He would have been written off as a simple fat man who had spent too many hours vegetating in a darkened tavern. Circumstance had transformed him into a man of regal power in our lives. I did not begrudge him his upward rise in the world. Considering what they might have given us, Verbin was a blessing.

5

The light had been out for hours, but I was unable to fall asleep. Perhaps it was the biting cold. In the darkness, the poet had been pacing back and forth in front of me. From the loud gurgling that came from his stomach, I knew that he was having dysentery again. His face had looked ashen the past few days. He roamed toward the door and then returned slowly to his bunk. I began to wonder if he, like so many of the others wracked with pain, might make a run for the tower and ask for a bullet. None of our many doctors had devised a better cure for dysentery.

I asked him how he was feeling.

He spoke in a weakened voice, but I was thankful his tongue was healthy. "I'm feeling fine," he said. "Can't you see that I'm taking my lice for a walk? They need to be exercised."

A few moments later the gurgling ceased and I heard the sounds of his sleep. His broken nose created a peculiar nasal quality to his snoring. I remained awake, wondering why I stayed near this man. So many times I could have moved nearer to Sheleen's bunk.

The tower beam swept through the hut, and Avron caught my eye. He was standing next to his window at the other end of the hut. His usually swaying body was strangely quiet as he peered out into the darkness.

I listened and for the first time heard what I knew was a violin. Intermixed with the sound of the wind and the coughing were the soft, unmistakable strains of a song. I could hear only a few scattered notes, but they were enough to warm my soul. I strained my ears, but his song faded into the wind.

Avron remained at the window long after the song had ended. A few moments later the tower light outlined his bent figure playing his own nonexistent violin. As he played, I heard him humming some of the same bits of music that had come from the boy.

Covering myself with another blanket, I got out of bed and walked slowly toward Avron. I paused for a moment in front of Sheleen's bunk to listen to the sound of his breathing. The past few days his coughing had worried us. I was thankful not to hear any trace of a rasp. I stopped a few feet from Avron and watched him playing. His back was to me as his body swayed to the rhythm of some silent song from his past. Like all violinists, he held his right wrist in that same twisted, unnatural position.

Without turning around, he spoke. "Every violinist must practice. Each year you must work harder and harder, just to keep what you once had. It all came so easy when I was younger. One has to keep his fingers limber. The violin has always been my life, and even here I must still play. One cannot stop breathing and still expect to live."

He finally turned around and looked at me. In the darkness I wasn't even sure if he knew to whom he had been speaking. His hands had dropped away from the void that cradled his lost violin. He walked toward me with his arms resting limply at his side.

"You heard the boy, didn't you?" he said with an air of excitement in his voice. "You'll hear him again. He will come back. The poet frightened him away. He is a very sensitive child, but soon he will forget and return to us. You will hear him play. No child has ever played with such genius. I've heard all the greats play, but none of them have what the boy has. None of them could play like this boy even when they were in their early twenties. The boy can't be more than eight years old, but he plays like a master. Such genius comes to the world only once in a lifetime."

Avron reached out in the darkness and grabbed my

arms. I couldn't believe such strength still existed in him. "Don't you see," he said with a fervor, "that such genius can only come from Heaven? God has been driven from this earth which man has drenched in blood. The only remaining spark of God lies buried in this boy. Why else would a child be roaming this wasteland? What other meaning could explain the presence of the boy?"

He released his grip on my arms and sat slowly down on his bunk. "Sheleen says the guards allow the boy to live only to humiliate us, to make us grieve over our lost children, to break our spirit. He is wrong. The guards and even the commandant could care less about our feelings. We are less than animals to them. The commandant only wants his spines, and the guards only want to stay warm and count the days until they'll be transferred. You can see that even Sheleen with all his answers can't really explain why the boy is allowed to live."

Avron's voice then became colored with bitterness. "Your friend the poet says that the boy is tolerated because he is the illegitimate son of the commandant and some whore from the city. Everyone knows this is just more of the madness that comes from the poet's mouth. The boy was obviously born before this war began. Everyone knows that the child has been here far longer than this commandant. What really bothers the poet is that the men give the boy a little food. He says the child is here to take our bread and starve us to death. He says the soldiers enjoy watching the boy take our food. The guards don't care if we starve to death. They can't even tell us apart. We are nothing to them, and they pay little attention to the boy."

The sweeping light illuminated Avron's tearstained face. He looked up and said, "The boy is here because it is God's will. The strings on his violin have never broken. Anyone should know that this is a miracle, the way he presses on them with his bow. The *E* string should have gone long ago. The boy must be fed. He must be kept alive. If he dies, then there is nothing left in this miserable world. God will have abandoned us."

Avron reached out and took my hand in his. "You will feed him, won't you? Just a little? Tell the poet to leave him alone."

After slowly releasing my hand from his grip, I asked him why he didn't feed the child as much as some of the others.

He was silent for a moment. I could barely hear him as he said, "Whoever feeds the boy his entire ration day after day will die soon. I know this. If I give everything to the child, I, too, will die, and then there will be no one to look after him. No one else cares about the child. How long do you think the boy would live if the poet had his way? He must get some food in the other compounds, but I doubt if it is enough. If I give him everything, then I will die and so will he. If you swear to look after the child, then I will give him all my bread. I've been here much longer than you, and I know that my remaining days are few. Somehow the boy must be taken out of here before he, too, dies. Our doctors tell me that the boy is sick and needs the food. Those men who have fed him have sacrificed their lives to God. What better meaning is there for life in this place?"

Avron was silent. I knew he was waiting for some promise from me. As I walked away, I told him that I would try to reason with the poet to leave the child alone. I said good night to him, but he did not answer.

The poet was waiting for me when I returned to my bunk. Before I even got under my coats, he started in. "Madness is a good thing in this place. Sheleen doesn't cause any real harm, but this Avron is a different story. No one has the right to have his own particular brand of madness harm another. As far as Avron is concerned, everyone can starve to death just to feed this miserable child. Even your Sheleen would say that everyone has the right to starve to death equally."

The poet suddenly became silent as his stomach began to rumble. I heard the rustle of his coats as he writhed in his bed. A few moments later the gurgling was replaced by his nasal snoring.

6 From my bench, I watched for the conductor to take up his position by the window. This routine of his at the start of each morning shift never varied. He stood motionless like a mannequin, only his eyes darting back and forth between the tower and the guard hut. Suddenly this mechanical man bolted from the window and raced toward the sleeping Verbin. This meant only one thing: The commandant was coming for his tour of inspection.

The conductor gently brought Verbin back to life from his deep slumber. He was always hardest to awaken in the morning. The red cap pried Verbin out of his chair, helped him to his feet, and made his usual vain attempt to fasten at least one of the buttons on the fat man's coat. I was certain that no button had found its way into a buttonhole in years. The conductor gave up the impossible and contented himself with brushing off the remnants of breakfast that littered Verbin's stained shirt. After straightening his soiled necktie, Verbin was finally prepared. He waddled toward the door to greet the commandant.

The conductor flung his arms into the air to speed up the orchestra. Then he pointed to the violin section, and they responded by screeching their machines. The high-pitched clamor pierced the ears of those guards who were still sleeping, and they rose slowly to attention. The ones who had been awake took quick drags from their cigarettes and then carefully snuffed them out. The precious butts were placed in pockets. By now all the soldiers had taken up positions at regular intervals and surrounded the perimeter of the orchestra.

The red cap then slowed down the orchestra to a steady rhythm, known to all of us as "the commandant's song." This tempo was most harmonious, and any machine could easily follow its beat. It was much too slow, however, to produce spines in any great quantity. The conductor then raced through the orchestra, looking for any prisoner who seemed as if he might die in the next half hour. His cold eyes were drawn to the erratic machine of the semicomatose man two benches from me. The man had once been kind of doctor. I had no idea where he was from; he was new.

The conductor propped him up in his chair and firmly placed his hands on his bench. "Hang on for just a little more," the red cap pleaded. "Just sit for a little more," he screamed into the unhearing ears. "I warn you, don't fall over while he's here. When he's gone, I'll carry you outside to the pile. The guards won't even touch you."

Perhaps the conductor's last words struck one of the few living chords in the doctor. The man nodded, and the red cap set the machine to the pace of the rest of the orchestra. The cutter beat in rhythm as it struck down on emptiness.

The conductor was out of breath as he rushed back to the window. Seconds later he signaled Verbin to open the door just as the commandant's boot touched the threshold of the shop.

Verbin, too, stood at attention with a broad smile covering his immense face. He had taken his black book from his pocket and placed it under his left arm in the fashion of the commandant. The book was lost in the rolls of fat.

The immaculate officer entered the shop with his book, as always, under his arm. Verbin made a futile attempt to bow before his superior. His beaming face was met by the monumental indifference of the officer.

I noticed that each time the commandant entered the shop, he had the foul look of a man being struck by a horrible odor. Even though he had been here but a few seconds, he looked at his watch. Standing in front of the orchestra, the conductor kept the machines playing on key. Verbin, cap in hand, began his incessant chatter. His bald head shone in the light that poured in through the open door.

Looking around at my fellow skeletons, it was as if three separate forms of animal life now inhabited the same room. As a child I had been taught that man had been created in God's image. I was certain that neither Verbin nor we resembled God, but it was painful to think that this officer, perfectly formed in every way, might be the chosen one.

The two men began their tour through the orchestra. Verbin's arms gestured up and down, pointing out his smoothly running machines. The commandant rarely spoke. I wondered if the officer even heard the torrent of words that flowed from Verbin's smiling mouth. As they walked through the cello section, Verbin reached into a canister and plucked out one of the musicians' spines. He shoved the spine in front of the commandant's face and seemed to plead with the officer to inspect this gem. Verbin's master held the spine up to the light, but his expression did not change as he beheld the work of art. The spine was returned to the fat man and carefully replaced in the canister.

They continued on through the aisles with Verbin in the lead. He held up a twisted piece of substandard scrap, trying to show the officer what his machines had to contend with. The commandant looked as if he could care less. He now walked on ahead, leaving Verbin behind holding the lump of metal.

The commandant's patience was wearing thin and he increased his pace. By the time Verbin caught up with him, the commandant had reached Sheleen's section. The guards, still standing at attention, banged their rifle butts to the floor as a show of respect befitting their colonel.

I saw Sheleen peer up from his machine, trying to make out the title of the commandant's book. Sheleen showed no look of surprise today; I still remember the astonishment on his face the day he saw our commandant reading Plato's *Republic.*

Verbin offered another spine to the commandant, but this one was brushed aside without a second glance. They emerged from the bass section and headed toward us through the percussion section. Verbin always avoided the center of the orchestra on these tours.

I looked over at the doctor, slumping further down in his chair. The man was about to die—ahead of schedule. The conductor raced to his side and held the body up. The veins bulged on the red cap's forehead as he called forth every bit of his remaining energy just to keep the body from crumpling to the floor. He went through the motions of making his visit look like a friendly chat.

Verbin tried to detour the officer around this obvious embarrassment. The commandant would have none of this and motioned the conductor away. The smiling red cap bowed and backed off into our corner, where he stood silently by the poet's machine. The conductor's hands were shaking. He stilled them by stuffing them into his pockets.

The doctor remained motionless for a moment, still clutching the bench as the impassive officer watched. The orchestra held its tempo while the doctor slowly descended to the floor. He was dead. The officer walked calmly over the body, followed by the perplexed Verbin who circled around the corpse. For the first time since his guest had arrived, Verbin's mouth was not in motion.

Verbin regained his voice as they stood by my bench. "I need new bearings," said the fat man as he pointed to my machine. "You can hear how they squeal. My shop produces the best. You see? I should have the new bearings. Give me the pick of the scrap. You can see what I do. You see? Good."

The conductor had grabbed the arms of the poet. His fingers dug deeply into the man's coats, and I could see his grip almost encircling the bones. As he squeezed, the red cap kept the same smile plastered on his face. Even though his arms were being strangled, the poet diligently continued making spines.

The conductor gained nothing; the poet had farted. The commandant's nose was overwhelmed by the unseen cloud of gas, his features twisted with a pained look of disgust. "Damnit, Verbin," he yelled, "this place stinks."

The commandant raced down the aisle trying to escape. He paid no attention to the saluting guards. Even in his haste, he carefully avoided the filth of the prisoners and the grease of the machines that lurked on either side of the narrow aisle. He finally made it out of the shop and breathed in the fresh air of the dock.

Verbin caught up with him. He opened his black book and read off the numbers of the neatly stacked canisters filled with spines. The commandant only looked upward, still sniffing in the clean air.

A few minutes later the two men returned inside and closeted themselves in Verbin's office. When they came out, the officer went straight for the main door. Verbin followed on his heels, still talking. His good-natured face kept pouring out words even after the commandant had departed. Verbin finally shut up when the conductor appeared and closed the door.

Verbin and his nervous conductor spoke for a few moments. By now the guards were relaxed around the stoves, puffing away again on their cigarettes. The conductor signaled the orchestra to double the tempo to make up for the losses incurred by the commandant's visit.

Verbin seemed unusually happy. Perhaps he had been promised new bearings or better scrap. In his joy he waddled up and down the aisles of the orchestra, singing his praises to his machines.

The poet's expression had not changed through the entire visit. I watched him now as his cutter fashioned an overly long, sharp spine. In his fantasies I was certain he was plunging the razor-sharp sliver into the commandant's black heart.

7

I looked through the windows and welcomed the coming darkness. The cold grayness of the day had slowly faded into the winter night. This late in the day the machines banged on only by sheer instinct. The conductor had mercifully slowed the rhythm of the orchestra. Soon all this would be over and I would have my bread and be with Sheleen and the group.

The guards loitered around the stoves, pacing back and forth. Now none of them slept. They were too busy counting the minutes until they would be free of us. The look of exhaustion covered their faces after another day filled with nothing. They showed no interest in the man lying on the floor in the woodwind section. Verbin had checked him off about an hour ago.

Only Verbin retained total enthusiasm for his orchestra. I'm sure that he would have added another shift to our long day if the commandant had given him the go-ahead. Today was a good day for Verbin; we had gone well over quota and none of his machines had broken down.

After the closing siren, I helped carry the man from the woodwind section out of the shop. Someone said he was from our hut. When we were outside, I sniffed the air, thinking I could smell the aroma of the bread from the food cart. The man was limp and very heavy. The dead always seemed to weigh more than the living. The food cart was nowhere to be seen. A slight cough rippled through the body—he was still barely alive. As we approached the hut, I could see the food cart outlined in the shadows. We rushed into the hut and deposited the man in his bunk. His body was relaxed, and now I knew he was gone. I went back out into the windswept night for my bread.

The peace of this night with Sheleen did not last long.

We had barely begun to talk when loud stomping was heard on the front step. The door burst open and a guard loomed in the doorway, glaring at us. I tensed. None of them had ever invaded the hut before. I glanced quickly to Sheleen and relaxed somewhat, seeing that there was no fear in his face, only the look of exasperation brought on by this intrusion.

The guard lumbered in and, before closing the door, scanned the outside of the hut. His rifle was slung over his shoulder. One hand carried a crumpled piece of paper and the other a half-broken pencil. Even in the semidarkness I could see the dull-witted look on his face.

He peered vacantly at our now silent group clustered around Sheleen. The soldier pointed toward us, and one of the men got up and automatically walked toward the table in the middle of the hut. The soldier left the doorway and joined the waiting prisoner. The two of them stood together, barely outlined by the faint glow of the light bulb. I didn't know what the hell was going on.

Sheleen's disciples from the other huts began to file slowly out into the darkness. They seemed to know that this soldier had ended for them any hope of peace that the night might have offered. I heard Sheleen say to someone, "It's so hard to keep the outside from smothering us."

The guard knelt by the table and attempted to smooth out the crumpled folds in the paper with his hand. Then, to my total amazement, the prisoner began slowly to recite what was obviously a letter to the guard's parents. The soldier was only semiliterate, and all but the simplest words had to be spelled for him. Even the content of the letter came from his tutor. The guard could contribute only the phrase, "Dear Mama and Papa." After that he was at a loss. He held his pencil in an awkward fashion, carefully scrawling each letter down on the paper as it was dictated to him.

He would leave the hut only when the light went out or

when he filled both sides of the paper. The letter would often end in midsentence, but this did not seem to bother him. Night after night this young guard began thrusting himself into our lives.

Sheleen was certain that the soldier had chosen us because he dreaded parading his ignorance before his own kind. With the exception of this soldier, the rest of the guards fortunately shunned any contact with us. Only when they beat us were they able bravely to surmount their horror of our filth. Our ferocious lice might descend upon them and desecrate their uniforms and bore into their bodies. Little did they realize that everyone in this place, including them, breathed in the same stale air that had filtered over and over again through our lungs.

I learned from the others who had tutored the guard that he had never been away from home. This camp was his first army post. He had absolutely nothing to say in his letters. In time, a new life was invented for him, and his letters became resplendent with military exploits that never occurred. His simple face beamed as his various tutors dictated the details of travels to places he had never visited, places we knew we would never see again.

It was quite clear that the guard thought he was dealing with the same tutor each evening. The few times I was chosen to dictate to him actually lifted my spirits. I was surprised how good it was to be asked for something. Here, a simple request was a rare thing; there was so little to give.

Actually, six or seven of Sheleen's group were involved with the soldier at different times. Sheleen was never a tutor. When the soldier happened to point to Sheleen, someone would always jump up and take his place. We wanted to spare him the ordeal of dealing with this simpleton.

It became necessary for each of us to compare notes in advance so as to keep the changing threads of his newly created life intact. In one session with the soldier, I was prepared to continue with the details of the story of his mythical two-day pass. As I stood over him, I began to recite where the last letter had ended. He put the pencil down and looked up at me. With difficulty he got out what he was trying to say. "How do I write that I am lonely and afraid? I don't know how to write such things. I don't want any more trips or things about the war. Tell me how to say that I want to go home. I don't talk good, but you understand me, don't you? Tell me slowly how to write what I want to say."

I asked him to tell me more so that I could help him write.

With a slight trace of a stutter he began. "I am by myself here. I haven't seen my family for a long time. I miss them very much. I don't know many of the other soldiers. The officers make me afraid. They yell at me. I don't know what I'm supposed to do in the shop. At night I lay in my bed and I am alone. I don't know why I'm here. I was only happy at home with my family. I ask the officers to send me home, but they don't listen to me. I don't like to be around this place. Everything is dirty here."

He paused for a moment and then went on. "Tell me how to say this. Go slow so I can write down what you tell me. Did you understand what I said? Did I talk good?"

This man had no idea how well I understood him. I recited back to him much that he had already said. I could have added reams about loneliness and fear, but my scribe soon ran out of paper. He folded the letter, placed it in his pocket, and walked out into the night. He never uttered a word to anyone when he left—never a thank you or even a cigarette butt.

The letters that he received were written by his father, and they, too, bore the mark of a tutor—the parish priest. The priest even complimented the young soldier on his great scholastic strides. He was obviously impressed by what the army had done for his once dull parishioner.

As the nights went on, the soldier acquired the best of instructors. His new chief tutor had once been the professor of literature at Stieden. The professor finally abandoned Sheleen's group and stationed himself each night by the table to await the soldier.

One night we had barely returned to the hut when the guard burst through the door. He had never before come this early in the evening. In his hand was an unopened letter. The professor rose up eagerly. By chance the poet happened to be nearest the soldier. Thinking the poet was his usual tutor, the guard thrust the letter into his hands. The poet, naturally, had never been a part of this. He held the letter for a moment and then placed it gently on the table and walked away. The guard seemed dumbfounded by this strange behavior. He picked up the letter and held it out again to the poet.

"Read it for me," he said, "you always have before. Why not now?"

"I won't," said the poet.

I waited in fear for the guard to go into a rage, but the expected explosion did not come. The soldier walked over to the poet and pleaded, "Why won't you help me? What will I do now?"

The poet roared back, "Listen, you, I slave for you all day —the nights are mine. Can you get that through your head?"

I doubted if the guard understood all of this, but at least his fists were not clenched. The professor started toward the guard but traveled only a few paces and then stopped. He looked to Sheleen for some gesture to guide him, but no sign came from the master's face.

The guard stuffed the unopened letter into his pocket and shuffled dejectedly toward the door. He turned and looked back at the poet who had still not retreated to his bunk. The guard, in a childlike manner, begged the poet again. "What did I ever do to you? Why are you doing this to me now?"

The poet, in a slow, measured voice, spoke so that each word would sink in. "Do you have any idea of what has happened to us or why we are here? What goes through that mind of yours when you bash one of us in the head with your rifle butt? I've seen you smash away at us in the shop just like all the others."

The soldier did not answer at first. "I never wanted to leave home," he murmured. "They sent me here. The only thing I want now is to go home." He looked back at the poet for a moment and then went out the door.

The professor raced over to the poet and, in a voice laced with curses, screamed, "You son of a bitch. Couldn't you have helped him just this once? What harm would there have been in going along with this? You've never gone along with a damn thing."

The poet roared back at him so loudly that even the half-dead among us raised their heads from their bunks. "Don't you tell me what to do," yelled the poet. "I've seen your prize pupil go wild in the shop like all the others. He's smashed me and I've seen him smash you. You can argue that your young idiot is only following the lead of the other guards. Perhaps your Sheleen would say that 'boys will be boys,' but even a club wielded by a boy still maims. Who the hell are you to tell me that I should guide the same hand that during the day grips a rifle and at night holds a pencil!"

The professor's curses continued unabated as the poet returned to his bunk. He sat in silence, his back resting against the wall. The professor raced over to him, shouting more abuse into his ears. Sheleen walked over, placed his hand on the professor's arm, and led the shaken man back to the group. He told the grief-stricken teacher to come and sit with us and all would be well.

The professor sat in numbed silence: I doubt if any student had ever meant so much to him. He began sobbing, knowing that the soldier would never return.

I was glad to be rid of this intruder. My soul desperately needed the nights with Sheleen just to keep from sinking into oblivion. To me, the coma of the mind was far more devastating than the constant cold and hunger.

Little was said during the remaining minutes of the evening. Sheleen was strangely quiet. He looked tired and worn out. A word or two from him could have uplifted us. The silence was broken by the light sputtering out. We shook hands in the darkness, but on this night I did not feel the usual firm handshakes. The exhaustion from our souls had filtered down into our hands. For the very first time, Sheleen had not revived us. I wondered what would become of me if anything ever happened to him.

I made my way through the darkness to the bunk. The poet began even before I covered my body with the pile of coats. In his shrill, nasal voice he said, "This professor has gone beyond the bounds of simple madness."

"Enough has already been said," I replied. No doubt Sheleen would take the professor aside and all would be well again.

The poet did not stop. Finally I left my bunk and went to my window in search of some peace. Looking out, I found the tower light at the far end of the compound and tried to lose myself in its wandering beam. The pencil of light cut a swath through the fog that clung to the ground. The beam coursed through the compound in an aimless fashion with no semblance of a destination. I pictured some desolate guard sitting alone in his windswept tower.

Loneliness blanketed this entire place just like the fog. I heard the sound of the machine guns off in the distance. The window offered me nothing this night, and I returned to my bunk. The poet had been silenced at last by sleep. I had the desperate desire to talk to Sheleen, but I would never think of awakening him.

I knew that Avron was standing in his corner. The beam crossed him for a moment, outlining his swaying body. I could not tell whether he was praying to God or playing his violin. It did not matter. Either of these motions was equally futile.

I looked up and saw that my window had been commandeered by someone else. My pane of glass held a fascination for only one other person in the hut. We knew him only as "the artist." No one had ever heard this strange man utter a word. His sanity had long ago fallen victim to this place. He and his machine were permanent members of the central woodwind section of the orchestra. The spines he made weren't worth a damn.

At night he would take his bread from the food cart and go directly to his bed. The poet sensed that this was a gifted man and on many occasions had tried to taunt him out of his bunk. The poet's caustic words fell on deaf ears as the artist remained motionless, buried in his covers. He was immune even to the soft words of Sheleen. Only when the lights went out did this man at times choose to come alive. The ice-coated window was his canvas, and one of the spines served as his brush. He would stand silently before the window, patiently waiting for the passing tower light to illuminate his canvas. His hand came to life during the few seconds that the light struck the window. The sharp metal spine quickly etched a line into the icy film that covered the glass. With each sweep of the light, more and more of his picture took form. He showed no signs of impatience, even when the beam was absent for long periods.

What was created on the glass was always the same. Slowly, ever so slowly, the face of a woman came to life before my eyes. The face was neither happy nor sad—just displaying the serene look that only a very feminine woman can possess. Her large, soft eyes would loom out at me from the fragile canvas. The face was full and bore the look of life.

I would stare back at the elegant face silhouetted in the semidarkness. Every woman is at the pinnacle of her beauty in the tender glow of the night. I always had a desperate desire to touch the soft faces that the artist created, but I knew my hand would erase them forever. I watched carefully as he put in the finishing lines. I made ready to jump from my bunk to stop him before he wiped the window clean. Like no other artist in the world, this one had no interest in standing back to marvel at what he had created.

I grabbed his arm before his sleeve could obliterate my woman. He offered no resistance as I led him away from the window; he never did. I covered him in his coats and thanked him for the picture. Many times I had offered him charcoal from the bottom of the stove, just to draw on the wall. His silence was his refusal. Even a chunk of bread could not entice him to create a permanent painting for me.

With the artist asleep, the window and its woman were mine now. My gaze did not leave her. She was at the height of her beauty during the few seconds before the light reached the window and immediately afterward. I was beholden to the tower for its light just to gaze upon this picture. As the night continued, the face in the window began to vanish. Her outline faded as the etched lines filled with new layers of ice. By morning all trace of her would be gone as if she had never existed.

I sat on the side of my bunk, staring up at her as I nibbled on the last of my bread. Finally only a single rye seed remained in my mouth.

The distant sound of the violin suddenly came through the air. Instinctively I looked toward Avron's corner, but he must have been asleep. I heard the child for only a few moments more, and then his song was stilled.

I fell asleep, thinking that this had been a good night

after all. I had been allowed a brief taste of all that is meaningful to want from life—a serene woman, a child, and a piece of bread.

8 Under the glow of the light, Sheleen looked like an emaciated old man. In the past few days his exhausted face had become even more deeply lined. Everyone aged so quickly here. Each week in this place drained the years from our lives.

Every night more and more men made the pilgrimage to Sheleen's bunk. Most of them were recent arrivals whose clothes and bodies were in the first stages of disintegration; others were veterans whose rags now hung limply on their dried-up bodies.

Sheleen was someone who would listen. He would not turn his head away upon hearing the same stories again and again. No question was too insignificant for him. He would nod sympathetically and then tell each man of our unique existence. I never tired of hearing him.

The heavy odor of ammonia clung to Sheleen. Much of his day was now spent in the latrine with the new men while his machine was allowed to remain idle. The conductor had chosen Sheleen to welcome the new arrivals to the orchestra. Sheleen accepted this unexpected opportunity with relish.

As always, Verbin recorded their numbers and then their heads were shaved. I was struck repeatedly by the dazed expressions on these men after the conductor had scalped them. They returned from the dock with the look of absolute defeat carved in their faces. The conductor even shaved the bald men, making certain that not a solitary hair survived.

Next, the red cap led the shorn men to Sheleen's bench, where a smile from him would soften their look of despair. Sheleen would hold out his hand, and it would be as eagerly grasped as a lifeline thrown to a drowning man. Together they would walk out of the shop to the latrine, a fitting place for one to learn the harsh details of life in the camp.

The conductor stood patiently by the door, awaiting their return. I knew that the longer the visit lasted, the better the chances were for the man's survival in this place. Amidst the acrid fumes, the new man would hear the basic rudiments of Sheleen's philosophy; here he would have the first of his many questions answered. Here he would learn to his amazement that a man such as Sheleen existed.

Sometimes the visits were very brief, meaning that the master could do little with the man. On one occasion Sheleen returned to the shop alone. The conductor raced over to his machine and they spoke for a few moments. Avron was then sent to the latrine to see what miracles the fear of God could work on the new man.

Sheleen seemed to thrive after the long visits in the latrine. He would return to his bench filled with new life, and even his machine sang out. Soon the entire bass section would follow. I, too, would try to pick up their exuberant rhythm.

A few of Sheleen's sessions ended in disaster. The sound of the tower's guns meant that the new man wanted no part of our world. The tower could always be counted on as a quick way out of here. The pounding of the guns brought a look of fear to Verbin's face. Seeing this, the conductor's mood turned black, and he would follow Sheleen back to his bench, yelling curses into his ears. The bass section would roar their machines to drown out the red cap's swearing and drive him away from their leader. The conductor would slink off and return to stand angrily beside the now placid Verbin.

The bonds that Sheleen forged in the latrine were further strengthened during the evenings in our hut. On one night the line waiting for Sheleen had formed even before we returned from the food cart. The pediatrician from

Torin was standing before Sheleen as he had many times before with the same problem. He wrang his hands in despair, pleading for answers to his dilemma.

The guard Paolo had suddenly begun favoring the pediatrician. Paolo was one of the soldiers detailed to watch over the night food cart. We would line up in front of our huts and await the bounty of the cart as it made its regular rounds. In single file we would pass the cart and be given our ration of rye bread and soup.

About a week before, Paolo had begun poking the prisoner who ladled out the soup to signify that the doctor's portion should be dredged up from the depths of the steaming cauldron. The bottom of the huge container was the hiding place of the potatoes, vegetables, and bits of stuff that we hoped might be meat.

Neither the doctor nor Sheleen could fathom this turn of events or even decide if it was to be considered good fortune. Not even Sheleen knew why the doctor had been singled out for this kindness. To know a guard's benevolence was unheard of. At best, we all hoped to be treated with equal indifference.

At first the pediatrician was sure that he had never seen Paolo before, but the continued richness of his soup made him uncertain. Perhaps before the war Paolo's father had been a diplomat stationed in Torin and he had treated the man's son. He soon became positive that he remembered ministering to a sick child who now resembled this grown-up soldier. It must have been during the great typhus epidemic.

This explanation was not to satisfy the pediatrician for long. He then struck upon the idea that he must have lived near Paolo during his medical school years. Perhaps Paolo was the child who used to run errands for him. He had always rewarded the boy handsomely.

I watched the deterioration of this doctor who, in the midst of sudden plenty, was now more miserable than ever before. He was aware that to be chosen for special favors would make him stand out from the rest of us, and this could bring the other guards down on him. To blend in with the group was everyone's goal. The guards could strike out like a pack of wolves at a lone straggler. On the other hand, he feared the consequences of Paolo's anger if he were to refuse the extra rations.

Sheleen had advised him repeatedly to accept what fate had bestowed upon him and forget the evils and uncertainties of the world. The vagaries of the outside were just not worth dwelling on.

On this night the pediatrician was more distraught than ever. The extra rations had suddenly ended. Paolo no longer poked the ladler; in fact, the soldier now totally ignored the doctor.

I had become accustomed to hearing the wailing of the pediatrician each night, but now I, too, became uneasy at this change in events. None of us liked a sudden deviation in any established routine.

The doctor begged Sheleen to tell him what he had done wrong. He didn't wait for an answer but cried out, "I was never forward with Paolo. At first I did nothing when I got the soup. Then I bowed my head a little. Just a little bow. Do you think this embarrassed him? Maybe he wanted me to give him something, but what could I possibly have given him? I have nothing. I never said thank you—that's it, I should have thanked him. Why didn't you tell me to thank him? Perhaps I should have asked him about the health of his father, the diplomat."

Sheleen did not voice what must have been obvious: The guard didn't want to waste any more food on a man who looked so near death.

The doctor screamed out to Sheleen, "I live with enough plagues. Why must I be burdened with another?"

Even if Sheleen had an answer, he had no chance to say a word. The conductor had barged into the hut suddenly, leading some wretch by the arm. I had never seen the red cap in here before. He shoved everyone aside, including the pediatrician, and stood before Sheleen. The man he held looked ready to collapse.

As always, the conductor came quickly to the point. "Sheleen, I want you to do something with this bastard. He has it in his head that he wants to run to the tower. Verbin's had enough of this. The tower has got to be quiet! Change his mind, or if you can't, get Avron to do it. Where's Avron?" The conductor scanned the shadowy figures in the hut until he was satisfied that he spotted Avron standing in his corner. "This tower business has got to stop!" he said in his nervous manner. "Do something with him!"

Sheleen rose slowly from his bunk and unlocked the conductor's grip on the man's arm. "I will talk to this man," he said, "but not with you in here. Leave us alone."

As the conductor approached the door, the silence was broken by the poet sneering after him, "How good of you to visit us. You must come more often." The red cap did not look around as he left the hut, but I knew that no one could ever mistake the owner of that voice.

Once again the pediatrician began reciting his entire story of the soup. Sheleen cut him off in midsentence and told him to go to bed.

Under the light I finally recognized the man whom the conductor had dragged in. It was the tailor from San Vincente who until recently had been a part of the orchestra's tympani section. In the past week he had retreated into the central woodwind area. At one time he had been a regular visitor to our evening sessions.

Sheleen beckoned the tailor to sit beside him on the bunk. The man was ashen; he was obviously sick. Both men looked down at the floor as if waiting for the other to talk first. The tailor opened his mouth a few times before actually speaking. "I know that you do not approve of what

I'm going to do, but I'm sick and spitting up blood. I've got only a day or so before I'm checked off. I want to die in my own way. I don't want to wait in the hut for the guards to come and slowly kill me off. You can understand this, can't you?" The tailor looked up at the rest of us as if seeking some sign of approval. He must have known that he had touched on something that we feared more than anything else. Everyone hoped that when his final day came he would simply drop dead, or be so comatose that his mind would not feel the blows of the guards smashing into his body.

Sheleen remained silent as the tailor spoke again. "I have been with you many times before when we talked of such things. I am a simple man, but I have understood you. I know you said that we cannot kill our own men when they are near death. I agree with you. If we killed each other, we would be no better than animals. I understand that if we are to live a noble life, our hands must be kept clean of the blood of our brothers. All I ask now is that you not pass judgment on me for what I'm about to do. Just leave me be so that I can go to the tower in peace. I know that I have disappointed you, but at least give me your hand and say good-bye to me. You have given me so much. I am so tired and I can't go on anymore. Just give me your hand and let me go."

I had never seen tears well up in Sheleen's eyes before this night. He held out his hand and together the two men stood up. Only the word "good-bye" came from Sheleen's lips.

The tailor walked slowly toward Avron. The violinist turned away from the man and stared out the window. Seeing this, the tailor stopped several bunks away and said, "I do not expect a man such as you who still believes in God to forgive me. What I am about to do is a sin against Heaven. I once had a wife and children and parents. I ask only that you say a prayer in memory of their lives. I myself have done this every day since they were taken from me. This has been my only contact with God. I ask only for you to add them to your list. I know that you cannot say anything for me, and I expect nothing."

The tailor hesitated a moment and then walked over to Avron. He put his hand gently on the stooped shoulder of the man gazing out the window. In a barely audible voice the tailor said, "You know, I have always envied the love you have for the little boy with the violin. You are a fortunate man. I hope that you have him with you all of your days. We all know what the pain is like to outlive our children. For your sake, I hope you don't outlive this new child of yours."

The tailor walked quickly away and headed toward the door. Avron did not turn around but threw his entire body into his prayers. Even before the tailor reached the door, the hut had emptied of all of this night's visitors. Everyone wanted to be lost in the safety of his bunk before the guns of the tower exploded.

The poet stood by the door as the tailor approached. "Listen to me," the poet begged. "If you're going, why not try to get through the wire? Go quietly and don't yell like those other idiots. What do you have to lose?"

"Where would I go?" answered the tailor. "I don't have the strength to run. When they caught me, they'd take it out on the rest of you. I'll leave going through the wire to you. Don't ask me to do what you won't do yourself."

For once, the poet was silent.

The tailor walked out into the night and, after a few moments of machine-gun fire, the tower was content.

There were no further questions of Sheleen that evening. The light went out, and I tried to find some peace in the cold of my bunk. I realized that even though we lived off the inner strength of Sheleen, he would not always be enough to sustain everyone. I knew that suicide would be a regular part of our daily lives. The voracious tower could always be counted upon to deliver anyone from this place.

Running to the tower was the most popular way out. Sometimes the tower did not notice, and it had become the custom to scream up at them and attract their attention. A burst of gunfire would then pierce the stillness of the night. The sound of each bullet cut through my soul like an ice pick.

Everything changed the night after the tailor's journey to the tower. The one area of certainty in our lives came to an abrupt end. From my window I watched the man from hut number three racing to the tower. He stood under it, cursing up into the night. The beam framed him in a circle of light, but the guns were silent.

The soldiers climbed down from the tower like black spiders descending from a web. The man tried to retreat back to his hut, but they caught him and beat him almost senseless. Finally the soldiers stopped and watched as he crawled slowly back through the mud to his hut.

I knew that from then on the tower had nothing to offer us. The guns roared on each night in the other compounds, but in ours there was only silence.

The nights went on as before for Sheleen and his long line of questioners. In time, the pediatrician found the peace he so desperately desired. He learned that Paolo was now similarly favoring a judge from the next hut with soup from the bottom of the cauldron. It then dawned on our doctor why he had been spurned by the guard. The richness of his soup had ended the day he traded his cap with the earflaps to the judge for a pair of gloves. The judge, upon learning the meaning of the hat, decided that the rich soup was not worth being singled out by a guard. The judge even offered to return the cap to the pediatrician. Together they decided to dump the hat in the nearest stove. The pediatrician's deep depression evaporated and was replaced by a rare euphoria.

For a time we were intrigued by Paolo's strange fascination with the hat. Naturally we were never to learn what memories it held for him.

9

I think there was the sound of a crash at first, but it was the screaming that must actually have awakened me. There was wild confusion throughout the hut. I knew in an instant that the end had finally come. I buried my head under the covers so I wouldn't have to witness the frenzied rampage of the guards. The screaming continued. I had always known that they would choose the dead of night to finish us off. They could smash us to pieces in our bunks. It would be easier than trying to shoot a moving target. My heart pounded as I awaited the coming of their blows.

Above the screams, I heard someone yell out that Sheleen was hurt. It all made sense; the guards knew what he meant to us, and now they had come to kill him.

I ripped the blankets away and raced down the darkened aisle in the direction of his bunk and all the screaming. I crashed into men and bunks as I tried to get to Sheleen. We could not let them take him from us.

Suddenly a match was struck, and I was able to make out Sheleen being helped to his feet. I looked around, but there were no guards anywhere.

The screaming still came from a man lying on the floor. No one showed any concern for him as he writhed back and forth in pain. All I heard were men asking Sheleen if he was all right.

I looked at Sheleen and could not believe what I saw. There was little doubt about what he had tried to do; he wore the evidence of his suicide attempt coiled around his neck like a scarf. The frayed rope dangled from his neck, almost touching the floor. I stared at the worn rope in total disbelief—suicide was not for a Sheleen but only for lesser men. Fortunately for us, a philosopher cannot tie a decent knot.

Sheleen had a bewildered expression on his face that I had never seen before. Looking at the weeping man on the floor, I realized that Sheleen's attempt had resulted only in his falling onto this prisoner.

Another precious match illuminated Sheleen's unintended victim. It was the writer from Anselm, who clutched at his limp right arm crying out that it was broken. "How can I run a machine with a broken arm?" he screamed.

We tried to lead Sheleen back to his bunk, but he brushed us away. He knelt down beside the writer and apologized to him for what he had done. Tenderly Sheleen tried to move the wounded arm. The arm was gently manipulated in all directions, and then slowly, on its own, it seemed to function again. Sheleen and the writer embraced when it was certain that the arm was unbroken. Had there been brandy, there would have been a toast of thanksgiving to the arm. A faint smile came over Sheleen's face. I feared the smile had more to do with the restoration of the writer's arm than Sheleen's relief in failing at suicide.

In the darkness, we led Sheleen back to his bunk and covered him with his coats. I wanted to untie the rope from his neck but feared that this might shame him even more. I longed to talk to him, but I remained silent; there was nothing I could have said that would not have come originally from his own lips.

I remained at his side until I was certain that he had fallen asleep. Then I groped my way through the darkness to my own bunk. My bed was cold and I lay there completely devastated. Sheleen had fashioned a home for us in this wilderness, and now with his rope he had tried to pull down all that he had created. We were devout in his new religion, but now he of all people was a doubter. I knew we could not breathe without his lungs.

I could not understand what had gone wrong in our

unique little world. I knew that the poet was still awake and asked him what he thought of Sheleen's strange act. He was quiet for a moment, and I was sorry I had said anything to him even before he spoke. "I never talk to any man about his mistress while she is still in favor." Fortunately, he said no more.

I lay in my bunk trying to remember exactly what had gone on during this night's meeting with Sheleen. More men came to him now than before. There were the usual questions, but there was also Sheleen's irritation with the banker from Margen. The frown on his face was something I had never seen before.

One of the men in hut five said he had actually witnessed the incident that now so troubled the banker. It was during the morning shift two days ago that a guard stood aimlessly alongside the banker's machine. A long cigarette jutted from from his mouth as he fumbled in his pocket for a match. Suddenly, before it was even lit, the soldier pulled the cigarette from his lips and flung it on the banker's bench. In an instant the guard raced down the aisle and smashed at one of the cellists who had fallen asleep at his bench.

Rather than return for his cigarette, the soldier sauntered off toward a stove and fell asleep.

As he told us later, the banker's first thought on seeing an unsmoked cigarette was that once again he was a rich man. A full cigarette could buy possibly two days' worth of bread—perhaps even three. He wasn't sure, for no one had ever found a whole cigarette before.

All morning long the banker waited for the soldier to return. On two separate occasions the guard actually walked right by his bench with the cigarette in plain sight. The soldier never stopped.

Thinking the guard might return at any time, the banker did not dare move the cigarette. It rested in the position normally reserved for his right hand while he controlled the speed of the machine, and he had great difficulty operating the cutter at its usual rhythm. He feared that Verbin would soon notice the machine's erratic behavior and check him off.

By the next day, he began to fear that one of us would steal the cigarette, and then there would be nothing when the guard finally came to reclaim what was his. He started racing to his bench the second we were allowed into the shop and was the last to leave at the end of each shift. The cigarette remained. The guard continued his aimless wanderings.

Naturally the banker discussed this with Sheleen each night. Sheleen asked, "Has the guard smoked since he threw the cigarette on your bench?"

"Yes, Sheleen, he has. They all do. They smoke constantly, every one of them. But, Sheleen, what should I do? Should I move to another bench?"

Sheleen's voice was filled with fatigue. "Would you, if you were a guard, just give something a throw if it was of value to you?"

"But, Sheleen, a full cigarette is worth two days' bread. Cigarettes are rationed even for the guards. I know they're rationed. But, Sheleen, what do you think? Should I put the cigarette on the next empty bench? I don't know what to do. You've told us how to live, but you've never said anything about a situation like this."

Sheleen sat slumped on his bunk. "How long have you been coming to our group?" he asked the banker who knelt on one knee before him.

"I've been coming from the day I arrived. You told me to come. You remember, don't you? It was in the latrine that first day. I've been with you almost every night." He paused a moment. "I've missed a few times, but you know that was when I had the dysentery. I think I've been here about four weeks, Sheleen. Yes, at least four weeks. I've learned much from you. You know that. You have given me..."

Sheleen actually interrupted him. "Tell me, what did you do before you came here?" His tone was devoid of its usual warmth.

The banker's voice rose with a certain pride and he spoke so all of us could hear. "I owned factories, Sheleen. My father left me with one, and through the years the business grew until I had plants in four different countries. I was considered a very successful man in those days, Sheleen. But from you I have learned the meaning of peace. You know I have been a faithful pupil. But tell me what I should do about the cigarette. Just say the word, Sheleen, and I will do it."

"How many men did you have under you in those days?" asked Sheleen.

The banker thought for a moment. "Before the end came, I must have had about four thousand people working for me in the four countries, but I'm not sure. I didn't spend much time with such details in those days. I had . . . but what of my problem, Sheleen? Just say the word."

Sheleen seemed lost in a trance. I waited for him to say something—either to tell the man what to do or at least lash out at him and make him shut up. Finally he spoke, but all he said was, "Let us end this evening. We will talk again tomorrow."

I was unable to sleep; the sight of Sheleen with the noose around his neck continued to tear through my mind. I lay awake, hoping that he had experienced only a momentary period of doubt. Soon all of this would be forgotten and he would continue on and so would we. The thought of the cigarette continued to run through my head. I kept wondering if such a thing as a cigarette had had a part in bringing down a kingdom.

By the next morning, everyone in the compound knew of Sheleen's attempt. Their disbelief was profound. A sorrow settled over the entire orchestra as the machines sang out a mournful dirge.

I could no longer sit still. Taking a chunk of scrap in my hand, I walked over to the banker's bench. I shoved his hand aside and smashed the steel down on the long cigarette. Two more blows left only shreds of garbage that were brushed over the side into the canister. The banker glanced quickly at the original owner of the cigarette who was sleeping peacefully in the corner, and then he looked up at me. A big smile crossed his miserable face as he said, "Thank you. Thank you."

I grabbed his collar and yelled into his ear, "Listen, you son of a bitch, don't ever ask Sheleen another question."

Men on their way to the latrine came to Sheleen's bench with offerings of bread. With his head down, he silently accepted their bits of rye and placed these gifts of thanksgiving in his pocket.

Partway through the morning, I saw the conductor go over to Sheleen. I could tell by the foul look on the red cap's face that he was yelling at Sheleen about his try with the rope. The conductor raged on. His monkeylike face was filled with contempt for this saddened man. Sheleen looked like a new prisoner who had just had his head shaved.

The conductor suddenly grabbed Sheleen by the arm and lifted him up from his bench. As the two of them headed for the latrine, the orchestra screamed out in agony with a screech so loud that Verbin and the guards were roused from their sleep.

No one had ever grabbed Sheleen before. Somehow even the guards seemed to know that this was no ordinary man. They had rarely trifled with him on their rampages.

Knowing Sheleen as I did, I could see that this was a changed man. His step was now slowed, and above all his eyes had lost their life. I watched as he came to resemble the rest of us; the metamorphosis was unsettling. My own spirit began to crumble as I beheld the disintegration of his soul.

That night, after the food cart had gone, we gathered together and agreed to go to Sheleen's bunk as if nothing had happened. Instead of his standing there as always to greet us, we found him hidden in his bunk. His body was still alive, but he appeared to be lying in state. His unblinking eyes gazed upward at the roof beam that had failed to grasp the rope firmly during his try at death.

This particular beam was unique in its own right. It was a beautifully hand-carved piece of oak that in a better age must have adorned a fine home. How it came to serve to bear the weight of this hovel was lost in the past. On its sides, carved in high relief, were clumps of grapes and vines. One could almost pluck out each solitary grape. I had seen Sheleen climb up to the beam and carefully clean the soot and dirt from each crevice. He had often referred to this one jewel in our midst as our frieze from the Parthenon.

We were still congregated around him, but Sheleen remained oblivious. One did not cross-examine a Sheleen, but finally the doctor from Rivos broke the silence and humbly asked the question that haunted each of us: "What has happened to change everything?" Sheleen slowly rose up out of his blankets and sat on the edge of the bunk. He leaned forward and supported the weight of his head in his bony hands. Now his eyes were fixed on the floor. He remained silent—perhaps hoping we would disappear.

He looked up slowly and appeared surprised at the size of the audience that had gathered around him. His voice seemed hoarse and I had to strain to hear him. "You know, I am now a stranger in what was once this special world that we created together. Go to sleep, all of you, I have no further answers left in me. I have done you a great injustice. You must now try to find your own answers to your own questions. Look at me. I am sucked dry. I have no answers. I do not even have any questions left in me."

He sank back into his bunk and stared up again at his

beloved beam. We continued our silent vigil over his body. He spoke again, but what he said seemed directed more to the beam than to any of us. "I just want to be free of my memories. I'm tired of the cold and the hunger and, above all, the lice. I can't stand these little beasts that are always draining the life from me. I can't stand the looks of the guards anymore. There's no room in my mind to wonder how long they will keep me. I don't have the strength to make my machine sing for these throwbacks from the Dark Ages. I cannot fashion any more answers for your questions. I am now afraid. When fear clutters the mind, no room remains for a creative thought. So many have died. So many books were never written. So many songs were never sung. So much that could have been will never be." He stopped for a moment, then pleaded, "Please let me sleep. Go to sleep."

The others walked away slowly. A cloud of remorse hung heavily over everyone's head.

I stared down at his parchment-like skin that outlined the contours of every bone in his skull. He and I were finally alone together. He looked up at me and said, "I so wanted to forge a brotherhood of men out of the ruins of these lost souls. Instead, I created a race of sniveling children. I tried so hard. You know that, don't you?"

Taking his hand, I said, "You have given us more than you can ever imagine. Please try to understand this. Surely at least you know that those around you live longer. Everyone has his doubts. You yourself have said this." I knew I was not breaking through his trance. With my other hand on his shoulder, I shook him. "Sheleen, listen to me, you have given us life!"

"But what kind of life have I given you?" he said. "It has been no life at all." He released his hand from mine. "I must atone for what I have done. You must know what I have done to you. Now, my brother, I must say good-bye."

I left him alone and walked slowly back to my bunk.

Surrounding myself in my coats and blankets was not enough to keep out the bitter cold and loneliness. As I had done many times before, I fixed my gaze up at the flickering light bulb and, with constant staring, tried to blur out my eyes and brain with its glare. This time the feeble glow of the light was not strong enough to erase my mind. I could no longer understand him. Perhaps he, too, had gone mad like so many of the others, but still I could not conceive of a Sheleen being struck down by such a common malady as madness.

The hut was silent; even the coughing was muted. Those who were alive, and even the half-dead, kept their gaze in the direction of Sheleen's bunk.

A few minutes later the quiet was broken by the scraping sound of the table being dragged across the uneven floor. It was Sheleen, positioning the table under the carved beam.

I sprang partway up from my bunk, but the poet grabbed my coat and shoved me back down. "Don't do anything foolish," he said. "Let him go. This is his will. Don't intrude yourself on a dead man's death."

In a quizzical manner the poet then asked, "You really don't understand what he's been doing to all of you, do you? This Sheleen of yours has been telling you bedtime stories so you wouldn't fear the night. I have learned that no one can keep the night from coming in and strangling us. Now the night is about to consume Sheleen."

I wanted to rip into the poet, but I did not. I just sat there.

The table was now centered exactly under the beam. Sheleen, who seemed to have found new strength, went about his preparations methodically. The long rope appeared from under one of his coats, and his fingers deftly tied the knot that created the noose. His thin fingers now moved with the facility of one well experienced in such arts.

With his work-stained hands, he went through the motions of cleaning the top of the table. Chunks of bread, once presented to him in celebration of his living, were deposited on a corner of the table. I had never seen any man here possess so much bread at one time. His tin cup, filled with the now congealed soup, was placed next to the bread.

The silence was broken by someone whispering, "Quickly, one of us must get the conductor." No one moved other than Avron, who turned his back on these proceedings. His head began rhythmically bobbing up and down as he recited one of his million prayers that must have been especially composed for such an occasion.

Time seemed to stand still as we watched. For once, a smirk did not cover the poet's face. All eyes were on the tragedy unfolding before us that no one could stop.

With great difficulty the frail man hoisted himself up onto the table and then stood erect. He reached upward, and his hands fondled the meandering ridges and furrows of the carved beam that he loved. The end of the rope was carefully tied around the beam and tested several times to make certain it would not fail him again.

The full impact of what I was witnessing struck me when he placed the noose around his thin neck. Avron's praying took on a frenzy, and the pediatrician began to cry. Everyone was absorbed in the last details of this catastrophe. The only nonparticipant was the pianist from Salonka, who must have died quietly sometime this evening. Even the artist had crawled out from under his rags to peer vacantly at the man on the table.

Standing there, Sheleen now looked imposing. The beautiful beam, the tattered rope, the frail man, and the old table fused themselves into an awe-inspiring monument.

From his commanding position atop the table, Sheleen gazed around the hut. As he spoke I was amazed to hear that the strength of old had returned to his voice. "You have come before me in the past for my help, and now I come before you for your help. I have given freely to you, and now I ask you to give to me. You can see that my soul is stone dead. Why else would I have a rope around my neck? My spirit has gone, and before you is a lost body. A body is nothing without a soul."

He looked around to see if his words were registering on his wretched audience. Perhaps he thought not, for he began to speak louder. "You can see that I am dead already. I have never lied to you before, and if I tell you I am dead then you know I am speaking the truth. My body wishes to join its departed soul."

The fire of old had returned to him, even though the tight cord around his neck seemed to limit the gesturing motions of his arms. "My dead body stands before you unburied. None of you was brought up to let a dead body rot out in the open. All I ask of you is just to push the table and allow my body to join my soul. It will be a simple act of mercy. There will be no blood on your hands. The God of old would have blessed you for such an act. I only ask of you what I failed to do myself. Come, rise up," he commanded.

He fell silent. His hollow eyes peered into the faces that still gazed at him in a dumbstruck fashion. Slowly his eyes made the rounds of the bunks. They were heading for me, and I looked to the floor to shield myself from his stare. I looked up moments later, but his piercing eyes were still fixed on me. I turned my head to seek the safety of my window. Fortunately, when I peered over at him again, his gaze had passed on.

No one moved; no one answered his plea. I felt numb. Maybe I should do this for him, but I could not make my body move. Perhaps one had to ask Sheleen for his advice before acting on anything. If only there were two Sheleens. Then I could ask the first if he agreed that I should push the table out from under the second.

Then his face came alive where only moments before there had been the look of utter hopelessness. He pointed down at the bread and soup that lay at his feet. "Look, my brothers, at this feast piled up before you. What does a dead man need with bread and soup? I know you are starving. There hasn't been a single day since you came here when your gnawing stomachs haven't cried out for more food. Bread is the currency of this realm, and before you is a treasure. Whoever pushes the table can have the bread. It will be a simple transaction devoid of any sentiment. I will get what I want, and one of you will fall asleep tonight free of hunger."

His voice now seemed to cut through our atrophied wills. There was a stirring. All eyes were on the beautiful mound of bread. "Come, one of you, rise up and take the bread. You know how it will taste. It is yours anyway. Most of it came from you, and now I am only returning it."

What had been a momentary stir in the audience died down to nothing. Sheleen shook his head and was silent. The soft chanting of Avron's prayers could be heard coming from his corner. Sheleen finally spoke. "Please help me. Don't let me stand here all night just to face the guards in the morning. We have been brothers. When the guards finish with me, all that will be left will be pools of blood. You will walk through my blood and your feet will stick to the floor. Wherever you go, my blood will remain stuck to you. My blood will cling to you forever."

The pleas of this man began cutting through me. His voice tore into me like someone scratching a fingernail deeply into a chalkboard. He stared at me, but I knew a brother could not kill a brother. This Abel wanted me to be his Cain.

Sheleen looked suddenly away from me and turned toward Avron's corner. I saw some man look furtively around and then, seeing no other signs of life, raise from his bunk and slowly walk toward Sheleen. Even though the noose was wound snugly around his neck, Sheleen still managed a broad smile.

I knew nothing of this would-be assistant other than that he had been a recent disciple of Sheleen's. He had never uttered a word in our sessions but had only listened. Until this night, the red roots on his shaven head had been his only distinguishing characteristic.

On his platform, Sheleen dwarfed the assistant who seemed to be waiting for some command, but none was forthcoming. This little man gazed greedily at his wages on the table at the feet of the master. He picked up the pieces of bread, and in the light they gleamed more brilliantly than the carved beam.

The assistant climbed up on the table and stared at the doomed man. Nothing was said as they stood together. Surprisingly, he offered a piece of bread to Sheleen, and it was quickly engulfed. Chunk after chunk was devoured by Sheleen and made safe passage past the constricting rope around his neck. Soon Sheleen had consumed all the bread. Then he pointed down to the soup, and his wish was granted. He drained the cup in such haste that precious globs of congealed soup ran down the sides of his chin and splattered on the floor.

The assistant peered once again into his eyes and asked, pleading, if he could untie the rope and help him down. I could not understand Sheleen's garbled reply; his mouth was still filled with food. He pointed to the table. Finally we all heard him speak. "Please shove the table."

The assistant descended from the heights but did not look up again. My compatriots climbed into their bunks and buried their heads in their rags.

The sound of the table grinding against the floor was followed by a gurgling noise from Sheleen's throat. I could hear the hollow banging as his arms struck his chest. Then there was nothing. The light went out soon afterward; we were plunged into total darkness.

10 I stand by my window, watching the dancing light from the tower reach out into the far corners of the compound. My gaze is drawn back to Sheleen's hanging body again and again. In the past I had tried never to peer into an open coffin, preferring to remember the dead when they were alive. The increasing light of the dawn shines on Sheleen's swollen blue face. I try to recall him as he was in life, but I cannot.

The artist shows no desire to take over the window and paint. I crave one of his beautiful faces. He shoves my hand away when I try to awaken him. I don't have the energy to pull him out of his bunk and make him draw on the window.

I feel as lost as the day I came to this place. I realize now that just knowing Sheleen was nearby helped me fall asleep. His hanging body offers no such solace.

The silence is broken by Avron reciting the ancient prayer for the dead. He stands before the body in the shadows. His hands seem to hold a nonexistent prayer book as he softly sings this dirge that has become our camp song. As with his violin, everything that fills Avron's hands resides only in his imagination.

When he finishes his prayers, he looks up in silence at Sheleen. Of all the men, only these two tried to give us an answer to this place. Few listened to Avron and his stories about the Almighty. Avron has outlasted Sheleen, but I know there is not the look of the victor on his face. I thank him for giving the final rites to this man who had always spurned God.

"Who am I to judge anyone," he says. "At first I would not say a prayer for a suicide. One night I heard the machine guns and said the prayer for the dead. The next day I found out that my prayers had been recited for a dog that had strayed too near the wire. Since that time, when a man dies, I say the prayer that any man deserves at death. I never tell anyone that I do this, for if I did, perhaps more would try to take their own lives. Who am I to pass a verdict on a man in times like these?"

I thank him once again.

"You know," he says, "it is strange. Men spend their entire day cursing God, and just before they are to die they want His blessing. Before coming here I was not a very religious man, but for some reason my faith increased while most of the rest of you lost yours. I don't understand this; perhaps I never will."

He pauses for a moment. "Your Sheleen was a decent man. He must have been magnificent on the outside. I am just a mere man reciting by rote a prayer to God. I say the prayers every time the guns go off, but I must confess something to you. Now the prayers are not only for the dead men. I plead to God that the bullets have not cut down the little boy. You heard him tonight, didn't you?" I nod that I did. "He will return, and you will see that God is within this child and the world has not been forgotten."

I am still drawn to Sheleen. His body sways from the end of the rope almost imperceptibly, as if touched gently by an unfelt breeze. I reach up and wipe away the globules of soup that stain his chin.

I stand before him and also try to say the prayers for the dead. I still know the words, but I cannot make myself utter them. I have only questions. I whisper up into his stone-deaf ears and ask, "Why have you done this to us? If you had to leave us, why couldn't you have died like everyone else of starvation and pneumonia? Why couldn't you have waited a little longer? Then at least we would have had a martyr to revere. We could have dwelled on your last words and recited them over and over as long as we lived.

When our time came to die, we would pass your message on to others so they would have known of you and the peace you brought."

I hear a harshness in my voice that I have never used with him before. "Why have you left us with nothing? How can we revere a man whose last words were, 'Please shove the table'? If you knew you were going to die, why did you eat your own bread and your own soup just like an animal!" I feel as though I want to strike out at him.

"What more do you want from him?" asks the poet. "I'm sure you have no idea in the world why he went through what he did tonight. Did it ever cross your mind that he could have jumped off the table in the middle of the night?" He places his hand on my shoulder and speaks softly, "You're just an ordinary man like the rest of the fools on this earth. You're always creating gods. As always, sooner or later your gods disappoint you and then you feel devastated. You spend your lives going from one god to another, always searching, but in the end the outcome is always the same." Gently he takes me by the arm and leads me to my bunk. "Go to bed, my friend, and get some sleep. To live, you must sleep, and here sleeping is the best part of living."

I sit on my bunk. I have neither the energy nor the words to answer him.

11 The light of day filters
through the windows. With the help of several men, Sheleen's body is freed from its rope. Great care is taken not
to stress the frayed cord further. It is secreted on top of the
carved beam, and, even though nothing is said, we all
know that it is now common property to be used by anyone
who desires it.

Sheleen's cold body is placed gently on his bunk. Hanging men are always taken down and put to bed. Everyone
fears the wrath of the guards if they were to discover a
hanging man. A violent storm might come down on our
heads if they were to learn that we failed to prevent the
destruction of a piece of their property. Our captors, however, readily accept our deaths without emotion if our
final end comes from starvation or their bullets.

Sheleen's remains are left intact. On this sorrowful occasion no one comes to appropriate his blankets or his
coats. Many of the men file by his bunk in silence to pay
their last respects; a few even recite a prayer for the dead.

I start toward his bunk with the same prayer on my lips
again. His bread flashes through my mind. Standing over
him, I realize that I am mouthing not the prayer for the
dead but the prayer before the bread. I do not finish the
prayer but turn away from him and walk outside into the
bitter cold.

The usual rows of shivering men stand in lines before
their huts. Their eyes are fixed on the emptiness of the
ground where Sheleen had always stood. I watch the anger
well up in the face of the red cap as he stares at the void
in our front row. None of us ever spoke during these line-
ups, but on this frozen morning the silence is more severe
than ever.

The sullen, half-asleep guard methodically records the

hole in our front line that had always contained Sheleen. Little does this soldier realize, as he makes his check mark, that our Golden Age has come to an end.

On this morning I march to the shop as if in a daze. Our four-abreast formation is still most precise. The man of the book, our commandant, watches today, and I know that with him present, the guards will lash out at anyone not in step. While we trudge on, I wonder why they expect perfect marching from men considered unfit to inhabit the earth.

As we enter the shop, each man must pass Sheleen's old bench, but no one claims it for his own. Verbin stands by the main switch, ready to pull the lever and breathe life into his machines. This man's fat face is always filled with the look of happiness.

Everyone is seated and the switch is pulled, but the machines bang up and down without direction. There is no rhythm. I realize now that it was Sheleen who set the tempo for our orchestra that even the musicians followed. Men stare at each other as if not knowing what to do. Only the dead ones in the woodwind section pound away in their usual discordant fashion. They are too far gone anyway to follow anyone's lead. The artist hammers away as always with the same faraway expression on his face.

Verbin knows instantly that something is wrong. The abundant folds of skin on his face constrict in a frown. He peers over at the conductor, whose eyes are fixed on Sheleen's empty bench.

The red cap races over and talks excitedly to Verbin. The black book comes out of Verbin's pocket, and they begin to march up and down the aisles. The conductor points to the black book as the two of them stop before each machine. Verbin's smile returns as his machines, one by one, roar off singing in near-perfect pitch.

The monkey and his master approach my machine. "Keep that tempo and never forget it," screams the conductor. They make the rounds of the orchestra but waste little time in the center. No threat on earth could ever make those men play in tune.

All morning the machines clang away, a slow, mournful song. The conductor stands in front of the orchestra smashing his fist up and down to guide our hammering. Still, no one has taken Sheleen's seat. His bass section has lost its old rhythm. Only the musicians follow in time to the conductor's beats. By the noon break the orchestra has regained some semblance of its usual rhythm.

We march out of the shop and head for the huts to await the noon food cart. Six or eight guards from the shop stand in the middle of our path and block the way. Since this day is not so cold, they play games with us. Our column is forced to detour around them and pass alongside the latrine. The contents of the latrine have oozed into the mud we must now march through.

The guards' eyes search out the weakest among us, and their rifle butts knock men into the slime. I straighten up, hoping they will leave me alone. The loss of Sheleen has thrown me into enough anguish that I doubt if I would have the strength to pull myself out of the mud.

The artist is flung into the filth. He, perhaps, is the most defenseless of all of us. We are not allowed to help him up. Slowly this bewildered man frees himself from the muck. The soldiers walk away; they've had their exercise for the morning. I hear the poet screech out at the professor from Steiden, "Ah, yes, Professor, boys will be boys." The professor has never been the same since his favorite pupil, the letter writer, stopped coming to our hut.

Occasionally Verbin would watch our exodus, and when he did, the guards were good boys. How I wished the fat little man's stare could have protected us each time we left the shop. We begged the conductor to tell Verbin what havoc was wreaked upon us, but nothing ever changed.

The noon food cart has come and gone. I nibble away on

my bread with some of the others. As if by habit, we congregate around Sheleen's bunk. No one utters a word.

The door opens and a man meekly steps into the hut. I know this is Sheleen's replacement. He whispers, "I am looking for the bunk of the man known as Sheleen." He is directed toward us. The writer from Anselm points, and the new man sits on the empty bunk.

At first the replacement seems repelled by all the filth, but then he smiles as he sees the group standing around him. This insignificant-looking man must think we are here to welcome him. There is a weakness to his face, and he looks too thin to last here more than a few weeks. I wonder what kind of selection officer would choose such a poor specimen.

The replacement makes a vain attempt to introduce himself to us but soon stops when he realizes that no one is paying attention to him. From what I can gather of his nervously told biography, our great philosopher has been replaced by an ordinary clerk. I know that the irony of this would intrigue the poet.

The members of the group look at one another, knowing that we have nothing more to say to each other. Sheleen has taken his world with him, and now both are gone forever. We walk away, leaving this clerk from somewhere or other sitting alone slumped on his bed.

I try to rest in my bunk and build up some strength for the next shift. Seconds later I look up and see the clerk standing beside me. He clears his throat several times, as if waiting for me to grant him permission to speak. He whispers, "What kind of place is this where no one even cares to know my name?" I ask. His name is Karl.

He rambles on and on. His story, naturally, is the same as everyone else's. Again a smile comes to his face when he realizes that he and I had lived about fifty miles apart and had once possessed children the same age. This lonely, frightened man grasps my hand as if I am his long-lost brother.

The poet is strangely quiet. He watches the man intently but says nothing. Perhaps he realizes that this simple clerk is not fair game for his tongue.

The now familiar sound of the table rasping against the floor interrupts Karl's incessant talking. He turns and looks in the direction of the noise. The joy on his face at finding a brother evaporates as he sees the man fix the noose around his neck. Karl stares at me with terror-filled eyes.

The first of Sheleen's disciples is about to join his master. Everything is the same: the carved beam, the rope, and the table. I maneuver Karl around so he will not have to see such things so early in his career.

The cellist from Stalten utters no last words before he jumps from the table.

Karl keeps his eyes closed throughout the entire episode. When the sounds of the cellist's agony are over, he stares first at the dead man and then at me. He seems to be in a trance.

I take him outside so he will not see the cellist unleashed from his rope and put to bed. We stand together in our places in line. Karl asks, "How long will it take for me to become just like you and all the others?"

I tell him that I possess no answers to anyone's questions and he is on his own. The others line up and we march off to the shop. He clings to my side.

Karl enters the shop with the same confused look that is the trademark of all new men. He seems the type who will flourish best in the center of the orchestra. I lead him to a vacant bench in the heart of the woodwind section. He stands by the bench until finally I tell him to sit down. I wonder how long this ill-equipped man can possibly last.

He begs me to stay with him. I hold up a spine to him and

say that we make shrapnel. I tell him that he is to watch the others and he will learn the machine. As I leave him, I tell him to expect Verbin and the red cap with his clippers. He is still pleading as I walk away.

Karl survives his visit with Verbin and the conductor. His machine makes futile attempts at striking the scrap. He obviously has no talent for such things.

The red cap still finds it necessary to watch carefully over the orchestra. He walks through our section and, as always, has a hateful look for the poet. The poet responds to him with an idiotic grin.

The conductor stands before my bench, but I do not look up. He reaches over and turns off my machine. "I need another Sheleen," he says. "I will make it worth your while. I'll shave your head every week so the lice won't bother you; I give you my word." After my first scalping, this bastard has always made me beg him for a shave. As punishment, the poet's head hasn't been shaved in weeks. "You won't have to work hard anymore. You can spend your time in the latrine with the new men. You will live longer. Take Sheleen's bench. You must know everything he ever said. This place must have a Sheleen if we are to survive. Take his bench." He points to the poet, who looks at us with his unchanging smirk. "You'll thank me for ridding you of that broken-nosed son of a bitch."

"Leave me alone," I plead. "How can I be a Sheleen? I'm not even sure anymore what he was. Even if I could be a Sheleen, I could never raise men up out of the mud and then throw them back down again. Now get out of here!"

The anger wells up in him. "You goddamn fool. We're drowning in a cesspool, and all you think about is ethics and morals. How the hell have you lived this long?" He shrugs his shoulders and says, "You've all become garbage. Even the best of you is worth nothing."

I hear him stop at the next bench and say, "Faster, faster —Verbin says we are behind quota."

Finally he returns to Verbin's side. The fat man has fallen asleep with a lit cigarette in his hand. The red cap gently removes the smoldering butt from between the puffy fingers. The butt is carefully put out on the sole of the conductor's shoe and the remains of the cigarette are secreted in his pocket.

Moments later the conductor reappears before me. "Take Sheleen's bench and I'll give you two cigarettes."

I shake my head no. He walks off again, cursing.

The shift comes to an end. The power is turned off and the machines come slowly to a halt. We have survived this day of mourning, and Karl still has all his fingers.

I walk toward the door of the shop. Avron waits for me. He grabs my coat. "The boy is out there. I heard him. He's in the compound. This is a special night for us. God is good," he says again and again. He is ecstatic. "God is good. Come with me. Tonight you will see him. Tell the poet to leave him alone. Give the child some bread. If we all give him a morsel, he will keep coming."

We march out into the night. Karl stares in wonderment at this beaten old man who proclaims, "God is good. God is good," over and over.

12   As we march through the
darkness, I search the night for some glimpse of the boy.
I listen for the sound of his violin but hear only the coughing around me as we breathe in the freezing air. The light
from the tower blazes a trail for our column as we walk
toward the huts.

The guards huddle around the flaming drum in the middle of the field. Fortunately, it is too cold for them to take
much notice of us. They stand together bundled in their
heavy overcoats, but still they look cold. Every few minutes they awaken from their frozen stupor and stomp their
feet up and down and then bang their gloved hands together.

I stand in line, waiting with Avron in front of our hut.
Karl, his body shivering violently, is as always at my side.
He doesn't know enough to wait in the hut for the food
cart. Avron and I scan the darkness for the boy. I begin to
wonder if the sound of the violin came from his imagination. He says, "He's out there. I know it. Just be quiet and
listen."

All I can hear is the squeak of the wheels of the food cart
as it enters the compound. The rest of the men respond to
the clatter by treking out of their huts and lining up. For
the first time the food cart means little to me. I just want
a sight of this child. I turn to Avron and ask, "Where the
hell is this boy of yours?" He says nothing but puts his
finger to his lips.

Through the night, above the wind, I finally hear the
violin. The lullaby is coming from the darkness by the old
tree. My heart races. I feel warm again as the high-pitched
sound courses through my body. It is the same song that I
have heard him play before. I become excited and grab
Avron by the arm and shake him. He looks up into the

darkened sky and says, "God is good. God is good."

The lullaby is played again, and I hum the same simple melody with the violin. Then there is only silence from the tree. I hum alone.

Turning to Avron, I ask why the boy doesn't appear. He only shrugs his shoulders. Then I wonder if perhaps the boy has spotted the poet and is still afraid. I step out of line and run to the poet. This idiot, Karl, follows my every step. I grab the poet and yell at him to leave the boy alone or I'll kill him. He acts surprised. "Where the hell is the boy? What the hell are you talking about?"

I walk away from him, wondering if I had actually heard the violin or if I am going mad. I look at Karl and ask him if he heard anything. All he says is, "Why does that man over there always say, 'God is good'?" I brush him aside and return to Avron.

Avron is annoyed. "Listen to me, I swear on the life of my dead children that the boy is out there."

The cart has now crossed the field to our side. I shove my way to the front of the line. I have never done this before. This time Karl does not follow me.

Half the compound has been fed, and still the boy has not appeared. The tin cup in my hand shakes, but on this night it is not from the cold. The cart is dragged to the next hut. One of the guards leaves the flaming barrel and screams at the cart ladlers, "Hurry up, you bastards. Don't you know it's freezing out here?" The men rush through. Their soup spills as they run to their hut.

All I can think of is the boy. In my thoughts I see the faces of my son and daughter. A million memories flash through my mind. My tongue reaches for the rye seed lodged in my teeth since the noon feeding. I can taste a last remnant of the rye flavor. I think of how my little daughter would run to me each time an ancestor of my rye seed got caught in her teeth. I would hold her in my arms and, with a toothpick, extract the seed from between her baby teeth.

She would bound from my grasp and return to her own beautiful world.

The cart approaches. My eyes are blinded by the tower lights that now surround us. I am ready to lunge for the cart even before it stops.

The chunk of bread is thrust into my hand. My cup is held over the cauldron, and in my haste I feel warm globs of soup run down my hand.

I strain to see the boy. I am terrified by the thought that he won't come out of the blackness. I rush to the edge of the circle of light. My eyes see nothing in the darkness. I hold my bread out into the night and call softly to him, "Come here, my son. Come to me. Here is some bread for you. Let me look at you just this once. No one will hurt you. Play for me. You can have the bread. Here, take it. You don't have to play if you don't want to."

I begin to hum his lullaby. I place one foot across the circle of light and stand halfway between the light and the darkness. I see nothing. I call to him again. I hum his song.

Then from out of the darkness the violin plays again. He must be just ahead of me. The sweetness of its sound melts away the ages of ice that have clung to me for so long. I am warm.

I look down and see that most of my soup has spilled onto the ground. The shaking cup is almost empty. My body strains to cross over to him. I call out again.

Finally I make out his small figure in the shadows. My arm thrusts the bread out to him. My eyes strain to see his face. All I can see are the features of my own son painted on the darkened silhouette. I cannot believe that anything as perfect as a child can occupy this same hell on earth with me.

The little figure does not move. I motion for him to come closer—only a little closer. He approaches slowly. I cannot believe that life can be so good.

The darkness fades away. I am crushed by what my eyes

see. Before me stands an exact replica of one of us. I stare at him. Everything is the same, only in miniature. I find myself backing away in horror from this ugly creature.

He comes up to the very edge of the circle but does not cross over. On his head he wears the oversized cap of a man. He looks up, and his sunken, unblinking eyes stare back at me. It is the head of a gargoyle. There is a reptilian quality to the gaunt face. Two separate rivers of snot lead out of each nostril and converge on his upper lip. They ripple back and forth in time with his breathing.

He keeps his gaze on my face but comes no closer. Still, those eyes do not blink. Then he looks at my bread. I shove the entire chunk at him, and a bony little hand grasps it. He wears at least two coats, one on top of the other. They reach down past his knees.

Mechanically he stuffs the bread into a cloth sack tied around the waist of his filthy coat. His dull expression does not change. There is no look of excitement at winning such a large piece of bread.

He reaches beneath his outer coat and produces a little violin and bow. The worn violin seems much too small, even for him. The beauty of the instrument contrasts violently with the grotesqueness of this little creature. For a moment I wonder if I am staring at a midget.

He places the violin under his chin lifelessly. The bow strikes the strings and a new song arises. I do not recognize what he plays, but I know it is more beautiful than any I have heard before.

As I watch him play, I am struck by the sight of the little fingers darting back and forth, up and down the strings. The hands are alive, but the face is dead, the body wooden. I wonder what they have done to him to produce what stands before me. There is no trace of sadness in his music; only his body is a picture of bereavement.

I reach out to hold him. My hands cradle his little head, and gently, I wipe his nose on my sleeve. The violin ceases

99

and we stand together for a moment. Suddenly he pushes me away, and with a hisslike, guttural cry, he races off into the darkness.

I have no time to let my eyes follow him into the night. I realize the cart has gone. Some guard is cursing me; I see him start to raise his rifle. The shivering cold in my body returns with a vengeance as each step brings me closer to the hut.

I run into the hut and slam the door behind me. I cannot move; I am out of breath. Avron greets me with out-stretched arms as if I am some returning hero. He runs to me, saying, "He let you hold him. He let you hold him. No one has ever been able to touch him before."

I shove him aside. The brief bit of happiness on Avron's face quickly fades and is replaced by his usual forlorn look. I ask him, "What the hell has happened to him? All that is beautiful in a child has been drained from this creature. There is nothing left of a childhood to salvage in this boy."

Avron follows me down the aisle to my bunk. He kneels before me as I stare up at the light bulb. "The boy does not look well," he says. "He is sicker than before, but he will look better; you will see. What color was the snot from his nose?"

I now wonder why snot is so damn important. I tell him I don't remember.

"The doctors tell me," he whispers, "that if the snot is clear or white, then the boy is reasonably well. But if it is yellow, then that is bad. Green means that he is very sick. Can't you even remember what color it was?"

I tell him to go away and leave me alone.

He does not move. "You heard him play. I have listened to music all my life, and what he plays has never been heard before. Don't you realize that he composes all that he plays? The life that God placed within him is still alive.

This is no mere child, and there's never been another quite like him before."

He pauses for a moment and I think he will finally go away, but, no, he continues. "I am worn out. I have lived beyond my time here. When I'm gone no one will look after him. He let you hold him. God has led him to you. You will be his Moses and lead him out of here. You will preserve the last remnant of God's presence on this miserable earth."

I sit up and tell him that everything that God has ever given to me has been wrenched away. He has left me with nothing but my lice. Only they have flourished and multiplied. I then demand to know why he himself hasn't become Moses and taken the boy into the Promised Land.

"I've never been able to get near him. Most of the time he even refuses my bread. When he does take it, he runs away if I try to even talk to him. He roams the camp. The guards let him go from compound to compound. I have never seen them harm him. God has shielded him from their bullets. The boy has walked by the commandant and no harm has come to him."

Avron stands and holds out his bread to me. "For every chunk of bread you give to him, I will give you a like amount of mine. Go to him when he returns and befriend him. His life is so fragile, and he is but a child. How can you refuse a child? Promise me that you will look after him." He points to his ragged coats. "I have nothing to give you other than my bread and soup. Perhaps I can find some cigarette butts. You will try to make the boy understand that he must walk out of here. They will never miss him. Most of the time they pay no attention to him. God placed the last spark of life on earth within him, but it is for us to preserve it."

I stand up beside him and push his bread away. "Leave me alone," I tell him. I let him know I'm well aware that he's given a similar damn speech to others and they've all starved to death feeding the boy. I say that I intend to live out every bit of miserable life left in me. He walks away when I say that he would make a better Moses than I.

He turns around for a moment. "No one has ever held him before." Then he is gone.

I lie with my head buried in my bunk, trying to avoid the poet. I have no desire to hear his commentary on anything. I feel a hand shaking me, but it is only Karl. With a few biting words, I try to send him back to his bunk. He is immune to my insults. Apparently persistence is this weak man's only strong characteristic. He does not go away. I hear his whining voice. "This man who blesses God all the time wants me to promise to feed the boy. What shall I say to him?"

I tell Karl to go to bed and I will give him an answer in the morning. When I look up again he is gone. I am surprised that my words have satisfied him.

The light flickers out. I am starving. I know that to miss a single meal can tip the balance from the side of living toward the side of death. I decide to go to my window and watch the light beam, but I am too exhausted to get out of bed. I stare at the glass, trying to produce the faces of my children. All my mind can see is the face of the little boy with the twin rivers of snot draining from his nose. For the life of me, I cannot remember their color.

13 The conductor goes from machine to machine. At each stop he beats his fists on the top of the bench, trying to make the erratic cutter follow his cadence. Then he stands aside and waits to make certain that his tempo is ingrained in the operator's mind. When he is satisfied, he swears under his breath and then goes to the next bench and pounds away again in the same manner. The red cap is paying dearly for the loss of Sheleen. Perhaps in his own twisted way he now grieves over Sheleen's death far more than I do.

It is difficult for me to keep up the rhythm of the machine. I find it almost impossible to lose myself in the monotony of the banging. Then it dawns on me that I am pounding out the beat of the boy's lullaby on the face of the scrap. The cutter slows and the spines barely flow into the canister.

Looking at the poet, I know that something is wrong with him. His face is more gaunt than usual. He has been strangely silent.

Karl gets up and moves a bench closer to me. Fortunately, he is still mired deep in the woodwinds. I begin to worry that sooner or later he will be next to me. I vow to myself that I will not let him become a weight around my neck. If he comes any nearer, I will keep moving one bench at a time, just to keep my distance from him.

Verbin wakes up and pulls himself out of his chair. He rises slowly to his feet and stretches. The broad expanse of his immense belly pours out between the top of his pants and his upraised shirt. He and his clothes are strangers to soap. He yawns continually as he makes the rounds of his machines from one end of the orchestra to the other.

I look at him, wondering if he knows anything of the boy. Surely he must have seen the child many times in the past.

When he passes by my bench, I breathe in deeply so my lungs can catch some of the smoke from his cigarette. He finishes them down to nothing. His spent butts are never left to clutter the floor. He loves the floor almost as much as his machines.

My mind forgets the cutter and drifts again to the boy. The machine becomes erratic and always balks at the first sign of inattention.

Then I realize that someone is standing behind me. I am sure it is a guard. They always wander aimlessly, but this one does not move on. I feel his eyes boring into the back of my head. He must have noticed that my machine hasn't produced worth a damn all morning.

My machine springs forward and gains power. The cutter rams into the scrap and the spines spew out in a regular rhythm. I am catching up; soon I'll be over quota. The machine and I are in perfect harmony. We are at our peak, but still the guard does not move.

My work is perfect. I speed up even further until I can go no faster without overheating the cylinder. Each spine is flawless. I have never produced so well—but the guard remains glued to me. Surely by now I have atoned for my half-hearted performance of the morning.

The poet is watching me. I can tell from his look that he knows I am in trouble. Instinctively I turn toward Sheleen's bench, even though I know it is empty.

I get a quick look at the guard when I reach down to the floor for another piece of scrap. It is the one they call Rollin. He has never paid any attention to me before. I can't even remember him ever going on a rampage. The other guards are sleeping peacefully, but this one has to hover over me.

He moves closer to me. His body partially blocks out the light filtering in from the dirty window. I think back, searching my mind, trying to fathom why he is singling me out.

The poet begins screeching his machine, but the rest of the orchestra plays on in the usual rhythm. They do not come to my rescue. I know that without Sheleen, each of us is on his own. Hearing the poet's clamor, Karl turns around and stares at me in stupid wonderment.

I, too, screech my machine, and the piercing noise finally reaches Verbin's ears. He wakes up and drowsily looks up at the conductor standing next to him. The red cap placidly watches me. He motions softly for Verbin to go back to sleep. With that the poet slows his machine to its normal wandering rhythm. I look at him, and we both know that he can do nothing more for me.

I still cannot understand what this Rollin wants from me. All I can hope for is a quick rifle butt to the head—maybe this will satisfy him and he will leave me alone. We all appear the same to them. How could he pick me out from the other skeletons?

Rollin looks older than the other guards. He is a corporal. Always before he paced up and back, enduring the long agony of the everlasting day. I never saw him pay attention to anyone. His mind usually seemed elsewhere—but now I have to fascinate him.

The face of the boy flashes into my mind. In an instant I know why all this is happening to me. It all makes sense. I have become a marked man because of last night's episode with the boy. I had violated a cardinal rule by standing out from the rest of the group. Rollin must have seen me with the child. I wonder if he was the guard who chased me back to the hut.

It then comes to me why the boy is allowed to wander at will. They keep him to ferret out the weak ones among us. Whoever succumbs to his violin is obviously not a fit worker. To try to make a decent spine and have your mind on the boy, all at the same time, is an impossible task. The selection process continues even here in the camp. The boy works for them; he is their final judge—the grand selector of the unsuitable. The poet had warned me about him, but I did not listen. Now I know why the men are indifferent to this little angel of death.

Rollin moves and now stands in front of my bench. I look up at him and see his grim face. He is a plain-looking man. His eyes are red. I wonder if he's been drinking.

He points first to the bar of scrap that I hold next to the cutter, and then his hand motions me to the dock. I think that he means for me to finish the bar and then go with him. The boy does the choosing, and then the guards do the killing. Even the brilliant mind of a Sheleen never figured this out.

The bar is slowly consumed. The spines that I create are as unfit as I am. The banging cutter edges closer and closer to my trembling fingers. I can barely hold the bar. I look up at Rollin; impatience is written across his face.

The last few slivers fall into the canister. I wonder if they really use our shrapnel. Perhaps having to make these spines is meant only to be our final humiliation. The commandant probably laughs as our life's work is dumped on some giant garbage heap to rust away to nothing in the pouring rain.

The last spine drops into the canister. I hear it clink as it lands among its brothers. The bar is gone; it is done. I want to cry out, but there is no one to hear me. I say nothing.

I let the machine idle down slowly until the cutting blade stops a safe distance from the surface of the bench. My heart pounds away against my chest. I grasp the sides of the bench and raise my drained body from the chair. I touch the machine for the last time. The poet does not look up. His head is buried in his work.

Rollin motions me toward the dock, and I follow behind him. My last tiny bit of bread is placed on the poet's bench; it is my only possession to give away. I hear his machine shriek out again to Verbin, but the fat man continues his slumber. Only the guards look up and then fall back to sleep. The blank faces of the orchestra watch me go to my end. No one is interested in anything so commonplace as death.

I give a pleading look to the conductor. He could easily awaken Verbin, but he does nothing. His sullen eyes just watch me. I wonder if he is satisfied, but I will never know since it is impossible to recognize the look of pleasure on his miserable face. He does not awaken the sleeping mound of fat wedged into the overstuffed chair. This must be the price for refusing to be the red cap's new Sheleen.

The dock is deserted except for the rows of filled canisters. The wind cuts right through me. In the distance a few trucks move slowly, plodding their way along the road.

I stand before him in silence. He doesn't look at me but stares off at the fog-shrouded hills. I wonder if he is waiting for me to confess. I wonder what the hell I'm supposed to do.

His rifle is still slung on his shoulder. His hands hang limply at his sides. The face has a troubled, faraway look. He has not shaved today, which is unusual for a guard. He looks uncomfortable—maybe he has not killed a man before.

Perhaps waiting in the cold and freezing to death is to be my punishment. Maybe he expects me to take his rifle and bash myself in the head with it. I feel nausea well up in my throat, and it begins to choke me. I could not speak even if I wanted to.

He turns and looks at me. I see the hate pour out of his eyes as he says, "My father once worked for your family. I remember you from when I was a child. My father hated most of your people, but he always told me that your family was decent to him. I know your family has important connections."

I am dumbfounded that anyone is able to recognize me. His face grows more somber. He speaks haltingly. "I have a little girl. She is my only child. She is very sick. My wife writes that the doctors can do nothing for her and that she is dying. I wrote my wife that she must take the child to the clinic at Canella, but she receives no reply from them. Her letters are returned unopened."

He lowers his head and slumps against the stacked canisters. He is oblivious to the grease that now stains his once spotless uniform. He says no more. I wonder why he is telling me all this. Perhaps he knows that I, too, have lost children. The silence is broken as I hear the machines in the shop. Their pounding is like a far-off roar.

He moves toward me again. There is anger in his voice. "I don't really give a damn about politics. I know what has happened to you, and, to be honest, I feel that the country is better off without you people. I know your family has important connections. Most of the doctors at the clinic are your people. You owe me nothing, but I have a child who is dying. I will deal with the devil himself if that will save her. She is an innocent child. I beg of you to have your family use its influence to have her examined at the clinic. She is a child. She is not part of all of this. Even you wouldn't refuse to help an innocent child."

He may have said more, but I am not sure. I am totally dumbfounded. I keep wondering how in hell he couldn't have known what has happened to us. I stare into his tormented face. I have never before seen the look of anguish on any of these invincible men. I am amazed to see the expression of hopelessness. I always thought that we alone had the patent on this look.

The strength to speak comes from some hidden recess in my body. I tell him that I would gladly ask my family to carry out this simple request, but the only connections they now have are to the ground they are buried in. I am all that is left of them.

His mouth drops in amazement as I tell him that the clinic does not answer his wife's letters because it, too, no longer exists. Most of its doctors have carried their healing powers into their graves. Perhaps some of them are here running machines. We are now of no use to anyone.

He turns away from me and stares into the wind. With its full force, the cold bites deeply into his grief-stricken face. He says nothing more. He does not answer when I ask for his permission to return to the shop. I leave him alone, still gazing into the dark gloom of the winter sky.

The conductor waits by the door as I enter the shop. He grabs me and asks gruffly, "What the hell did he want?"

I push him aside and walk back toward my bench. I hear the ringing tempo of the orchestra. They are greeting my return. My stooped shoulders rise and I walk upright. Avron stares at me as his mouth recites one of his prayers. Everyone looks up as they race their machines faster and faster. Karl peers back and forth around the orchestra, without the slightest idea of what's going on. The poet's face breaks out into a broad, twisted smile as he reaches over to my bench to replace the lump of bread.

My machine welcomes me back and roars off under full power. I have returned home safely and relish the feeling of strength within me.

The red cap, standing in front of the orchestra, brings the machines back under his control. My hunger returns, and I long for the end of the shift. My mind is filled with visions of the bread stacked on the food cart. As a child I dreamed of doing magnificent things and being hailed by all the world. Now all I desire is to be able to sit in a corner and gobble up all the bread on this earth, and maybe if I'm lucky find a cigarette butt.

14 The men carefully gather around me as we march out of the shop. They all want to know what happened with Rollin on the dock. The poet's bitterness pours out. "What the hell could you expect from the likes of him? Compassion is what men always expect to receive but never learn to give."

The red cap shoves his way into the line and marches beside me. He gives me a jab in the ribs with his fist. "What did this guard want of you?" he yells. "You tell me now or I'll make it hard on you!"

The poet grabs the conductor and pushes him away from me. He puts on his twisted, idiotic grin that is reserved especially for the red cap and shrieks, "Rollin told him that Verbin is going to replace you as the conductor!"

The red cap shouts back, "Listen, you bastards, you'd all be dead without me!" He says no more; the guards are looking in our direction.

Steam pours from the cauldron as the food is passed out to the first hut across from us. I tell Avron about the incident with Rollin. At first he says nothing. He does not look at me when he speaks. "You would have helped a child who belonged to one of them, wouldn't you, but you refuse to do anything for the child who is ours."

I tell him to leave me alone with his damn Moses speech. Karl starts in, and I move away from both of them and walk to the back of the line. I find the artist standing there in his usual stupor. This man berates no one. I button his jacket to try to shield him from the cold and then place his hands in his pockets. I tell him how much his pictures mean to me, but my words never seem to register in his head. There is always an air of melancholy serenity to this man. I find myself asking him questions about his past, even though I know he will not answer. In a way, I find all this satisfying. No one here ever has a trivial conversation.

The wheels of the cart cut through the thin layer of snow and churn up the mud in their wake. The lines of men pass before the cart and humbly accept what is offered. Flames dart from the oil drum that warms only the guards. Periodically, without even looking up, the soldiers scream out for us to hurry up. They are always in a rush to go nowhere.

A sudden commotion overtakes the food cart. The men run by, grab their bread, and race to their hut. My first thought is that the guards have waded in and are bashing skulls. Quickly I look toward the shop, hoping Verbin might be watching, but he is nowhere to be seen. Next, I peer over at the fire, but the guards have not moved.

Then I see the boy standing under the old tree. He looks smaller in the light of day than he did last night. He begins walking slowly toward the food cart. Some of the guards look up at him briefly but then return to the spouting flames. He seems to hold no special attraction for them— just a part of the usual dull scenery.

I am struck by the boy's nose, which is too large for his head. His ears peek out between the strands of his matted hair. The ragged coats that cover him are the same color as the mud. He is even filthier than I am.

As he walks along toward the cart, I see that each step seems difficult for him. His overlarge shoes sink into the mud with every step, and his feet slide out of each shoe as he plods along. His bare, sticklike legs stand out between the end of the long coat and his untied shoes.

There is the look of pride on Avron's face as he watches the boy trudge on. The child walks mechanically; the arms do not swing as he moves. I notice that his right sleeve is covered by a glasslike coating that shines in the light. He raises his arm to wipe his nose, and then I know why one sleeve glistens.

The cart is pulled to the next hut, the boy following

closely behind. The ladlers try to wave him away, but he pays no attention to them. Each man grabs his food and makes a wide detour around the boy who has now moved between the cart and the hut. No one, however, can make it home without first passing the child. Some of the men begin to gulp down the bread the second it is deposited in their hands. The soup spills out of their cups as they run past him. He watches impassively without moving a muscle. From beneath his cap come long wisps of hair that flutter in the wind.

Suddenly the violin comes out from under his coat and springs to life. The same lullaby begins. He moves with the speed of a cat and blocks the way of a hapless man. By the look of his clothes, I know this prisoner is a newcomer. The trapped man moves first to his right and then to his left, but the boy follows his every step. The violin sings out ever louder and faster. The prisoner can go nowhere, and finally he stops. It is as if the strings of the violin have tethered his feet to the ground.

The guards look up and watch this strange duel for a few moments. The red cap stands on the doorstep of his hut, shaking his fist at the boy. He tries to motion the child away from his prey. The boy does not look up; his eyes are fixed on his prisoner. The man looks confused as he stands there, clutching his soup and bread close to his chest. The violin stops as the boy stares into his face. I look at the man; I can feel his hunger.

They stand motionless, facing each other. The boy can easily grab the bread but does not. In an instant the man makes a sudden dash for freedom and runs around the boy to the safety of his hut. Much of his soup has been lost in his flight. He slams the door shut behind him. The boy does not look around or try to follow him. There is no look of disappointment on his unchanging face. Only Avron is sorrowful.

The boy wipes his nose on the sleeve and coughs a few

times. Each cough seems to send tremors through the frail body. The delicate little violin is shoved back under his coat as he slowly follows the moving food cart.

The boy traps another new man at the next hut, but he too, escapes without losing his bread. The boy's sack is still empty. The entire compound, with the exception of the guards, is overtaken by a frenzy. Even men on our side of the field move nervously about in expectation of their forthcoming combat with the boy.

I see no guilt in the men as they run past the boy. As they rush by him, there is only a look of relief. Guilt seems to be a foreigner in this land of ours. The screams of an empty stomach drown out all feelings of pity, even for a child. In my own hunger, I pass judgment on no one.

The cart crosses over to our side, and with it comes the boy. One of the ladlers, after glancing over toward the guards, tries to shoo the boy away but fails once more. The song of the violin starts up again almost immediately. He seems to have the uncanny ability to know whose soul is alive and whose is dead. The lullaby is not wasted on those men whose souls have departed from this earth.

He catches another man at the next hut. This one shows no inclination to escape. The song has totally disarmed him. The lullaby stops, and the boy peers into the man's empty face as if waiting for some words of congratulation from his victim. The man remains motionless. The boy then drops his gaze to the bread. Totally ignoring the soup, he points his bow toward the rye. The man hands the entire chunk to the boy, who barely glances at it as he stuffs it into his cloth sack. The sack now bulges with the outline of the man's lost meal. No sign of happiness crosses the boy's face to mark his victory.

With the sack satisfied, the violin begins softly to play another, totally different melody. Now there is none of the simplicity of the lullaby. I strain to hear what he plays, and I am rewarded with a song that sends a feeling of peace through me. My mind flies upward with each rising note. I feel as though I am being lifted up from the mud that binds me to this earth. Hunger is forgotten as my soul rises higher than the towers. I can imagine the earth to be as beautiful as the day of man's creation. I am warm.

The song of the violin slowly descends from the heavens back to the earth. The boy walks away and abandons his dazed victim, whose feet still linger in the mud while his shaking hands hold the half-empty cup.

The cart now stands in front of our hut as our line gets ready to be fed. The boy takes up his usual position and gazes intently as each man rushes by him. We have many new men, but the violin attacks none of them. They seem to hold no interest for the child's silent stare.

I guide the artist along as the line continues to pass the cart. Avron holds out a minuscule piece of bread to the boy, which is accepted in a perfunctory manner. No song is played for this generous man of God. Avron then stops a few yards away and watches as Karl is given his bread and soup. I hear Avron call softly to Karl, "Give him something. Anything is enough. Just give him something." Karl races by the boy without stopping and makes it safely into the hut. He should have saved his energy, for the boy showed no curiosity in him or his bread.

I make sure the artist is given his ration and then point him in the direction of the hut. The boy lets this easy prey pass by without molesting him.

A guard walks over to one of the ladlers and smacks him in the back with his rifle. "Finish this goddamn thing up in the next few minutes!" he screams. "We're freezing out here!" Before returning to the fire he glances over at the boy, and the hint of a smile crosses his face. I think to myself how much better tolerated the young of accursed races are than the adult forms.

With my bread and soup, I walk slowly by the boy. He watches my every move. I stare into his face and try to smile at him. That gaunt face never changes. He walks away and follows the food cart on its journey to the next hut. I stare after him. He stops, turns around, and looks back at me for a moment. Then he's off again to the next hut.

Avron waits for me by the doorway as I climb the two steps up to the hut. I have no desire to listen to him. My bread interests me more than what I know he's about to say.

"Did you see the way he looked at you?" he says, filled with excitement.

I tell him that he looked at everyone the same way. He speaks no more after I ask him if this creature is a midget. He walks slowly away from me.

Sitting on the side of my bunk, I begin my feast by drinking the soup. It is cold and brackish. I save the best for the last. The bread is always good. I let each bit roll around in my mouth and chew it over and over again before swallowing. I am pleased to feel a rye seed safely tucked away between two of my back teeth.

I ask the poet why the boy goes after some of the new men, but not all of them. "Don't worry," he assures me. "He'll get them all. Sooner or later he'll get them all. Save your bread; you know you need every bit of it. I think Avron fed him today just for your benefit; or maybe it was to show Karl the exact technique of handing bread to the boy. Avron probably wanted you to give him your whole chunk again. I know how he works. I've never trusted these religious ones. They always want something. Their damned hands are always out for something."

Lying in my bunk, I think of the boy's song. I had never heard anything so beautiful before. The child seemed so dead. The only sign of life about him was the rippling snot from his nose. The violin, however, was another story. I could almost believe that there was a tiny music box inside the violin creating the song. I try to remember the strains of the melody, but I cannot recall them. Only his trademark, the lullaby, sticks in my head. I realize that in my mind the devastated boy and the beautiful violin are always separate; I cannot conceive of them as being one.

Rising up out of my bed, I question the poet again and ask if the boy has numbers on his chest.

"Why don't you get him off your mind?" he growls. Then there is a change in his voice. "Oh, well, I wondered the same thing when I came here. The numbers are there. I saw them myself. One day I gave him a piece of bread. When he took it, I grabbed him by the arm and shoved his collar open. Beneath the dirt I saw the numbers. He's one of us, there's no doubt about it."

My mind becomes filled with questions about the child, but the siren for the second shift sounds. I drag the artist up out of his bunk and lead him outside. I doubt if his crippled brain has any idea where in the hell I am taking him.

15 No one talks. Without She-
leen, the nights in the hut are as silent as a tomb, except
for the coughing. Each man is an island.

I lie on my bunk, totally exhausted. The episode with
Rollin has drained everything out of me. I barely have the
strength to gaze into the light bulb.

The poet says nothing. I even miss the venom that used
to pour out of his mouth. After a few attempts, I give up
trying to talk to him. He does not answer. His mind is off
somewhere else.

I notice the pediatrician standing beside me. Without an
invitation, he sits down on the edge of my bunk. He looks
at me for a moment and then peers quickly over at Avron,
who watches us from his corner. "The boy is not a midget,"
he says in a voice loud enough for Avron to hear. "I swear
to you that this is a child. When I came here the boy had
no front teeth. I thought that maybe the guards had kicked
them out, but I was wrong. Gradually I noticed, as the
weeks passed, that his permanent teeth came in. He's
probably eight years old by now. It's hard to tell, though;
his growth has been stunted. He's very small for his age,
but I promise you that this is not a midget."

He gets up. He has done his duty. Furtively he looks
toward Avron and then bends over and whispers to me, "A
child cannot be a child without a mother or a father. You
know what I mean. I have seen children all my life, but I
have never run across anything like this boy. Even a child
raised in the worst of orphanages is better off than this
one. The boy has paid dearly for his time in here. Perhaps
he is a little mad like all the rest of us. What else can you
expect this place to produce? I've never seen him cry or
even talk, but I have heard him scream out like an animal.
He is alone all the time. I don't even know where he sleeps

117

in the camp. I don't even know *if* he sleeps. I have heard the violin play in the middle of the night. The food-cart men say they see him all over the camp, preying on the prisoners. This is a very sad child, but what can you expect?"

He looks back at Avron again and then, with obvious difficulty, says softly, "Don't tell Avron I said this, but I think the boy would be better off dead. He can never be reclaimed. I have always loved children, but I must tell you that this is the first child I have no feeling for. I tried, but all this little animal wants is our bread. He swoops down on the new men like a thief who attacks only the helpless. I love what comes from his violin, but I actually hate this child."

He pauses. "If Avron asks you, tell him that I told you that the child is a child."

As he walks away, I realize that my own children have been blessed by their quick deaths. Fortunately for them, they did not have to linger on this miserable earth and become like the boy.

I find myself listening for his violin. I hear nothing but Karl's voice. Sheleen's grand replacement now takes his turn sitting on the edge of my bunk. He talks, but I have learned to shunt his voice off into some back corner of my mind.

I hear the name "Sheleen," and suddenly I begin to listen to what he says. "I have been told that you always talked to Sheleen. Maybe you will talk to me like you did to him." He has the habit of spitting as he speaks, which I find even more annoying than the words that come from his mouth. His face has a hurt look when I do not reply to his offer.

"I must talk to someone," he pleads. "I cannot lay in my bunk and stare at the wall." Then his face lights up. "Do you think things would be better for me if I took Sheleen's bench? I have his bunk now, and if I'm also behind his bench maybe everyone will talk again like they used to. What do you think? Please don't tell me to wait until tomorrow for your answer."

I tell him to do what he thinks is best.

He reflects for a moment. "Do you think anyone holds it against me because I was the one who replaced this Sheleen? Everyone should know that it was by chance that I was given his bunk."

I turn over and try to bury my head in a blanket, but Karl's whine never stops. "Let me talk to you," he begs. "You don't have to answer me. You don't even have to listen. Just let me speak; it takes away the loneliness." He talks and talks, and my mind soon wanders off.

The poet stares in amazement as Karl continues his monologue. I am surprised that the poet has never unleashed his tongue on this simple clerk who owns the philosopher's bed and now wants his machine.

Karl becomes silent as the doctor from Rivosk begins his final preparations with the table and the rope. Since the night Sheleen left us, his method of escape has been copied many times in the huts throughout the compound. No one tries to stop these men. No one says a word. We just look the other way until the sounds of life are over. Tonight is no exception. It is done so quickly. This is all Sheleen has left us.

Somehow even Karl has come to regard these miserable episodes as part of life here. He asks, "Do we take him down now or in the morning?" He is satisfied when I tell him that we will do it in the morning. As soon as the light goes out, he is gone and I am left in peace.

I awaken suddenly and realize that I have been dreaming. Moments before, Rollin was beating me to death with his rifle. His gun was crashing down on me while the boy, standing a few paces away, played his violin. The rifle smashed down on me to the beat of the boy's song.

I am glad to rid myself of this dream and welcome the

tower's beam swinging through the blackened hut. For once, the reality of this place is preferable to dreaming.

In the darkness I notice the poet sitting stooped over on his bunk. I ask him why the hell he's been so quiet. "Tomorrow is a very special day for me," he says. I am struck by the sound of his voice; it is different. The nasal twang is gone. In the reflection of the light, I see his hand pushing against his twisted nose. That strange nasal sound disappears as his fingers partially realign his nose. "I have kept track and I'm sure that tomorrow is my fortieth birthday. I've spent the last forty years wandering in the desert."

He pauses for a moment as if it is painful to keep up the pressure on his bent nose. His hand returns again before he speaks. "It's odd," he says. "Only when I came here did I become what I always wanted to be. When I arrived, I told everyone that I was a poet from Vilna. These idiots accepted me for what I was not."

He reaches out and slaps my arm and in a laughing voice says, "Do you know what I was? I was a measly clerk —just like that goddamn fool, Karl. I was the son of a clerk who was also the son of a clerk. I sat at a goddamn little desk all my life, dreaming of being a poet. Someday I was going to kick over the desk and go to Vilna. For me, Vilna was the nearest Athens. I never had the courage to leave my desk until one day, when this all began, the soldiers came and kicked over the desk for me as they carried me off."

There is a silence as the tower light comes through again. Then he resumes. "Now Vilna is gone. I'm sure the city is there, but the people who gave it life are dead. It's strange, but I've even met some of its former inhabitants here. Vilna actually came to me, but the men who are here have had the life extracted from them.

"It's all so utterly absurd," he says. "Once again I am chained to a bench. What I now create has as much meaning as the entries I made in my old ledger books. I allowed myself to work for faceless creatures then as I do now. I went from job to job. I could never sit still, but I never went to Vilna. I spent my life wandering in circles through the wilderness. Maybe I was like Avron—always looking for a Moses to lead me out. I never found a Moses, nor did I become my own Moses. I never took a goddamn risk in my entire life. All I did was spend my life sitting first behind a wooden desk and now behind a wooden bench, creating nothing. I have been an insult to myself, but the forty years are over. I am going to leave here tonight. The first day of my forty-first year will not dawn in this place."

I am stunned for a moment and then ask if he, too, is going to try Sheleen's way out.

"I would never imitate that fraud," he sneers. "I want a victory for once in my wretched life. I'm going to try for the wire. If I get one hand through the fence before the bullets, then it will be a victory. If I get my whole body through before they cut me to pieces, then I will be satisfied. If I make it all the way to the outside, then it will be a monumental triumph."

I ask him how far he thinks he will get without papers. Surely he must know that he doesn't look like an ordinary citizen.

He then shuts me up as only he can. "If I make it out of here, you fool, I will get what I want. This time I will have what I want. If a man has a clean pair of pants that I need, then I'll kill him for the pants. I will keep running, and this time nothing will stop me. I will spend the rest of my life drinking up the milk and honey of the Promised Land. I will live away from the rest of the miserable world. I will find a woman to love, and I will sit in the sunlight and watch our children grow. Then and only then will I become a poet."

In the darkness he reaches out and hands me something. From the feel, I know instantly that he has made a long, razor-sharp spine. "Keep it," he says. "It's the best thing

I've ever made in my entire life. I've had one of my own for a long time. Yours I made today when you survived your meeting with Rollin."

He moves across and sits beside me. "I want you to come with me. Together we will try the fence. There's nothing here for you. Take the risk with me. What the hell do you have to lose? You'll be dead anyway inside of a month."

I say nothing to him. My fingers slide back and forth along the sharp edges of the dagger. I hand back the spine and tell him that I cannot go with him.

His nasal voice returns as he tears into me. "It's that goddamn boy, isn't it? Avron has filled your head with the nonsense of you becoming the new Moses. All his garbage has settled into your brain, hasn't it? Avron will have his Moses, and you will have nothing. If you think you're going to make a son out of that little bastard of a child, then you're crazy. Mark my words, you'll never have that boy. For all I know, you'll lead him to Avron's Promised Land, and then do you know what you'll get? A hail of bullets will be your reward. The boy will run off and won't even look back at you as you bleed to death in the mud."

He takes my hand and gives me the dagger again. "Take it, you damn fool, and come with me. Don't you know what happened to Moses? He followed every one of God's commandments, and still he wasn't allowed into the Promised Land. He lies buried in an unmarked grave on some damn mountain that no one can even remember. Who the hell celebrates *his* birthday?"

There is exasperation in his voice. "You're always tying yourself up to someone else's life. You haven't gotten over the loss of Sheleen, and now you're making a god out of this damn child. I told you that you're like all the others. You'll never be satisfied with the gods you yourself create."

He grabs me by both shoulders. "Listen, my friend, come with me. I beg you. I'll even carry your luggage."

Nothing more is said. Slowly he gets up. I cover myself

with the blankets. The dagger that he made for me falls to the floor as he walks away. I watch him as he stands by the door, trying to time the intervals of the passing light. I look out through the window and see the falling snow. At least his tracks will be covered if he makes it to the fence.

His ragged body stands motionless by the door as the light glints off the dagger clutched in his hand. I get up and walk toward him. As I approach, I know that someone else is by his side. The voice is Avron's. I hear him say, "I wish you luck." Avron is obviously smart enough not to call out aloud to God to bless the poet on his journey. Avron holds out his hand and they shake rather coolly. "I hope you make it out of here," Avron whispers. "I beg of you but one thing, and that is to tell the world what has happened to us. Tell them of the horrors that we have been through. Tell them what has happened to our children. Above all, tell them that the boy still lives and that while he is alive there is hope for the world."

The poet brushes him aside. "What makes you think the world gives a goddamn about us? If I were to tell them our story, I know they would believe me. They would even grieve for all of two minutes, but then when the two minutes of mourning were over, they would be wondering whether they should dine at home tonight or go out to a restaurant. Their next concern would be with the type of wine that would most suit their dinner. At best, a man will show deep concern for his own family; after that the rest of the world can go to hell."

The poet shakes his head as he looks at Avron. "You know nothing of men. Where have you been hiding all your life?"

Then he turns and stares at me. "What on earth do you have to lose by coming with me? Take this risk with me."

I hold out my hand to him, but he reaches only for the doorknob. When the light passes, he opens the door and he is gone. Avron and I rush to the window but see nothing of him. I hear Avron say, "May God bless you."

We listen for the guns, but they are silent. No one climbs down from the tower.

Avron stands beside me, going through his prayers. I look out and wonder where the poet is. He must be near the wire by now. I have always heard stories that they patrolled the outside with guard dogs at night, but I do not hear barking. I start back toward the door, thinking that his beaten body might be lying there freezing in the snow. My hand grasps the knob, but I am afraid to open the door.

Avron has followed me and speaks. "I want to thank you for what you've done." In the darkness he holds out what I am sure is a piece of bread. I stuff my hands in my pockets.

"You stayed because of the boy, didn't you?" he asks.

I curse out at him. "Goddammit, Avron, can't you get it through your head why I stayed? It was for just one reason. Do you know what that noble reason was? It was because I didn't have the guts to go with the poet. It's easier to rot here than take a risk at getting out."

I know now that I deserve everything that this place has to offer—the cold, the lice, the hunger.

I look around and find that Avron is gone. He is in his corner, swaying back and forth as he goes through his useless motions. In the darkness I cannot tell whether his corner has become a house of worship for his praying or a concert hall for his lost violin.

The total quiet of the outside world gives me hope that the poet has made it through the wire. I am all alone now. Any scrap of hope that resided within me has escaped with the poet. I know that I have allowed any chance for a human life to slip through my open hands. Had the guns gone off, I would have found it easier to go on living here. Their silence makes remaining here excruciatingly painful. The cold tension races through me as I feel the emptiness of being alone. I am drowning—a hand was offered to me, but I didn't reach out for it.

I find myself standing by the artist's bunk. With all my strength I drag his sleeping body up out of bed. I know that I am getting weaker, for I can barely guide his stuporous body to the window. He leans propped against the wall next to his blank canvas.

I pick up the steel dagger from the floor and place it in his hand. The feel of the strange object seems to awaken him somewhat from his sleep. I ask him to draw something for me—anything.

As if by rote he begins his etching with the tip of the long spine. I stand back and watch him as the figure begins to form slowly on the window. On this night, I am not to see one of his women. After the first few lines appear on his canvas, I know exactly what he is creating. He captures every last detail of the face of the boy. I am tempted to stop him and put him back to bed, but I let him finish. The boy pictured on the thin coating of ice is as real as the child I saw today.

When his painting is complete, I take the dagger from his hand and lead him back to his bunk. He stumbles around like a drunkard and falls lifelessly into bed. As I cover him with his blankets, I stare back at the picture of the boy on the window. I realize that the artist's empty eyes see more of this world than I thought possible.

With each sweep of tower light, the child's face recedes more and more into the ice. Finally each line is lost, and all that remains is the emptiness of the frozen window. Now it is my mind that creates the boy's face on the window. Perhaps it was more than just fear that kept me from leaving with the poet.

16

The shriek of the morning siren flings me out of bed. I stare at the poet's empty bunk and shudder to think of what will happen when the guards find him missing. There is an unusual murmuring in the hut as, one by one, the others learn that the poet is gone. They come to his bunk and fling the covers off his bed, hoping that his body is hidden somewhere beneath the pile of coats. I hear and see the strange foreign sound of the word "escape" form on their lips. The feeling of panic runs rampant through the hut. Karl scurries over to me, wailing, "What will happen now? Will they kill us?"

The cellist from Pavan berates me in a seething voice. "You could have stopped him. You know what they will do to us."

The men take the hanging body of the doctor from Rivosk down from the beam and place his remains in the poet's bunk. Now in the minds of my fellow prisoners, the poet has not escaped. One of them even tries to push the doctor's nose off to one side but gives up when the dead nose refuses to move.

Someone yells out that he is sure the poet's body lies sprawled out in front of the hut. Hearing this, my heart sinks. I wonder if his dead face will be frozen into a permanent smirk that will glare up at us as we walk by his body. Perhaps he didn't even get to the wire. Maybe they have him hanging from the tower for everyone to see. He might even be kneeling before the commandant at this very moment in the center of the field. I can visualize the officer beating him to death with this book. This time there would be no question about what lesson we were to learn from this death.

I get the artist up out of bed and shove him toward the men who are all congregated by the door. No one wants to

126

be the first one out of the hut. I hear the guards screaming for us to come out, but no one moves. Someone whispers, "Send the artist out first. He doesn't know what's going on."

They begin to look at me. Avron remains in his corner sanctuary, praying. I wonder if he is trying to get in touch with God to see if He will go out first.

Karl stands at my side and assures me that he will follow me. I hand the artist over to Karl. Wondering again if I should have grabbed it last night, I reach for the knob and fling the door open.

The poet is not to be seen—not on the step, not hanging from the tower, nowhere. This dark morning is like all other mornings.

I wait in the line next to the poet's empty space. The guards are counting the men at the next hut. I look around and grab Karl who is standing behind me and shove him into what was always the poet's position. He smiles and whispers, "Thank you for wanting me to be beside you."

The guards' boots make a crunching sound on the thin, frozen layer of snow as they approach. One of them walks up the steps of the hut holding his kerosene lantern in front of him and peers inside. "There's one of them who looks dead over in the corner," he yells. "Make a note to check on him later."

Another of the guards counts us with his waving finger. My heart pounds in time with the finger that points at each of us. His eyes are bleary-looking as he trudges along in front of the line. He mumbles to his comrade, "They are all here." Without looking back, the guards move on to the next hut. I cannot believe it. I cannot believe that he miscounted.

We continue to stand in formation, waiting for the tally to end. As we breathe, the warm air pours out of our mouths and forms white smokelike puffs in the cold wind. The red cap stands in his own line with his usual foreboding look. I begin to dread what he will do when he discovers that the poet has escaped.

As we march to the shop, I search the ground for any sign of the poet's tracks. The snow appears undisturbed along the fences. There is no break in any of the wires. Then I see something on a strand of wire at the corner of the compound by the shop. A small dark piece of cloth impaled on a barb in the wire dances back and forth in the wind. It flutters like a tiny flag pointing always away from the camp out toward the distant hills. Hope wells up within me—perhaps the poet has entered the Promised Land unscathed except for a rip in his coat.

The conductor's eyes never leave the poet's empty bench as the machines start up. I see him talk first to Avron and then to the pediatrician. He makes the rounds of the entire orchestra, searching out all of the men from our hut. His glaring eyes always return to the poet's bench. Then he stares at me with his hate-filled look. I know that he will soon descend on me.

The red cap takes up his position by the window to watch for the commandant. Verbin, too, is waiting by the door, holding his black book. With his stubby finger he scans the pages. He attempts to straighten his tie and tuck its frayed end inside his shirt. His face is animated and full of expression as he practices what he will say to his superior.

The guards stand around the stove, warming their hands. One of them, looking over at the poet's bench, takes his finger and shoves his nose over to one side. Several of the soldiers laugh. I am amazed that they even remember him. Gradually, one by one, they settle into their chairs and fall asleep. Looking around the shop, I see no sign of Rollin anywhere.

The machines bang away with no particular rhythm. Verbin and the red cap are still waiting at the door. When the song of the machines becomes erratic, the conductor waves his fists in the air and brings them back into harmony.

Another guard ambles by and stares at the poet's silent machine. I am uncomfortable with the thought that the soldiers know something is different about my corner. When the soldier is gone, I put my machine in neutral and move over to become the new owner of what was once the poet's bench. I motion to the lawyer from Traden to take my bench, and he does so after a long period of hesitation.

Perhaps Karl has seen me move, for he rises up and walks toward Sheleen's vacant bench. He sits down and starts up the machine. His always weak face lights up with a tinge of self-respect. His look of pride does not last. Loud shrieking comes from the machines surrounding Karl. Sheleen's section will not accept such a man to sit in their master's old chair. They shake their fists at Karl who now looks as if he is on the verge of tears.

The red cap hurriedly leaves his window and races toward the bass section. He tips his hat to the sleeping guards and then grabs Karl by the collar. Karl is dragged back to his seat in the woodwinds. The red cap shoves him against his machine and then returns to Verbin, who is still practicing his welcoming speech. The bass section is now quiet and sings in tune. Karl sits slumped over his bench.

Finally the conductor points to Verbin's pocket. The glasses come out and Verbin fumbles for his watch. He stares at it and then shows it to the conductor. The fat man shrugs his shoulders. His face is filled with disappointment as he waddles back to his easy chair. The commandant will not visit us this morning.

My period of grace is over. The red cap stands by my machine, holding a large bar of scrap in his hand. He shoves my throttle lever down. As the machine winds to a halt, I see his face twisting in anger. "With this bar I could make your nose look just like the poet's," he says. "Come on outside, I want to shave your head."

I raise the throttle bar and tell him that I don't need my head shaved. "I don't give a damn what you think you need," he says. "You're coming to the dock with me."

I stare out at the old stone houses of Verbin's city perched in the far distance along the hillside. Clustered among them is the church with its steeple rising upward into the gray sky. The conductor's voice is strangely calm, but I feel his bitterness as the clippers dig into my scalp. "I always wanted to be rid of him, but why the hell couldn't he just have dropped dead?" I feel a warm trickle down the side of my face. I know it is blood. "Do you know what will happen when they catch him? They will swoop down on us and we'll all be shot. How far did that idiot think he could get? Anyone spotting him, even a child, would know that he escaped either from a camp or a mortuary. Either way, he's a dead man. Our only hope is that he will freeze to death and not be found until spring, or that he's shot dead before that big mouth of his tells them where he's from."

The clippers continue making furrows in my head. "Don't you try anything like this. One man can spoil everything for us."

I can't take any more of the pain and shove his hand away. The clippers fall on the floor of the dock. Picking them up, he inspects them carefully and seems pleased that they still work. Then they are placed in his pocket. He sighs. "Your broken-nosed friend will probably get us all killed. Avron tells me that you are interested in the boy. That is good. Forget any thoughts of imitating the poet or I'll kill you. Become Sheleen, become religious, become interested in the boy, become anything—but don't get us all killed!" He walks back into the shop.

My head is too raw to wear my cap. I enter the shop, feeling like a beaten child. The machines do not applaud me this time. My bleeding scalp is the conductor's lesson for everyone. As I pass a half-awake guard, he stares at my head for a moment and then turns away with a green, nauseated look on his face.

The east gate at the other end of the compound opens and the cart enters. Following a safe distance behind comes the boy. The gate is locked after him.

Avron is excited. "It is unusual for him to come two days in a row," he says as he grabs my arm. "God is good. God is still with us." Avron looks at my head and then pleads, "Put your hat on. I don't want you to frighten the boy."

I wonder how the hell I can possibly frighten this child whose eyes have probably witnessed every conceivable abomination. My head feels better with the hat on—the bite of the wind had the same effect as pouring salt on an open wound.

Karl is beside me, but he says nothing. He is hunched over, staring into a puddle of muddy water.

Avron watches the boy as he takes up his position by the cart. The violin strikes; a man is cornered. Avron's body imitates the child's every motion, whispering encouragement under his breath. "Don't press so hard on the strings. Play slowly now, slowly—reach for the bread. Take it. Take it. He's offering it. Take it." The boy finally points with his bow, but at that moment the man makes a run for it and gets away. Avron is beside himself and smashes his fist into the palm of his hand. "Why do you always hesitate? What are you waiting for? Take the bread when they stop. You'll starve to death if you wait. Why do you always wait?"

On his third try, the boy wins his prize and the sack bulges. "That's it," says Avron. "Now play him a little song and follow the cart." The violin plays a piece that I can barely hear. Avron nudges me. "It is some Brahms."

The song continues and Avron becomes anxious. "Why

do you have to play him a symphony? Go on and follow the cart," he whispers. "Why play him a symphony for such a small morsel of bread? The more they give you, the more you play. When are you going to learn this?"

The cart crosses over to us, and with it comes the boy whose sack is almost filled. He starts his routine at the next hut, but then he begins coughing. The violin ceases and the potential victim escapes easily. Avron, too, begins coughing. Between gasps Avron says, "Why don't you ever take the soup? It is good for you. It will keep you alive—but no, all you take is the bread. The soup will keep you from coughing."

The boy recovers and takes the bread from another man. Avron is happy. "This is a good day for him," he tells me. "Some days he gets nothing."

The boy's eyes watch each of us go through the line. Avron peels the crust off a small piece of rye and walks carefully over to the child. The boy backs away after taking the bread. The violin does not come out. I pass by next and feel his cold stare.

Karl walks a few steps toward the child and holds out his entire chunk of bread. The boy pulls out his violin, but then, after looking at Karl, replaces the instrument under his coat and walks away. Karl breaks into tears and slowly returns to the hut. It is one thing to be spurned by one's fellowmen, but the hurt cuts even deeper when one is rejected by a child.

I stand with Avron on the steps as the food cart finishes its rounds and is dragged out through the gate. Mechanically, the boy returns to the midfield opposite our hut. Avron leaves me and walks toward him. He stops several feet from the child. Avron holds out another small piece of rye, which he grabs and stuffs safely in the sack. Avron then hums a piece that I recognize as Mozart. The violin plays the exact same song—note for note. Avron then buys another lesson for the boy with his bread. This time the violin reproduces some of Avron's Beethoven. It is the same each time—first the bread, then the humming, and then the violin mimics Avron's song.

The violin stops suddenly in the middle of some Mozart. My first thought is that perhaps Avron tried to get too close. I notice that the boy has his eyes fixed on the group of guards by the fire. He abandons Avron, who tries to entice him back with more bread, and trudges off toward the soldiers.

The violin begins to play a lullaby similar to his usual song, but with an earthier ring to it. Broad smiles cross the faces of the soldiers. One of them seems drawn away from the fire by the lullaby. He is not smiling. The violin plays on and on, and as it does the soldier begins to cry. The boy peers into the tearstained face of the grown man who stands before him. The boy's expression does not change.

The other guards are convulsed with laughter as they taunt their crying comrade. They yell, "Get him. Get him." I don't know who they're talking to—the boy or the weeping soldier.

Avron races over to me and grabs the bread right out of my hand. He holds it up in the air and waves at the boy who is still playing the same tune. The boy doesn't even look at us. Avron whispers, "Run away. Come here and I'll give you all this bread. You won't have to play. Run away from him or he'll hurt you."

The soldiers keep up their taunts and suddenly the crying stops. "Get him," they yell again. The soldier wipes his eyes and reaches for his rifle. The violin is hurriedly stuffed under the coat as the boy begins to walk away. The soldier raises his rifle over his head and follows the child. I watch horror-struck, but the soldier makes no real effort to overtake the boy. It is like some macabre charade. The soldier could easily crush the child if only he ran after him instead of walking. The boy does not look back as he heads toward the east gate. The soldier finally stops and walks back to the flaming barrel.

The boy stands before the east gate and plays his lullaby. The gate is opened and he is gone.

I look at Avron and ask him what is going on. He is visibly upset. He watches the boy disappear into the other compound. "I don't know why he does this," he says. "It's always the same guard. I don't know what it means. One of these days he is going to get killed. The child won't listen to me when I tell him to stay away from him. I don't know what pleasure he gets from seeing him cry. He won't listen to me. The best I can do with him is to teach him the music that he should be learning if he were on the outside. Sometimes he won't even take my bread. I can't get near him. If I step an inch closer, he runs off." He looks at me, and I see a calm come over his face. "You must agree that no child has ever played like this."

I take my bread back from Avron. He follows me into the hut but then goes over to Karl. I hear him telling him to try giving the boy some bread another day.

I try to sleep, but my scalp is still too raw. I can barely lay my head down on the bunk. All I hear is the talking around me. It is as if Sheleen were still alive. This night, however, only the poet's name is mentioned. His escape has thrown those who still have the ability to think into complete turmoil.

Of all the speakers this night, the writer from Anselm is most eloquent in his funeral oration. "He is dead," he intones to the others, who nod in agreement. "He got out, but he couldn't have gone far. They must have shot him not far from here, and in his weakened condition he died instantly. Yes, he is dead. He probably crawled into a thicket and bled to death. They'll never find him, and if they do, no one will be able to tie him to us. He was crazy to do what he did. He thought only of himself. Where did he think he could go? Vilna is no more. If he showed himself back in Vilna, they'd shoot him on the spot. We don't have to worry about him being brought back here. The conductor is right; we're better off without him. What he did was the work of a madman. If the rope was good enough for Sheleen, then it should have been good enough for the poet."

Sleep finally comes easily for my brothers. They are convinced that the poet is no more. They, too, could not continue this way of life if they knew he were alive. They are fortunate if they can believe he is dead.

The quiet of the night is broken as Karl approaches, his arms laden with blankets and coats. He has given up trying to follow in the footsteps of Sheleen. Now he takes over the poet's bed.

I watch him straighten his coats and lie down. He needs somebody. I wonder if I was placed on this earth to end my days being the nursemaid to this lost soul. I am sure I was destined for a better fate than to be the Sheleen for this fool. I think of Avron's offer to fill the vacant position of Moses. There must be a reason why the job has gone begging for over 3,000 years. I remember the poet's parting words about the fate of Moses.

I think of awakening the artist, but I'm afraid he will paint the boy again. I would run to the wire, but I'm afraid I will get shot. I try to fall asleep, but I cannot lay my raw head down on the bunk.

17

We watch as the cart is dragged into the compound. The guards follow, lashing out at the three prisoners shoving the wheels through the mud. These cart men never seem to last very long. The boy follows them in but remains a safe distance behind. When the cart moves, he moves, as if bound to it by an invisible rope.

The boy's routine never varies. He ensnares the second man he goes after. The bread is easily within his grasp, but his gaze never leaves the man's face. The boy's eyes then shift from the man who offers his bread for the warmth of a song to the guards standing by the fire.

As the boy walks away from his prisoner, the violin begins to play the guard's lullaby. The same soldier moves a few steps away from the others toward the child. Everything is on schedule—each of the players knows his role in this same drama.

Avron's face takes on the look of panic. He turns to me with his hopeless eyes. "He's starting up with the guard again." He stares up toward heaven. "Why God, why do you let him do this? Why can't he just take Your bread?"

The violin draws the soldier further and further away from the fire. Slowly they approach—the grown man with his gun and the child with his violin. The violin sings, and the tears well up in the soldier's eyes.

Only the men dragging the food cart to the next hut are oblivious to what is happening.

They now stand a few paces from each other. I see the tears run down the soldier's cheeks. The boy's expression is always the same—the days change, the seasons change, but his face never changes. The boy stares into the man's reddened eyes as the tiny fingers race up and down the strings of the violin.

136

The taunts begin coming from the other soldiers. Had they remained silent, the violin would have probably drained every last drop of water out of the body of the crying soldier.

The laughter of the guards increases, and finally the crying soldier turns and looks at his jeering friends. He sniffs several times and wipes each eye as the rage builds up on his face. With the encouraging shouts from his comrades, he unslings his rifle from his shoulder. They start their laugh-filled cries, "Get him. Get him."

The violin stops just before the rifle is raised into the air. The child backs away as the swinging rifle butt barely misses crashing into the violin. I am terrorized by what would happen if the violin was smashed.

I am surprised by Avron's screams. None of us have ever yelled out before. Screaming was meant only for men begging for a bullet from the tower. At the top of his lungs he yells, "Run away! Run away from him! For the sake of God —run away!"

The boy studies the wild face of the guard and scurries off. I have seen him run faster, though, when he's been after a man whose hands are filled with bread. This time the soldier follows closely behind, swinging his rifle as he goes.

The boy stops suddenly—his body is wracked by a fit of coughing. Phlegm spews from his mouth as he doubles over. He falls to the ground. His upraised arms protect the violin and bow from the mud.

The soldier stands over the fallen little body; his tormenter is cornered. The other soldiers laugh and yell as their bewildered comrade holds his rifle high above the boy. The child lies on his back anchored in the mud—his body sinking ever deeper into the ooze with each cough. He holds the violin off to the side, away from the rifle butt poised over him.

The shouting from the guards suddenly stops. Their

faces become serious. They even look worried. Then one of them, in a voice filled with contempt, yells out, "You damn fool." With that the butt of the gun crashes down on the boy.

I do not see where it lands. Avron's racing figure flashes in front of me and blocks my view of the sprawled-out child. As he runs toward the boy, Avron's clenched fists strike up toward the sky. I hear him scream, "God, God! Why are you letting them take him? You've closed your eyes to everything!" Avron reaches the dazed-looking guard who still stares down at the lifeless body and, with all his might, pushes the soldier away.

I am running. I am running toward Avron and the boy. Another guard reaches Avron first and, with one swing of his rifle, smashes him in the face. Another blow of the rifle butt crashes into Avron's hand as he tries to protect his head. Avron drops to his knees.

I yell at the guard to leave Avron alone. My body shields Avron as I scream at the soldier that this is Verbin's best worker. If he kills him, he will be sorry he was ever born.

The guard shoulders his rifle and walks away. The commandant rushes out of the guard hut and orders the food cart out of the compound. The lines of unfed prisoners begin running toward the shop. Today no one gives a damn about orderly rows.

The commandant draws his pistol and starts toward us. I grab Avron and lift him up off his knees He reaches out to touch the body of the boy, but I pull him away and half carry him to the shop. The same guard who smashed the boy still stands gazing down at the motionless child. Finally he, too, walks off.

The commandant holsters his pistol as the soldiers herd the men through the narrow door into the shop.

Avron cries as I drag him ever further from the child. He keeps looking at the boy, whose half-closed eyes face upward into the overcast sky. The violin rests on his chest.

As I pull Avron up the steps of the shop, I see blood pouring out of his left ear. The entire left side of his face seems pushed in, and the eye is swollen shut. With his one good eye, he looks back at the body lying in the mud in the center of the field.

Avron fights being shoved into the shop. One hand clutches the door frame and will not let go of it. The red cap comes over and bangs Avron's fingers. His hand then drops away from the door. I lead Avron to his bench. Blood flows out of his mouth. In a garbled voice he repeats over and over again, "Why did God let this happen? Why did God let this happen?"

I place him in his chair next to his machine. His right hand is blue and swollen. I wonder if the violinist's hand will ever move again.

I look into his devastated face. I stand beside him for a moment, then bend down and whisper in his good ear. "Listen to me," I say. "Can you hear me?" He nods slowly. "If the boy lives, I will be your Moses. Do you hear me? I will try to get him out of here. You have my word."

A slight smile forms on the uninjured side of his face. He lays his head down on the bench. I wonder if he has passed out.

"Get back to your goddamn machine," swears the red cap. "You know, you're more trouble than you're worth."

I brush past him and head for Verbin, who is about to settle into his chair for his afternoon nap. I gaze down on his good-natured face. Only he in the midst of this hell retains a constant warm smile etched in all that fat. I point over to Avron and say, "That man is your best operator. He is sick, but he will soon be well. We need to follow his machine if we are to make good spines. Don't mark him off. He has always taken good care of his machine. He will be well soon."

I feel the red cap's hand clamp around my neck. I stop talking. Verbin's pleasant expression does not change. He says nothing. Gradually his puffy eyelids close.

The conductor intersperses his curses with the warning that he and he alone does the talking to Verbin.

Avron remains slumped over his bench. The guards seem fidgety. The one who struck the boy stands alone, staring out the window at the road. At regular intervals one or another of the string players makes quick trips to the window by the doorway to peer out at the boy. From their look I know that he has not moved.

I find that my machine bangs out his lullaby and then strays off to play that special soaring song of his. I wonder what will happen to me if he lives—then I wonder what will happen to me if he dies.

About an hour later I see the cellist from Pavan race from the window to Avron's machine. Avron listens to him and then pulls himself up from his bench. With difficulty he begins to walk in my direction. His body weaves down the aisles through the orchestra. Using his good hand for support, he grabs onto each bench as he makes his way toward me. He falls once and is helped up by the pediatrician. The entire left side of his face is a mass of black and blue. Only one eye guides him on his journey.

He grasps my bench with his hand. He speaks with difficulty. "The boy is alive," he says haltingly. "The cellist saw him get up and crawl toward the east gate." He pauses. "Did you mean what you said to me?"

I say that I did.

Avron drops to one knee and takes my filthy, grease-stained hand. He kisses it. There is an awe in his voice as he says, "I will do anything you ask of me. God has chosen you. God is good. You are Moses."

I help him to his feet and ask him how he feels. "I have never felt better," he answers. "We all have a purpose in life. Today my purpose has been fulfilled. God gave me life for only one reason, and that was to place the boy in your hands."

He stumbles off in search of his bench. The orchestra roars out as it gives Avron its salute.

I have been officially crowned the new Moses, but my head is still too raw even to wear my own dirty cap. Only my lice rejoice at my elevation to Avron's version of sainthood. The lice dance wildly across my body to mark their happiness at their master's good fortune.

I look around at the many pharaohs I will have to overcome. Inside the shop I stare at the gleaming guns, the sleeping Verbin, and one of the greatest bastards of all time—the red cap. Outside, I know there are more guns, fences, towers, and the commandant.

My machine pounds away, wondering where the poet is at this moment. I push the poet out of my mind and wonder where the boy is.

18

The days pass, but there is no sign of the child. The food cart comes and goes, but he is never part of the entourage. Without him, our feedings are peaceful, except for occasional smashes from the guards.

Each night I listen for the violin, but there is nothing. Only the distant chattering of the machine guns breaks the silence. The boy never leaves my mind. I wonder if he has crawled into some far-off corner of the camp and just died. I ask the food cart men about him, but they only shrug their shoulders.

I am supposed to be the new Moses, but my soul does not feel uplifted. In fact, I feel worse than before—I am growing weaker each day. This place continues to drain the years out of me. I am now an old man. The new men look at me with a kind of wonder usually reserved for the very old.

I came here taking it for granted that I was still young, but now this is gone. In the past, I was always intrigued when I heard people refer to themselves as being "old." I always wondered what one event in their lives had the power to tip their self-image from the side of youth over to the bonds of old age. I knew my own youth was doomed the moment I walked through these gates. Now I realize that I had become "old" the moment Avron kissed my hand.

I am now Avron's Moses, but I have no one to lead out of the wilderness. I lie in my bunk wondering if the child still exists. Neither God nor anyone else gives me instructions on how to proceed out of this Egypt. Only Karl babbles on.

I lie in filth, bound to this place. Only the poet could see things for what they really were. He was right—Sheleen and his world were all madness. Now I begin to wonder about Avron and the boy. Was the poet also right about them? I can't help wondering where the poet is at this moment.

Avron screams out again from his bunk. Ever since he was bashed in the head he has alternated between periods of lucidity and delirium. The doctors think his skull is fractured. They debate among themselves in words that I cannot understand about how long he will last. I know, however, that Verbin, and not our doctors, will be the ultimate judge.

Each day we drag Avron back and forth to the shop. He spends most of his time with his head resting on the bench. The musicians come by frequently and turn his face so that the injured side does not lie in the pool of blood oozing from his wounds. From time to time he raises up and makes pitiful attempts to run his machine. Only two fingers on his battered hand continue to function. With them, he guides the scrap into the pounding cutter and makes enough spines to let the world know he is still alive.

Verbin keeps a steady eye on Avron. Other men are checked off, but somehow Avron is spared.

We hold Avron up as we go through the food line. I ask one of the doctors about his left ear, and he says he thinks he will be permanently deaf. He is unsure about the fate of the eye.

At first Avron lives only on the soup; he cannot bite into the bread. We can easily trade his rye for more soup. The cellist from Pavan chews Avron's bread, and, when it is soft enough, he pushes it tenderly into Avron's mouth, coaxing the violinist to swallow.

In his delirium, Avron talks of the boy. Above the noise of the machines I hear him scream out to him. The orchestra speeds up to drown out his cries so the guards will not take notice. The soldiers hear nothing as they sleep on.

Throughout the commandant's brief visit, the red cap stands by Avron and holds him up by the shoulders. The officer's tour is uneventful. When he leaves, the conductor lets go of Avron's head and it drops back on the bench. The violinist screams out in pain. I could believe again in God if a lightning bolt would crash through the window and strike the red cap dead.

After the lights go out, I take some of my soup to Avron. He talks with difficulty, and what he says makes little sense. I ask him how he feels, but he doesn't answer. Even when I mention the boy, he says nothing. When he does speak, it is only of his violin. "Where is my violin? I must find it. You must practice each day just to keep what you have. Please have Anna find my violin."

I cradle his head in my arms and put the cup up to his lips. I wonder where this Anna fits into his past. She must have been his wife. He sips the soup and slowly drinks up what little is left. Whispering in his good ear, I plead to him, "Avron, do you hear me? If the boy does not return in a few days, I must leave here. I want to join the poet while there's still some life left in me. Look at me, I'm an old man. Soon I'll be too old to run. There is so little time left for me. I cannot be your Moses without the child."

His only reply is to ask me again to find his lost violin. I cover him up and stand beside his bunk, listening for the sound of the boy. All I hear is Avron shouting out for his Anna.

When I return to my bunk, Karl asks, "Who is Anna?"

I tell him I will find out in the morning. He talks on for a while and then drifts off to sleep.

The poet comes into my mind, and as always I wonder where he is now. I have so little imagination left in me that I can't even invent a suitable place for him to be. I wrack my brain to dream up something. It is hardly surprising that my famished mind conjures up the poet sitting in a fine restaurant. A waiter in a spotless tuxedo takes the order from my friend, who is still dressed in his filthy clothes. The poet and the waiter discuss the merits of the different wines, and finally he settles on a bottle from a good vintage year.

No one sits in the empty chair opposite the poet. The other waiters clear the half-eaten food from the plates on the other tables. I visualize the poet reaching into his pocket for a cigarette. The waiter rushes over to light it. I laugh for a moment, realizing that I have placed a half-crushed butt in his mouth. My imagination replaces the butt with an unsmoked long white cigarette that just came out of a silver cigarette case.

My mind does not leave the poet. I get up and search for his dagger, which I have kept hidden under Karl's bunk. Its edge is like a razor and sharp enough, I hope, to cut through the wire. I find myself buttoning my outer coat and putting on my gloves. I have finally decided to say to hell with all of this. I'm going out to have dinner with the poet.

As I pass the sleeping artist, I pat his head in farewell. He looks up and for once begins to get up on his own. He reaches into his pocket for his spine, thinking that I have commissioned him to do another painting. I tuck him back in his bunk and he falls asleep.

The soldier in his tower handles his light beam without any sense of rhythm. The sound of machine guns sets my heart racing even faster until I realize that the firing is far off in the distance. I stand waiting by the door, holding my ticket of admission to the outside—the poet's long spine.

I reach for the knob and turn it, but I go no further. From out of the darkness he calls, "Is he out there? Do you hear the violin?" It is Avron. He stands in the darkness a few feet away from me, draped in his blanket.

My hand slowly leaves the knob. I slump against the door and let the dagger fall into my pocket. "No, he is not out there," I answer.

"He will return soon—he always has before," says

Avron. "Why are you up so late? You need your strength. God has given you a mission. Please go to bed." He takes my hand. "I feel better now. I have lost track of the days. I remember you and the others feeding me. I will be better now. I think I can manage on my own."

I walk slowly back to my bunk, knowing that I am destined never to dine with the poet. The best I can hope for is to grab some of the manna from Avron's heaven if and when it ever begins to fall.

19

Avron is now able to chew small bits of bread. For the first time he walks to the shop on his own. He stumbles a few times but brushes us away when we attempt to help him.

When he tries his machine, it is obvious that he is not the masterful operator of old. He cocks his head to one side to give the one good eye the best possible view of the cutter. The battered hand hampers his rhythm. The doctor from Wiven made a splint for the hand, but Avron will not wear it. As I watch him try to play his machine, I can see that he is now no better than any of the men in the woodwind section.

Avron makes several trips to the window in hope of seeing the boy. The red cap sends him back to his bench as the time draws near for the commandant's tour of inspection. The officer's visits have become less frequent the past few weeks.

Today is different. Verbin's face lights up as the conductor, standing by the window, signals the imminent approach of the commandant.

Try as he might, Verbin cannot coax the officer beyond the cello section. Verbin's mouth moves quickly back and forth as he tries to say everything in the short time he knows is allotted to him. Within a few minutes it is apparent that the officer has had enough of the shop. He begins walking toward the door. He takes only a few steps when one of the cello players half rises from his machine and points to him. The sight of such a foolhardy thing sends the orchestra into a frenzy of wild banging. I recognize the man as the writer from Anselm.

The writer's hand reaches out and points first to the commandant's book and then back to himself. I realize that the goddamn fool must once have written this book.

The officer seems puzzled as he looks at the book and then slowly up at this man who should, long ago, have lost all traces of such impudence. Rage comes over the officer's perfect face. He takes the book and flings it into the nearest canister. When he sees this, the writer realizes what he has done and buries his head in his hands.

Verbin, with an apologetic look and arms flailing in the air, follows the commandant, hoping to lure him back into the shop. All he gets for his efforts is the door slammed in his face.

Several of the guards start toward the writer, but the red cap rushes over and gets there first. The soldiers watch and seem satisfied as the conductor does their work. Blow after blow comes down on the writer's head until he drops to the floor. The red cap then smiles and bows toward the guards.

The conductor drags the writer out of the cello section and pushes him through the aisles to an empty seat in the woodwinds. The guards go back to sleep, but Verbin, with a worried look on his face, wrings his fat little hands as he stares out the window toward the guard hut.

The conductor settles the orchestra down to the standard tempo. He grabs a frightened new man—pulls him out of his chair and leads him to the writer's old bench. I look at the writer and know he is lucky to be alive.

Moments later the door opens and the commandant's adjutant—a young lieutenant—walks into the shop. He ignores Verbin's attempt at a greeting and goes over to the nearest guard. A quick shove brings the dozing soldier out of his stupor.

Together they walk up and down the aisles of the cello section, peering into each canister. Finally, they stop. The adjutant nudges the soldier, who bends down and lifts out the grease-covered book.

The red cap produces a rag and cleans the cover. Each of the crumpled pages is carefully straightened. Then the book is handed to the lieutenant, who quickly places it under his arm and heads toward the door. Verbin's smiling words of farewell to the officer are ignored, just as was his greeting.

When the officer is gone, an exuberant song comes from the writer's machine honoring his book, resurrected from the garbage. He has little time to rejoice as the conductor paces back and forth behind him, pouring curses into the writer's ears.

Verbin remains brooding by the door. I am sure that he is terror-struck that he will lose his beloved job after the incident with the book. He tries to find solace in his easy chair, but he is unable to fall asleep. The fat man bounces up and down, waddling between the chair and his office. The faithful red cap follows Verbin's every step, trying to soothe his troubled master. Then they closet themselves in the office.

The orchestra slows down as fear settles over each machine. I begin to wonder what will happen to us if Verbin is replaced. Everyone has heard the stories of entire shops being emptied out and the men shot. The song of the crying machines begins to rise. My own cutter follows the buildup of the clanging until the entire orchestra screams out in terror.

Verbin follows closely behind as the conductor runs out of the office. They proceed to the nearest machine where the red cap, with one fling of his arm, pushes the operator off his chair onto the floor. The conductor hurriedly makes a few spines, which Verbin catches in his hands before they can fall into the canister. They are handed back to the red cap, who runs the finished spines once again under the blade of the cutter.

Verbin grabs these reworked spines and runs out of the shop as fast as his stubby legs will permit. The conductor waits nervously by the window, fingering the brim of his cap. With all the noise, the guards begin to stir. The conductor turns around and, with the lowering of his arm, the orchestra slows to a normal pace. We now play in hushed tones, waiting for the fat man's return from the guard hut. I shrug my shoulders when the lawyer from Traden leans over and asks, "What is going on? What is he telling the commandant? What if the commandant is gone?"

An eternity seems to pass before the door bursts open. Verbin is smiling as he holds the spines up in the air. His round face is the picture of happiness. I don't exactly know the reason for his pleasure, but it is enough for me to see him settle into his chair and fall asleep with his moronic grin still covering his face.

The red cap spends no time in exultation. He races from bench to bench, barking out orders. A spine is shoved in front of everyone's face as he goes through his explanation. It is obvious that the conductor has just dreamed up some new technique in the fine art of making spines that has pleased the commandant.

He spends little time in the center of the orchestra. For a few seconds I see him trying to explain the new technique to the artist. After realizing what type of men he is dealing with in the woodwinds, he abandons the area, but not before giving the writer another smash to the head.

Slowly he makes his way from bench to bench through the orchestra until it is my turn for his lesson. He is out of breath and seems exhausted. Rather than have him shove me aside, I get up and let him sit down. His shaking hand bangs out the usual spine, but then he adds the modification that could have come only from his brain. The cutting blade barely nicks the sides, creating barbs along the entire length of the spine. He glares up at me and yells, "Look at it, you bastard, this is how you'll make them all now! You'll turn out the same number as before, but now they'll be barbed!"

I pick up one of his new spines and stare intently at its irregular sides. Before, the sharp spines would pierce through a man. Now, they will tear the guts out of anyone they hit. I look at him as he gets up from my machine. His parting words to me are, "Don't give me your goddamn look of righteous indignation." He points to the writer who brought on his stroke of creative genius. "That son of a bitch will barb every damn spine made in the woodwinds." He leaves me and goes on to the next machine.

One of the guards reaches into my canister and picks up a new spine. He shows it to his comrades, but they only shrug their shoulders and go back to sleep.

Within an hour, adding the barbs to the spines becomes almost routine. I wonder if history will regard the red cap's invention on a par with the discovery of the wheel or the invention of the light bulb.

Even before we reach the hut, I see some of the men at the head of the line pointing toward the tree. I am gripped with excitement as I see the boy standing there, holding onto the trunk for support.

The gate opens, letting the cart through, but the boy does not move. Everyone stares at him, even the guards. One of the soldiers yells at the guard who smashed the boy. I cannot hear what the soldier says to this simple bastard, but the guard walks away from the others toward the guard hut. He opens the door and goes inside.

The usual feeling of tension is missing as the men go through the food line. It is apparent to everyone that the boy is in no condition to separate a man from his bread.

The cart passes tranquilly from hut to hut. Each man takes his bread in peace. The boy starts toward the cart, but there is little life in his steps. The violin is produced, but no song comes forth. He stops, perhaps knowing that he cannot keep up with the cart. I am sure he doesn't have the strength to trap a man.

The boy does not cross over with the cart when it comes

to our side. I hear the rumble of a cough as it reverberates through his chest. He sits down very slowly on the ground in the middle of the field and stares blankly into a pool of murky water. The back of his coat is caked with dried mud. When he looks up, I am shocked that his gaunt face is even thinner than before.

The cart feeds our huts and then is gone. The soldiers rush off to the warmth of the guard hut. The boy remains sitting bent over on the ground like a little bird shivering on its perch.

Avron hands me his bread and says, "Now he is yours. Go to him." I tear off a small chunk and hand the rest back to him. He gives me a gentle shove and I start toward the boy.

The red cap's eyes never leave me as I head toward midfield. He stands in the doorway of his hut, nibbling on his bread and sipping his soup. He does not wave me back to my hut.

I stop a few feet from the child—his back is to me. The battered coat, always too large even in the best of times, now hangs from him. I hear his breathing and intermittent moist coughing. He kneels on the ground; with each breath his head bobs up and down.

He turns slowly and looks up at me. He has the same emotionless expression, but now his lids are drooped with fatigue. An angry hiss comes from his mouth as he makes a vain effort to get up and run away. He falls back on his knees and begins to crawl toward the east gate.

I run around and block his escape. He lies at my feet totally exhausted—his head rests in the mud. His little body begins to writhe violently as I try to pick him up. The hissing begins again. I grip him by the arms and raise the shaking body to its feet. He is nothing but skin and bones. His hands grab onto my coat for support.

Kneeling down, I hold him up beside me. He looks away, and his eyes will not meet mine. With my sleeve, I reach around and gently wipe his nose. He shows no interest in the piece of bread that I wave in front of him. I put my arms around him and feel him trembling within my grasp. Whispering to him in the softest voice I can muster, I say, "I will not hurt you. Do you understand me? I want to feed you. You are hungry, aren't you? Do you know what I'm saying? I will take care of you. I will give you bread. See, look at the bread."

I turn his face toward me, but still he looks down. I bring the piece of bread to his lips, but the mouth does not open. He lunges to free himself, but I tighten my grip on him. He can go nowhere and I think he knows it. I try to get the bread down again. Finally he opens his mouth a little and takes tiny bites of the bread. He eats from the side of his mouth like most of the men here. Everyone's gums are sore, and I'm sure his are too. After another few bites, he refuses to take anything more.

I hold the cup up to his mouth and beg him to take a sip. "Take some of the soup. It will make you feel well. I once fed my children soup."

Gently, I place the edge of the cup to his closed lips until I can feel his teeth. Holding the back of his head, I shove the cup up against his mouth. He takes a little sip and, with the first swallow, the most beautiful fantastic look of revulsion crosses his face. Only a child can possess such a look of total disgust. I hug him as I get more and more of the soup down him. Then he starts gagging like any ordinary child being forced to eat his vegetables. I cannot take my eyes off his face, so filled is it with loathing for the soup. For the first time I see the face of a child. Finally he pushes my hand away and I drink from the same cup, all the while being careful to hide my own similar feelings for the soup.

With some dirty water from a nearby pool, I wash the mud off his legs. The siren for the second shift sounds. Hurriedly I say, "Come back tomorrow during the day.

153

Don't come at night; it's too cold. Come again tomorrow and I will give you some more bread." His usual blank expression remains. He says nothing, but I take heart that his hissing has stopped and the trembling of his body is stilled.

The boy remains standing where I left him as we march to the shop. I look back and see him watching me. From his place in line Avron asks, "Did you tell him about God?"

I stare in amazement at this one-eyed man who is still possessed by only one idea in his beaten head. Trying to hold back my anger, I say, "Avron, how can I talk about something like God when I don't even know if he understands what the hell I'm saying to him? Who knows what goes on in that mind of his!"

Avron watches the child from the window until he is again waved away by the conductor. I can tell by the steady way Avron plays his machine that the boy must not have fallen back down into the mud.

My hand reaches for the poet's dagger, still hidden in my inside pocket. I slip it out when no one is looking and place it before the cutter. With each bang of the machine, the long sharp spine becomes smaller and smaller. From the metal of the once gleaming knife comes one spine after another until there is nothing left. My onetime ticket to the outside lies torn to shreds at the bottom of the canister.

I see the conductor walking toward my bench and immediately wonder what plague is about to befall me. He never wastes words. "Meet me in the latrine. I want to talk to you about the boy—it will be worth your while."

As I enter this stinking place, the conductor is in the process of throwing everyone else out. When we are finally alone, he motions for me to sit down. I turn my collar up to protect my neck from the biting cold.

He nibbles away on a crust of bread. I wonder how anyone except him could eat in such a place without throwing up.

He continues chewing on his crust as he speaks. "You and I have something in common. I talked to Avron, and I find that we both want that damn child out of here. Our reasons are different, but the end result is the same. I thought I saw the last of him the day the guard smashed him, but that little bastard must have nine lives. I don't have the strength to live through any more of them. I can't have him taunting that guard or making a shambles out of the food line. I don't want anyone disrupting anything, and that goes for you too."

Angrily I ask him, "What the hell are you trying to preserve by all this? The guards may honor your red cap, but the pneumonia and the dysentery won't. They'll finally get to you just like they'll get to the rest of us."

For the first time I see something that I can call a human look come over his monkeylike face. His voice loses its iron-hard cast. "Someday this will all come to an end, and I expect to be alive on that day. I will walk out of here. Those of you who follow me now will follow me on that day out through the main gate. Someday I will be free of this place."

There is a knock on the door and a voice pleads to be let in. The conductor yells, "Stay out of here! If you have to piss, then piss in the mud!"

The conductor levels the same harsh voice at me. "I don't give a damn about this Moses business you have going with Avron. It's fine with me any way you get rid of the boy. All that matters is that I want him out of here, and so do you. The boy is an untamed mongrel who will only cause trouble. The average dog is more civilized than this little bastard. He can probably squeeze through the wire to the outside and be gone without them ever knowing the difference. I want you to convince him to get the hell out of here. Tell him anything you want—I don't give a damn. I can control the men, but I never know what this little animal will do. I don't know why the guards put up with his roaming around this place."

He thinks for a while and then says, "You'll be the one to feed the boy. The only one. In time you'll get him to eat out of your hand. Then you'll kick his butt out of here, and we'll have some peace. I want more time to live, and you need more time to convince him to leave."

I yell back at him, "How the hell are you going to keep him from going after the new men?"

He shakes his head. "Oh, I won't—you will. You will talk to all the new men. You will greet each and every one of them. You will convince them to accept this place. This time you *will* become the new Sheleen. This latrine will be your seat of higher learning, just as it was for Sheleen. You will tell them not to feed the boy. I don't care what you tell them, just so they behave. I don't want any running to the fence or any more escapes. You remember all of Sheleen's answers, don't you? You will tell them about the 'noble life' or whatever the hell he called it."

Then he laughs as he says, "If you're smart, you won't take anything you say too seriously. I think Sheleen believed some of that garbage he talked about every night. I want you to last longer than Sheleen. While he was here, things ran smoothly. You will do just as he did. The men will come to visit you each night. You will charge them a little bread for their lessons. If you're smart, you'll keep some for yourself and give the rest to the boy. Keep the boy out of here at night; there's too much chance for shooting."

He takes a flattened cigarette butt from his pocket and lights it. The smell of the smoke is a welcome relief from the ammonia. The smoldering butt is held out to me. There are just one or two drags left in it. "If you are a good Sheleen," he says, "I think I can convince Verbin not to check off Avron. You and I know that Avron will never be worth a damn with that hand of his. I think I can arrange to keep Avron alive. Do you understand what I mean? Is it a deal?"

He holds the cigarette out and waves it in front of my face. "You'll become Sheleen, OK?" He hesitates for a moment. "All right, goddammit, take Sheleen's bench and I'll keep you in butts every single day."

I grab the butt and then realize that my first puff is the equivalent of a handshake. We have made our deal.

His voice is filled with contempt. "Goddammit, I bet I could have had you as the new Sheleen the first time I offered. I just didn't know your price was as high as a butt a day." As he walks out, several waiting men rush into the latrine.

I get one last drag from the cigarette before it burns my fingers. My back slumps up against the wall. So much has happened between the red cap's first offer and now.

I am immune to the stench of the latrine. This is good, for I know I will be spending much of my life in here. I realize that now I know what to do with the boy. The instructions I have awaited have not come down from heaven but have been presented to me by the devil himself.

20

I walk over and stand beside Sheleen's silent machine. As I look around at the members of the bass section, I wonder if they will think that I am invading their holy ground. This section is still filled with many of his original disciples. They stare up at me, but it is only with indifference. There are many new faces in the group. Several of the old ones I remembered so well have just faded away without my realizing they have gone. For them it was easy not to find the strength to get out of their bunks in the morning.

Finally I sit down and start up the cutter. As with every machine in the orchestra, Sheleen's sings with its own characteristic pitch. The cutter moves effortlessly. Someone has taken good care of it in his absence.

The man next to me reaches over and asks, "Does it run well?"

I nod that it does.

There is something familiar about him. I look at the face carefully and then realize that he is the one who pushed the table out from under Sheleen. All of us have thought of this man many times when hunger gnaws through us. Everyone's dreams are filled with eating Sheleen's mound of bread, which once stood within easy reach on the table. I have heard men curse this man who now works beside me for not sharing Sheleen's legacy instead of squandering it on a dying man.

Sheleen's assistant looks up and asks, "Are the bearings running smoothly? I have oiled them every day."

I tell him that he did a good job. The man sits back with a satisfied look. He has tended the grave of his master quite well. Perhaps he had expected Sheleen to return. I wonder if he is disappointed that now only I run the machine.

I enjoy the tranquillity around me. This corner is populated by a more somnolent group of guards. They are less edgy than the ones I have left behind. Above the noise I hear bits and pieces of their conversation. From what I can gather, Rollin's daughter has died and he has been given leave for the funeral. Two of the guards have a somber look as they talk about the child's death. They are silent for a while but then begin to laugh about something I can't make out. All of us strain to hear what comes from their mouths. Anything they say seems fascinating; servants are always caught up in every detail of their masters' lives. I listen constantly to the guards for any mention of the boy, but never once do they even say a word about him.

Verbin goes over to the new man in the woodwinds, and I know that my official duties as the new Sheleen are soon to begin. The man's number is registered in his black book, and then the red cap has his turn at the man's head. The man returns from the dock appropriately degraded and is brought over to me by the conductor. He stands listlessly by my machine, running his hand across his smooth scalp. The conductor motions us toward the door. I get up and reach my open hand out to the conductor. Unwillingly he drops a butt into my palm and says, "Save this one for tomorrow—you've already had one today."

I gesture to the new man to follow me. Automatically he does what I tell him. From the looks of him, he would jump off a cliff if I told him to do so.

We sit in silence in the latrine. He keeps touching his head. I myself have forgotten what it's like not to have hair. The man only stares at the floor. I pull out the butt the red cap gave me and see that at most it has only one puff left in it. Then I realize that I don't have a match. I catch myself starting to ask the man for a light but, after looking at him, decide that this is not the time for such things. He probably doesn't have one anyway.

He remains hunched over with a terrified look on his

face. He is exhausted. I stare at his miserable figure, but my thoughts are on the cigarette in my pocket. Then I comprehend how fully I have adapted to this place.

A torrent of words suddenly pours when I ask of his family. His story is the same as my own and all the others. Tears stream down his face as he talks of his lost children. When he mentions children, I find it strange that I do not think of my own; only the boy fills my mind. I no longer hear this crying man. I keep wondering if the boy can be reached, or if this place has destroyed him. How can I teach him to walk out of here? I am afraid that someday I will lead him to the fence but he will refuse to crawl through the wire to the outside.

The smell of the ammonia begins to overwhelm me, and hot tears drip from my eyes. The crying man looks up, and I am certain that he thinks I am grieving with him over his lost life. He begins to sob uncontrollably. "Thank you," he cries, "for listening to me. For the very first time some-one has taken the time to listen to me."

As we walk out, I tell him to come to my hut tonight after the food cart and we will talk some more. He goes back to his bench with more life to his walk. I realize that being a Sheleen need not be a fatal occupation. It seems an easier calling than that of a Moses.

When I return to my bench, I see that Karl has moved two spaces closer to me. I don't even give a damn any more.

Through the cold night air the boy's lullaby drifts to-ward me as we wait in line for the food cart. Avron listens with his head cocked first to the north and then to the east. He points toward the east gate and, in a disappointed voice, says, "He's over there tonight—two compounds over. He will not come to you tonight." He looks at me and, in a consoling manner, says, "Don't worry, God will bring him back. Never fear, God will aid you. God will give you the wisdom to bring out the spark within the boy." He pauses for a moment and whispers out of the uninjured side of his mouth, "Look how God has shielded me from Verbin. I know that I can't run the machine like I used to, but still God keeps Verbin's pencil mark from striking the black book. My faith protects me while I live in the valley of the shadow of death." I say nothing as he repeats again and again how God keeps Verbin's pencil away from him.

As we pass through the food line, I grab the prisoner who is passing out the bread. He backs away quickly and looks around for the guards, but they are huddled by the fire. I grip his arm with all my strength and say, "Listen to me and remember what the hell I'm telling you." He tries to free himself, but I hold onto his bony arm. "The boy is not to be fed in any of the other compounds during the noon feeding. He must learn that he will get nothing there." I squeeze his arm even harder. "You tell this to all the other ladlers. The boy is to get nothing from anyone at noon except here. At night anyone can feed him. Do you understand me?"

As I release his arm, he still looks skeptical. Swearing at him a few times brings a worried look to his face. "Don't cross me," I say, "or I'll get the red cap to ship you out of here!" When he hands me a bigger share of bread than usual, I know that what I've said has gotten through to him and his insides are probably churning with fear.

The crying man from the latrine comes to my bunk. He has brought another new man with him. I motion for them to sit beside me. They never take their eyes off me as I drink my soup. Without the boy around I can gag on the soup in peace.

Karl starts talking to them, and suddenly the three of them are all talking at once. Each one is using different words to say the same thing: "Why did all of this have to happen to me?" They soon tire of each other's tragedy.

I ask them if they know anything of what is happening

on the outside. They can tell me nothing more than the little we all know—the war is still raging. One thing said does strike me—they talk of seeing bomb damage. This surprises me, for I cannot imagine an enemy plane being able to get through unscathed and slap at the invincible giants that cage us in.

They take turns telling me disjointed incidents of their past. Their own talking seems to soothe their inner misery. As if by an unspoken rule, each man, including Karl, speaks for a few moments and then allows the others equal time. Now and then they dwell on the happy portions of their pasts. They still look at me as they speak, and periodically I nod my head. This satisfies them and they continue. I find it hard to believe, but they seem to be enjoying themselves.

Avron comes over and interrupts them. I know him well enough to predict that he will try to reawaken their interest in God. His battered, grotesque face makes it hard to extol what God will do for those who still trust in Him.

Karl begins some story of his own, but Avron does not let him go on. Cradling his broken hand, he starts in with the preaching I have heard so many times before. "There is a child here in the camp whom God has placed among us. We must feed him to keep the spirit of God alive."

The new men show little interest in his sermon. I gently nudge Avron, who then stops. I begin to talk and hear myself speak with the firmness of Sheleen. "What this man is trying to say to you is that the child is the only reason to go on living. There is the seed of humanity left buried within him. You would never know this by looking at him, but you will when you hear him play his violin. As long as he survives, the memories of your children will live. I shall get this boy out of here someday, and his life will be a memorial to all of those we have lost. This will take time, and I will need a little of your bread each day to add to mine to keep him alive. As long as the child lives, we will keep our dead alive."

The siren blows, and I tell them to go back to their huts. I shake their hands and they thank me. "Come back again tomorrow night," I tell them, "and bring me a little bread for the boy."

When the light goes out, I walk Avron back to his bunk. He keeps massaging his crippled hand. "I can no longer play," he says in a worn-out voice. "I thought that I outwitted them when they took my violin—I still played. I was so sure they could never take this away from me, but they did. I could have played with one eye and one ear, but they took my hand. I thought I could rise above them, but they have finally whipped me. The violin meant so much to me. God works in such strange ways—but who are we to question Him?"

I cover Avron with his blankets and say, "The boy will go on playing for you and for all the rest of us. In your mind you will continue to guide his hands. He will still learn from your humming."

He reaches out and grasps my hand. "Do you really mean all the things you say? Did you really mean what you told the new men when you spoke of the boy? You sound like Sheleen, and I never knew if what he said really came from his heart. I fear a man if I am not sure of his heart. I fear a man who is too glib with his tongue."

"Do you fear me?" I ask.

Perhaps the length of his pause is his answer. I lie in my bunk, asking myself Avron's same questions.

The violin has none of its old force as the boy tries to ply his trade. He can barely keep up with the cart. He takes a few futile steps toward the new men, but he hasn't the strength to trap anyone.

Finally he stops one man. Avron cries out under his breath, "Run away from the child! Don't give him anything! Run!"

The man stands there with his bread. I recognize him as the one I cried with in the latrine. When he looks toward me, I raise my fist at him. That's all the encouragement he needs to escape from the boy. The red cap watches me and nods his head in approval. I always wonder if I am doing something wrong when I see this man look pleased.

The cart continues on, but the sack remains empty. Each man makes a mad dash for his hut the minute the ration reaches his hand. The boy soon gives up the chase and rests his tired body on the ground of the midfield.

Slowly, the boy gets up and follows the cart over to our side. The violin screams out in desperation. Everyone is now fair game—veterans as well as new men.

At the next hut, an old man is immobilized by the violin. The ladler steps away from the cart and gives the man a shove that propels him halfway to his hut. The boy with his never-changing face watches the man and his bread fly past him.

The boy gives up and sits on the ground. He does not follow the cart on the remainder of its rounds.

With the cart and the soldiers gone, the boy and I are alone in the compound. He walks over and stands by the fire that the guards have deserted. I sit on the step of my hut, gazing at him. He knows that I'm here, but he will not look at me. With the start of the rain, he shoves his violin and bow under his coat.

I place three large chunks of bread on top of my hat at the other end of the step, but still he ignores me. The rain runs down my face, and soon both the boy and I are wiping our noses on our sleeves. His eyes finally fix on the bread that is getting soggier by the minute.

I hear the creak of the door as it opens behind me. Avron

yells impatiently, "In the name of God, call out to him. Give him some bread. He's starving."

I hum his lullaby loud enough so that I'm sure he can hear me. He does not move but continues to stare at the bread. He blinks as the rain drips off the bill of his cap into his sunken eyes. Slowly he comes toward me but stops every few feet to cough. Each step he takes is heavy with fatigue. His coat and mine are now totally drenched by the rain.

He stands a few feet in front of me and stares down at the bread. Then he looks at me with his weary face.

Pointing to the bread, I say softly, "Take it. Eat some and put the rest in your sack. Sit down with me and we will eat together."

He reaches out for the bread and quickly stuffs each piece into his waterlogged sack. Walking away, he stops every few feet to look back at me. His blank stare is the same.

The boy watches us from the shelter of the tree as we march off in the pouring rain for the shop. Avron nudges me. "He looks so sick. In the name of God, how long is this going to take you?"

I shoot back, "I don't know how long it will take. I can't tell you and you can't tell Him."

21

The man has been silent the entire time. I ask him again where he is from, but still he says nothing. I begin to wonder whether it's ammonia or sorrow that has dulled his mind.

I am well prepared today. The match lights the cigarette butt, and it almost singes my nose in the process. After I take a few quick drags, the man comes out of his stupor. I hand it to him, and he gets one last puff out of the butt before it's gone.

"Where is the boy?" he says in a dull, matter-of-fact voice.

I am shocked and shoot back, "What do you know of the boy?"

"I heard an officer tell the driver of the truck to take us to 'the camp with the boy,' and we were brought here."

I begin to tell him of the boy, but the man falls back into his stupor.

The door opens and it is the conductor. He points to the man and screams, "You! Get the hell out of here! Your time's up! Get out!" By the way the man shuffles out the door, I know that he will fit well into this place.

The red cap's face is covered by his angriest look that is reserved for black occasions. "We've just received some bastard who looks like he's going to be trouble. He's been here fifteen minutes, and already he tells me he's going to kill all the guards." Then he grabs me by the arm. "You work him over with your damn mouth and calm him down." I can tell by the way he paces back and forth that his nimble brain hasn't yet figured out what to do with such a man. He mumbles under his breath, "Why the hell did we have to get this bastard! Why couldn't somebody else have gotten him!"

My first glance at this new man makes me wonder how

he got past the selection officers. The usual look of complete desolation is nowhere on his face. He seethes with anger as he kicks at the door after the red cap leaves.

I hold out my hand to him, but he brushes it away. His head is only half shaved. The red cap's clippers must have been thrown to the floor after the first few cuts.

"What the hell are you for?" he asks in a voice dripping with scorn. "What is going on in this place?"

I scream above him and tell him to sit down. He doesn't. I get up and shove him down on a seat. Giving him my coldest look, I tell him, "I'm here so that you can have someone to talk to. I don't sit here because I like the accommodations. We've all had to adapt—perhaps we can talk for a while and things will be easier for you."

He looks me up and down, and it is obvious that I do not impress him. "You've been here a long time, haven't you? I gather that you and that son of a bitch with the red hat want me to become just like you. That shop is filled with a bunch of eunuchs making shrapnel for the very bastards who killed our people. Do you realize what you're doing? You're helping them kill even more! You're prolonging your useless lives a little longer for nothing. I can't believe my eyes as I see you pounding away while the guards sleep. You could slit the throat of every guard without them knowing the difference. They'd even die of astonishment if they saw you act like men. You could take their guns and kill off half the other guards in this place before they got you. You could put a knife into the fat gut of that slob who sleeps in that big chair."

I grab him by the arm and shout, "Listen, you, the whole world's mad and so are we. Do you think I like living like this? All I know is that I'm still breathing. Forget about killing the guards. Don't get us killed with you."

I feel that there is little use talking to him. He smashes his hand against the wall until his knuckles begin to bleed. Then, for the first time, he sits quietly.

I try talking gently to him. "Listen, my friend, we all have our needs, and mine is to keep things as they are for just a little longer—a few weeks at the most. Then I will get out of here myself. We can even try the wire together. Trust me. We are of the same people. Who can you trust if you can't trust me?"

He looks down and, in a drained voice, says, "They killed four of mine and I want to kill four of them. If I can kill more, all the better. I have no interest in escaping." He rambles on that four guards are not enough. He must avenge his parents also. He keeps raising the stakes. Now he won't be satisfied until he avenges everyone.

The conductor peeks his head in through the door. He looks at me and I shake my head. Then he is gone.

I keep wondering why this man didn't do his killing at the selection camp. I think that he would have gained more pleasure in strangling an officer there rather than any of our privates or corporals.

I whisper to him, "Listen, we don't have much time. This won't last forever. Go along with me for a few weeks—a month at the most. If you go after the guards, you'll end up dead without taking a single one with you. At most you'll anger them when your blood and guts dirty their uniforms. Live with me now so that someday you can live again on the outside."

The man stares up at me, and momentarily I think that I have reached through to him. Then his spit covers my face and for an instant I am blinded. When I look up, I see the red cap leading him out. As I follow behind them, I'm surprised at first that the man offers no resistance. Then I realize how anxious he is to get at the guards.

The man sits at his bench and makes no effort to work his machine. The conductor stands behind him with his hands locked on the man's shoulders to keep him from jumping up.

When Verbin rises out of the chair, I expect him to walk

over and check the man off. He glances at the man for a moment, then walks into his office and half closes the door.

The conductor raises one fist high in the air, and the orchestra speeds up in answer to his command. The fist is raised again and again until the machines scream out in an ear-piercing clatter.

The guards awaken. Some of them hold their hands over their ears to stifle the screeching. Others, seeing Verbin's chair empty, start on a rampage through the aisles. I look over and see the pediatrician knocked to the floor.

The red cap then takes his restraining hands off the man's shoulders and quickly backs away from him. The man immediately jumps up and goes after the nearest guard with a long piece of scrap iron. From the four corners of the orchestra, the guards descend upon him. When the soldiers return to the stoves, their uniforms are as spotless as before.

As the conductor lowers his hands, the orchestra slowly calms. When the banging stops, Verbin comes out of his office and returns to his chair. He sits down and looks as good-natured as ever as he gazes at the empty bench of the once-angry man. Then Verbin dozes off.

The conductor walks through the aisles trying to steady the tempo, but he cannot smooth out the orchestra. He slumps against the wall with a morose look as he stares out over the shop. The machines, too, are worn out after playing this wild symphony.

The conductor comes over and says, "Play your machine louder and try to get some order back into this place." I bang the cutter in a regular tempo, and soon the others follow. Now everything is as it was except for my mind. It is still out of order. I wonder about this man whose only desire was to kill the guards. I look out over the orchestra at the rows of men pounding their lives away and take some comfort from the fact that I have convinced myself that the boy is reason enough to go on living. Avron, too, has the boy and his God to give him meaning. But what of the others?

I look up at the conductor and wonder about him. Of all people, he is the one I cannot figure out. What keeps him going?

He watches over me as I barb a spine. "We can't survive any more men like the last one," he says. "I don't want anyone else to get such ideas into his head." He looks around at the men and seems satisfied that no one among us has such inclinations. The guards, also, must not be too worried for they have returned to their usual stupor.

I look up and ask him, "I have the boy, but what do you have? What drives you on? I don't think you were like this all your life. Do you have someone waiting for you on the outside?"

"No," he says. Then he shuffles off to the front of the shop to stand watch over the orchestra.

No one comes to my bunk this night. The death of the man has further blackened everyone's spirit. Karl goes on and on about the foolish thing the man did. Finally I've had enough of him and tell him to shut up. He becomes silent and covers his head in his blankets. I tell him to talk about something else, and immediately he begins recounting some episode of his boyhood. He keeps this up, non-stop, until the light flickers out.

I listen, almost desperately, for the sound of the violin, but I hear nothing.

Avron comes over and, in the darkness, asks, "What was the name of the man the guards finished off? I want to say a prayer for him."

"I don't know."

"You mean you talked to him all that time and never asked his name?"

"That's right," I tell him.

"Was there no other way of handling him?" he asks in a sad manner.

"No."

He wanders off through the darkened hut to his corner and says his prayers for the nameless man.

I sit on my bunk, still hoping to hear the boy, but there is nothing. When everyone is finally asleep, I drag myself over to the artist's bunk. Nudging him awake, I beg him, "Draw me something beautiful. Do you understand me? Dredge up something from when the times were good. Draw me one of your women—one with a soft face."

He rewards me with one of his serene women; the eyes are large and soft. When he finishes, I put him back to bed and thank him. Whispering to him, I say, "Don't ever die on me. Keep on living so that my soul will not drown. I will take care of you."

I stare at the beautiful face until it dissolves into the frost.

22 The violin sings out, but the boy is not rewarded with bread. His steps are surer now and he can run faster, but he captures no one. The ladlers have listened to me well. They tell everyone—those who are fully alive and those who are in a half-stupor—to run past the boy without stopping until they reach their hut.

The boy seems to sense the change, but still he attacks the new men with his violin. He stares intently at them as they run by him. The boy races after them almost to the steps of their huts before abandoning the chase. Finally he gives up altogether and just watches the cart giving away the bread that he can no longer trade for a song. Probably he could easily grab the bread out of the frail hands of one of the old men, but he doesn't try.

From time to time the guards look up and watch the boy, who now stands alone in the midfield. I wonder if the soldiers miss the old struggles between the bread and the violin. If they do, they don't show it. Most of the time they just face the fire. Occasionally one of them will slowly turn around—like a suckling pig on a spit—and let the spouting flames warm his entire body. The reflection of the fire shimmers off their slick black raincoats.

The boy watches me as I am given my ration. He remains there, shivering away as the cold rain beats down on all of us.

The cart and the soldiers go off on their separate ways. The boy and I are alone once again. No one ventures out of the huts as the rain continues to pour down. I sit on the corner of the step and we eye each other.

I place some bread on a square piece of once-white cloth that Avron has given me for this occasion. The bread is just a foot away from me. I take a drink from the cup and then place it near the bread.

He starts to come toward me with carefully measured steps. I sit silently, fearing that any false move on my part will send him running away. His eyes never leave me as he comes closer. I have to cough but hold it in. I force my face to smile at him, but I have no idea if I look benign to him. His expression does not change. With the crystalline sleeve, he wipes his nose.

He is only a few feet away when he begins coughing. His body shakes so much that drops of water fly off his coat like a wet dog shaking his fur.

He walks to the far side of the step and stands there, gazing into a puddle of water. I gently whisper to him, "Sit down, my son. You're tired and wet. Sit down and we will eat together."

Looking around at the huts across the field, I see each window filled with faces staring out at us.

The boy watches the flaming drum for a while and then sits on the farthest edge of the step. Even with his collar turned up, the rain runs off his hair and down his neck. His bare knees shiver up and down from the cold—or is it from fright?

Carefully, I move Avron's cloth with its bread a little bit closer to him, but he ignores me. "Do you want to come inside with me? It's dry in there." He starts to fidget as if he's about to get up and head for the gate. "We can stay out here —it's all right, but let's eat the bread before it gets wet."

I pick up a piece of rye and hold it out to him.

He turns toward me and, without looking up, takes the bread. He carefully peels the crust off and then holds the bread up to his mouth. He nibbles on it like a child eating candy. He eats as if he wants the bread to last forever. Each bite is still taken from the side of his mouth.

I look behind me as the door opens slowly. Avron's hand carefully eases a steaming cup of the soup through the door. I wonder how much of his bread he had to trade to get the matches to reheat the soup.

I pass the warm cup toward the boy, but he shows no interest in it. Instead, he reaches over for another piece of bread. He takes a few bites and then places the remainder in his sack.

We are both thoroughly drenched. I watch the drops of rain fall into the cup. Holding the soup out to him, I say, "Go ahead, take some." I take a few sips and pass the cup to him. "Take it. It tastes bad, but it will warm you up." He reaches for the cup but sets it down before it comes near his lips.

I, too, am shivering and start coughing. He picks up the cup and hands it to me. The horrible-tasting stuff soothes my throat.

What is left of the bread is now a soggy mess. The boy begins his coughing again, and I am quick to shove the soup over to him. He looks down at the bile-colored liquid as his coughing continues.

"Go ahead and take some. It tastes bad, but it is good for your cough. You saw me drink it." He puts it up to his lips and takes a few swallows. As he drinks the soup, the same beautiful bitter look comes across his face again. This time I know I am smiling. In my happiness, I cry out to him, "It's bad, isn't it? It's really bad, but it's good for both of us." He looks at me and his head actually nods. I have never seen him do this before. The remembrance of my son taking his first steps crosses my mind.

When the siren sounds, he gets up and walks slowly off toward the tree. I wring the water out of Avron's tablecloth and carefully fold it and place it in my pocket.

The boy stands under the tree as we march off. I turn to Avron and whisper, "It's been a good day."

Avron looks over his shoulder at the boy still standing in the pouring rain and says, "The very first day of creation could not have been more beautiful." A broad smile remains on his maimed face as we enter the shop.

A few men come by my machine and, when the guards are not looking, place tiny morsels of bread on my bench. They say nothing. These men are mainly the new ones I have met in the latrine. However, I receive a few pieces from the writer from Anselm and Sheleen's assistant. The bread that I am given is always free of crust. It strikes me as strange that everyone knows the child's likes and dislikes.

I spend much of the afternoon shift in the latrine with two new men. Their level of hope has been so demolished that I know they will cause no trouble. One of them gives me a bit of bread for the boy. I wrap their offerings in Avron's cloth. Now I, too, carry a sack just like the boy.

After the night feeding, the hut begins to fill just as it did in the days of Sheleen. Karl goes to each man and collects their bits of bread. "For the boy," he says as he holds out his hand. The men do not object. In fact, I sense a certain feeling of pride as they give him a tiny piece of their ration.

Karl places the collection on a corner of my bunk. He makes a great show of adding his own chunk to the little pile.

The men look to me. They have paid their admission, and now I am to perform for them. I am expected to give them sustenance for the bread that they have donated. Even though I remember all of Sheleen's words, I have neither the strength nor the will to try to fill their heads with his stories of the "noble life." I am, however, too worn out to conjure up anything else.

I find myself talking to them of the boy. The words come out naturally. It is obvious that they desperately want to hear something, but I am still surprised that they come to me. Perhaps I could babble in some foreign tongue and they would still make the trip. Some of the members of my audience are not very discriminating—they are only half alive, but others were once well educated and had heard and seen almost everything. Still, they listen.

Sheleen's assistant watches me as I speak. I look at him and wonder if someday he will be the one to kick the table out from under me.

I tell them what the boy means to me. They continue to listen, and by the looks on their faces, I know that they hear me.

Avron walks over to my side and places his maimed hand on my shoulder. He pleads to them, "Hear this man. God has placed him among us to be the Moses for this child. Like Moses, this man will not walk into the Promised Land. God has ordained this. God, in his infinite wisdom, has kept us here in captivity to sustain the boy until he is ready to enter the Promised Land. God has kept me alive—you all see that Verbin has not checked me off. God, with our help, will look after the boy."

The siren blows and the evening is over. No one says a word as I shake the hands of each of them. Many are from the other huts.

Avron remains behind and whispers, "Each day I find your faith in God more restored."

I grab him as he starts to walk away. "Listen, Avron, I, too, am going to walk out of here. I don't intend to be like Moses and only look out on the Promised Land. My feet will walk on that ground and I will live again. Don't you try to order my life so that it follows the Bible word for word. I don't plan on dropping dead the minute the boy is free. I am just an ordinary man chained to this place. After I get the boy out, I'm on my own—you, your God, and the red cap can make all the pronouncements you want—but I'm on my own!"

He says nothing for a moment. In a quiet voice he tells me, "The boy is everything and we are nothing. Whether you like it or not, you are following God's will. Man plans, but God decides. Go to sleep, my friend, you need your strength."

In the darkness Karl continues his meandering chatter. I begin to wonder, "If I am Moses, then who the hell is Karl?"

The talking stops and I think he's fallen asleep, but he starts up again. Karl asks, "Why didn't you shake my hand tonight like you did with all the others?"

I get up and shake his hand, hoping that he will fall asleep. My own hunger now keeps me awake. There is plenty of bread in my pocket, but I can't sleep because I'm starving. Reaching into my pocket, I finger the little chunks of bread collected in the name of the boy. Under my breath I taunt God to keep the bread from reaching my mouth. He does not intervene and I savor a few pieces. I let them roll around and melt in my mouth. Even swallowing them is pleasurable. Surely the real Moses would not have taken bread destined for the mouth of a child.

I am still chewing the boy's bread when Karl starts in about being hungry. "Damnit, go to sleep," I tell him.

"I can't sleep—I'm too hungry," comes his whining reply. After a few quiet moments he asks, "What can I do for the boy?"

I try to think what the hell will finally shut him up. "If it is raining when I sit with the boy, you can pass some dry coats out to us. You've got to do this quietly or you might frighten him away."

"Good, good," he replies in an excited manner. "I want to be a part of what you're doing with him." He sits up. "Here is the piece of bread I always save for the morning. You take it and give it to the boy."

I refuse it and push his hand away. He persists and keeps shoving the bread at me. I finally place his offering in my pocket. He says, "Good night."

I lie here in my bunk, thinking that I am no better than the red cap. I had always prided myself on the fact that I lived on a higher plane of humanity than he. Now I know we are brothers. Perhaps life is easier to live as a bastard.

All thoughts of being a bastard suddenly end as the sky lights up as bright as the day. My bunk trembles in time with the explosions. Sirens pierce the air all around us. In the distance I hear the drone of planes.

From the back window, I watch the buildings of the far-distant city outlined by the flames. The church steeple stands bolt upright, as always, pointing toward the fiery sky. Searchlights crisscross the night, looking for planes.

The ground under me rumbles with each exploding bomb. I look around the hut, bathed in the eerie light pulsating through the windows. Most of the men are hiding under their bunks, but some huddle together by the stove, shouting and waving their hands. I hear them screaming at the top of their lungs. Men who have hardly ever uttered a word thrust their voices up toward heaven. I hear their cries, "God, God, bring the temple down on us! Bury us under the same rubble with those who have killed our children!" Men who have always damned the name of God now cry out to Him to end this hell. Avron is not among them—he stands in his corner, praying silently.

I stare at these strange, pleading men and see an unfamiliar look of strength coming from their hollow faces. The sound of each bomb blast seems to raise the level of their prayers as they beg to be consumed by an explosion.

Only one man makes good use of the opportunities that this night provides. The artist stands by my window, painting wildly on the glass. For once in his life his canvas is continuously illuminated. For once he doesn't have to wait patiently for the wandering tower beam to light up the frosted pane. The spine in his hand races madly across the window. From where I stand, I cannot make out what he is drawing.

Another explosion shakes the foundations of the hut. Then there is silence. The fires die down to nothing. The church steeple is silhouetted in a smoky haze. Distant sparks fly upward and then die out in the night.

I walk over to the artist who stands by his etching waiting for more light—but the tower beams do not come on. I try to lead him back to his bed, but for once he wishes to remain in the darkness by his painting.

The night returns to its usual blackness. Moments later the tower light comes on and the beam makes its rounds. The prayers slowly cease. Now none of them call out to God for anything. They shuffle through the darkness to find their bunks. They must know that the camp still remains intact, and so do their miserable lives. This place is not a temple, and even if it were, they cannot pull the pillars down around their heads.

The rays of the tower light poke through the windows. Nothing remains of the artist's drawing; he must have wiped the window clean.

I peer out and see the camp looking exactly as it did before the raid. Nothing is out of place. I sit on my bunk gazing out the window, waiting for the dawn. For me, after the dawn will come the shop, and after the shop will come the boy.

I hear men around me crying. Unfortunately, tomorrow will bring them only another day.

23 The wind cuts through me the instant I step out of the hut. My eyes are drawn instinctively to the city, which this morning is veiled in a smoky haze. After all the bombing, I am surprised that the steeple and most of the houses are still standing. A line of people trickles out of the town and heads down the road toward the south. They walk slowly, laden down with their few possessions.

We sit silently behind our benches waiting for the power switch to be thrown, but nothing happens. Verbin is sprawled in his chair, staring at the floor. I have never seen him so oblivious to his machines. I don't like the strange silence that hangs over the shop. The men stare at me with that "Is this the end?" look.

The red cap stands beside Verbin and points over and over again to the switch. The fat man will not budge. The conductor makes an attempt to lift Verbin up out of the chair but is shoved aside. The immense round head is minus its usual good-natured look. The conductor doffs his cap and goes through some of his usual groveling, but none of his antics brings a smile to our master's face.

I look around and can see that everyone wonders what is going on. Even the guards look puzzled as they wait impatiently for the start-up of the machines to lull them to sleep. For the first time I notice that Rollin has returned. He stands with a group of guards next to the cello stove. He looks thinner than before.

Finally Verbin lifts himself up out of the chair after more coaxing from the red cap, who leads him in the direction of the power switch. Then suddenly Verbin changes course and walks slowly toward the front of the orchestra. The conductor stands by the switch with a flabbergasted look on his face.

All of a sudden I realize that Verbin is screaming at us. I am shocked to hear his always soft singsong voice raised in anger. What comes out of his mouth is disjointed at first until finally I understand what he is trying to say. "My city was beautiful. My city has nothing to do with the war." Then he points his finger out across the stunned orchestra and screams, "Why did you bomb my city? Why did you let them bomb my city?"

We look at each other in amazement. This morning when we talked among ourselves about the raid, the planes were always referred to as "enemy planes." What more does this idiot want from us?

Verbin rails on, repeating himself again and again. Gently the red cap tries to lead him over to the switch. Verbin lashes out with his fists at his faithful servant. The conductor backs away into a corner as the screaming continues. "This place is my home. How could you do this? There are women and little children there." Finally the storm sputters out and Verbin stops in midsentence. With his head down, he shuffles into his office. The door slams with a bang that echoes throughout the shop.

The red cap runs over and pulls the switch. His hands gently rise into the air and the machines beat in a slow, even tempo. Even the woodwinds keep up fairly well as the orchestra sings out in perfect pitch. The conductor does not tolerate a single machine to be off-key. He points to the artist, and someone gets up and turns off his cutter so that he will not ruin the harmony. We bang away in perfect rhythm, trying to placate Verbin's ears, but the door remains closed. He will not come out.

Another storm begins. The guards race through the aisles and start their rioting. A club strikes me across the shoulders, but I keep playing. Rollin turns and looks out the window as the others roam through the orchestra, knocking men off their chairs.

The rhythm of the orchestra begins to break down as the

guards go wild without Verbin's restraining eyes. Seeing the havoc, the conductor races over to the office door and knocks gently. Then he begins banging harder as the soldiers' fury increases, but the door does not open.

After a moment of indecision, the conductor makes a mad dash for the nearest machine and turns up the power full blast. The high-pitched screech of the racing cutter rings throughout the shop. With the piercing sound of the machine blasting through everyone's ears, the rampage of the guards ends. They stop their smashing and slowly file back to their corners.

The red cap continues pounding away on the overheated machine until he sees the door open. Verbin enters the shop, and the machines give him a thunderous ovation. Wild joy runs through the orchestra as the frown evaporates from Verbin's face and is replaced by a smile. He returns to his overstuffed throne. Apparently his period of mourning is over.

The conductor returns the orchestra to a steady pace. Contentment reigns throughout the shop—all except for the man whose machine has the bent shaft after the red cap's wild screeching. I know that this man is wondering how he can possibly remain anonymous to the guards with his off-key machine. He soon abandons his bench and moves to a vacant chair in the woodwinds.

Verbin walks over to the maimed machine and, with his hands, moves the cutting cylinder up and down. His round face takes on a sorrowful look as he surveys the damage. The black book is produced and his pencil makes a few notes in it. I wonder if the guards will descend on this sick machine that can no longer work. Will they now beat the hell out of it with their rifle butts? The soldiers take no notice of the helpless machine.

I can hear some of the soldiers around me talking about the raid. They are laughing. From what I can gather, the enemy planes must have bombed the wrong target. Verbin's city had nothing of military value worth destroying. To the guards, the whole raid was a monumental joke on the enemy. They wasted their bombs on a few houses and a herd of cows.

The laughter eventually dies down, and their faces return to the usual morbid state. Sometimes everyone in this place has the same lost expression—guards and prisoners alike. Only the discussion of women can be counted on to bring some life to their faces. They revel in the details of past, present, and future seductions. One of them laughs as he wonders out loud whether the town's one decent whorehouse has survived the raid unscathed by a bomb.

I can always identify with their conversations when they talk of food or tell stories of their boyhoods. Their stories of seductions, however, seem as foreign as if they were part of another world. I realize that such thoughts are an early casualty of this bondage. The lice, the fear, and the hunger eat away at our self-images as well as our bodies.

The soldiers' laughter begins again but stops the moment Rollin walks by. He spends the day pacing back and forth along the periphery of the orchestra. His comrades nod to him as he passes, but he does not respond. His head always turns away when he comes near me.

When Rollin is gone, I hear the guards resume their talking, but now their conversation is about the war. I keep thinking about the planes and wonder how they were allowed to bomb anything without first being blasted out of the sky. The war always seemed a million miles away, but now I know it is coming closer. As I etch the barbs into a spine, I wonder where we fit into the struggle between the warring giants. I doubt if anyone even knows we exist— and what if they did? Do we mean anything to anyone? The war is coming nearer. We will probably end up being trampled under the feet of these giants as they battle around us. The pounding of the cutter is like the seconds ticking off on a clock; I know that I do not have much more time to get the boy to walk out of here.

The machines pound on and the morning continues.

The boy watches from the tree as the food cart is dragged to each hut. As soon as the gate closes behind the cart, he starts walking toward me. He walks in a straight line directly through the mud puddles and takes his seat on the far end of the step. His nose is plugged again, and it is difficult for him to breathe. I doubt if he even knows how to blow his nose. A steaming cup of the soup is slowly passed out to me. I take the cup and place it on the cloth. The boy watches as I empty my pockets of the bits of bread and drop them, one by one, into the cup. When he sees the bread being immersed in the soup, he looks up at me as if I have just cheated him out of his inheritance.

I hand the cup to him, but he ignores me and shifts his bleary eyes to gaze at the trucks passing on the road. "Here, take the soup," I tell him, "it will taste better with the bread in it." He watches my face for any sign of nausea as I take a sip. I smile at him, and, with a disbelieving look, he takes the cup. After a few swallows he puts the cup down and gives me a look that tells me he knows I'm a damn liar.

I dig out a few large chunks of rye from my pocket. When I hold them up to him, I see a glimmer of life come to his eyes for the very first time. "Finish the soup," I promise, "and I'll give you the bread."

With both hands he picks up the cup and, even before drinking it, begins to gag. He takes several swallows and then hands the cup to me. I see that it is empty. Hoping to get him to say something, I ask, "Did you finish it?" He looks up at me as if I am an idiot but then nods his head up and down.

He nibbles on the bread. When I move closer to him, he

184

slides away from me until he is sitting on the extreme edge of the step. I reach into my pocket for some more rye but feel a stone mixed in with the bread. I give the stone a flick, and it lands in the center of a puddle of water next to the step. The boy puts the bread down and stares into the pool. His eyes never leave the circular ripples that radiate from the center of the pool where the stone struck the water. When the surface of the puddle is smooth again, I reach down and find another pebble in the mud. The boy is transfixed again by the ripples. I hand a pebble to him and he gives it a throw. He wipes his nose, and when the sleeve leaves his face, I see the first trace of a smile on his lips. It is fleeting, but I know it was a smile.

He bolts from the step as his eyes search the ground. He races back with a handful of stones. Several are placed on Avron's cloth. He motions for me to take them. Alternately, we throw stones into the pool, creating the undulating ripples.

As he raises his arm to throw another stone, I ask, "What is your name?"

Still clutching the stone, he slowly lowers his hand and sits hunched over in his old stuporous fashion. I vow then and there never again to ask him anything about himself.

He sits and watches as I fling my last stone into the pool. The siren rings. He gets up and heads toward the tree. I yell, "Come back again tomorrow. Please come back tomorrow. I will have a lot more bread. We will throw stones again."

He keeps walking without looking back. Suddenly he stops, and I see him stoop over and pick up a stone. He stands over a puddle, drops the stone and watches the ripples.

Before entering the shop, I get one last look at him. He is a few yards from the tree, dropping a pebble into one of the many pools that dot our muddy landscape.

24

In the morning the machine is always sluggish until the banging of the cutter warms the oil in the cylinder. It takes about a half hour before the orchestra can play a decent song.

The tempo suddenly speeds up—I look around and see one of the violinists slumping to the floor. He makes no effort to raise himself back up. I know he is finished.

The conductor gently awakens Verbin. The mound of fat oozes out of the chair and makes its way to the man lying on the floor. The violinist is checked off.

Even before Verbin can carry himself back to his chair, the red cap signals the coming of the commandant. Everyone makes ready for his visit. His brief marching in and out of the shop is the only bit of change that courses through our world. Two of the men pick the violinist up off the floor and prop him in his chair. All will now look in order for our colonel. The soldiers stand at attention. Of all of them, only Rollin slouches next to the stove in the cello section.

Verbin opens the door. Even though I detest this officer, I am always awed by his magnificent clean uniform. The purple of the book he has chosen today clashes with the brown of his gleaming jacket.

The officer marches into the shop past Verbin, who is talking already, and heads directly for the office. He disappears inside. Verbin, still standing by the door, looks dumbfounded and finally rushes after him.

The soldiers remain at attention as the conductor keeps our machines at a steady tempo. Nervously he fingers the brim of his red cap while he inches ever closer to the office door.

Everyone's eyes are glued to the office. I give up trying to imagine what the hell is going on in there. The com-

186

mandant has never spent this much time here before. The minutes move slowly on. I see the soldiers steal glances at their watches as they try to remain at attention. Hardly anyone notices that the violinist has once again fallen to the floor.

Finally the commandant comes out and, in his imperial manner, walks toward the main door. The red cap bows as he opens the door to let him out. The second the door is closed, the bowing man straightens up and races into Verbin's office. Neither man comes out. We become more and more nervous. The guards can sleep and so can those men in the woodwinds, but the rest of us cannot control our machines. The orchestra begins to play faster and faster. Seeing that the guards are beginning to stir, I try to slow the machines down, but I cannot.

First the red cap's menacing head peeks out from the office and then comes his raised fist; the machines slow down.

I long to see the fat man return to his chair, but the two of them remain closeted in the office. Several times during the morning the orchestra goes wild again. The conductor's shaking fist then appears and brings us back into some semblance of order.

Avron stops his machine every few minutes, and I see his head bobbing up and down in prayer. Many of the men look at me with deep frowns etched in their skull-like faces. Our cutters bang on. We all seem to know that some major change is about to befall us, but what will it be?

Even the blast of the siren that ends the shift does not extricate Verbin or the conductor from the office. The soldiers crowd the doorway to be the first ones out of the stinking shop. They rush to the guard hut for their food.

Slowly, one by one, the men get up and head for the door. I walk over to the artist and help him up out of his chair. Karl then leads him to the door, jabbering some of his nonsense in the stuporous man's ears.

The cellist from Pavan and I carry the violinist out of the shop and place the body next to the scrap pile. Avron follows behind us, murmuring the necessary words to help ease the musician's passage into heaven.

I watch the door of the shop, but the red cap does not come out.

The boy stands waiting again by the tree. He and his violin no longer interfere with the food cart. He has no way of knowing that on this day he would have little trouble getting all the bread he wants. No one's mind is on food —everyone's thoughts are still in Verbin's office. My pockets fill with the bread of men who are too terrified to be hungry.

The rain begins even before the food cart leaves. The boy and I sit in our usual places on the step. I huddle over, shivering, as the downpour covers us. The boy seems oblivious to the water flowing off the roof onto his back.

My mind drifts momentarily back to the shop. I hear Karl's voice coming from behind me, "Here, take the coats." I bundle myself in one of them and start to hand the other to the boy. He pays no attention to my offering but busies himself by making two piles of stones on the worn cloth that separates us. Each little pebble is almost identical in size to the next one. His hand darts back and forth into his pocket, pulling each stone out one at a time. Alternately he places them on my pile and then his. Finally each little pile contains an equal number of stones.

He looks down at the pool and picks up a stone from his stack and gives it a throw. He seems disheartened that his ripples are distorted by the falling raindrops which dot the puddle.

The hot soup is shoved out to me with Avron's warnings, "Talk to him. I think your time is running short." The boy watches as I fill the cup again with the bits of bread. I hand the cup to him, but, instead of taking it or shoving it aside, he reaches into his pocket and pulls out a large chunk of bread. Half is broken off and given to me.

I tell him, "I'll take some of your bread if you take some of my soup." Ignoring my offer, he stares off into the distance and nibbles on his chunk of rye.

Thankfully, the rain lets up. I take a sip and hand the cup to him, saying, "Let's finish the soup. Then we will throw the rocks." He takes the cup and drinks about half of it. I down the rest.

The surface of the pool becomes smooth and reflects the brightening sky. The two of us take turns throwing the pebbles. He waits impatiently for me to throw my stone. I hold it in my hand and whisper softly, "I was once a boy like you. I remember going to a big park. There was no mud at the park. I ran all over. It was warm. I jumped high in the air and tried to touch the sky. There were other children in the park. I would run with them. Together we would jump into the air." I stop and look across at him. His eyes are lost in the distance. The stone bounces up and down in his little hand.

"Do you understand what I am saying? Tell me if you do."

He keeps gazing up into the sky.

I move slightly closer to him and continue. "There was a pond in the park—much, much bigger than this little pool. The water was clear and warm. I would take pebbles just like yours and throw them into the water. The pond was so clear that sometimes I could even see fish swimming in the water. Do you know what fish are? Someday you will run in a park like I did. You will run and jump. Someday you . . . "

I look up and see him walking away from me. He is heading toward the main gate. The walk becomes a run. The truck filled with new men is parked at the gate. The guards kick one of the men off the truck and lead him into the compound. The boy closes in on this man who is being shoved along by the guards. They all stop as the first strains of the violin sing out. The guards laugh as the lullaby is played before the terrified new man. The soldiers seem to enjoy the man's bewilderment at this strange reception to hell. The boy stares at the man as he repeats his lullaby louder and louder.

Finally the man is given such a kick that he falls face-first into the mud. He picks himself up to escape the rifle butts. The guards point to the second hut across the field from me, and the man rushes toward it.

The violin is silent. The boy starts to saunter away when one of the guards walks over to him and hands him something. Whatever it is, the boy takes it and places it in his sack.

Moments later he returns to me and sits in his usual spot on the far end of the step.

"What did the soldier give you?" I ask.

He reaches into his sack and pulls out what looks like a small piece of candy.

I look at him and say, "Give it to me."

He hesitates for a moment and then places it next to my pile of rocks. I pick it up and see that it is a piece of hard candy. "Do you know what this is? Do the guards feed you?"

He reaches out for the candy. For a moment I am tempted to throw it into the puddle. I don't want these bastards to start feeding him, nor do I want him to take a damn thing from them. He grabs the candy from my hand and this time hides it in a pocket of his inner coat next to the violin.

I start to slide closer to him, but as I approach, he stands up and walks a few paces away. When I return to my edge of the step, he sits down again. "Someday you will leave here," I tell him. "This is a very bad place. This is not a place for a child like you. There are no other children here. You can see that, can't you? The other children are outside these fences. They are running together. They are running in a park where there is grass. It is cold here." I point toward the road in the distance. "Just over that hill is where the children are. Beyond that hill is where the park is—the one with the children and the green grass. The park is warm and the children are not hungry."

I say nothing more to him. We take turns throwing a few stones into the pool, but then the siren blares out. Quickly, the boy picks up the remaining pebbles and stuffs them into his pocket before walking away. Again he stops at every puddle to drop an offering into the muddy water.

Avron is silent as we march to the shop. I shake my head and say, "I reach out to him, but I don't know if all this is really getting anywhere. I don't think there's enough time left. It's just like in the days of Sheleen; just when I think I'm making some progress, the outside world ruins everything. Just when I think the boy understands me, he runs off to try to get some food from that new man. The camp will end before I can ever reach the boy."

Avron places his hand on my shoulder as we enter the shop and, in a consoling voice, says, "Trust in God."

His words are never satisfying—I trust only in Verbin's mood, and, staring at him, I see that his usual grin is gone. There is a worried look on his face as he stands by the switch, waiting for everyone in the orchestra to find their chairs. His expression is like a storm warning, and I know we are in for bad times. I cannot get the red cap's attention to find out what the hell is going on. Finally the switch is thrown and the machines roar off.

The red cap brings a now-shaven new man to my bench. I look up and ask the conductor, "What's happening? What went on this morning?" He does not answer.

I turn to the new man who stands beside me, looking half dead already. I nudge him. "Go to your bench. We'll talk later." The man looks blank and continues to stand there. I motion across to Sheleen's assistant, who then gets up and leads the man to his machine.

The red cap bends down and, with a tremor in his voice, says, "They're phasing out the camp—at least part of it. I can't get the whole story straight from Verbin. Something is going on with the war. Verbin doesn't even know if they're winning or losing. He doesn't even know that the rest of the world exists. One thing I do know: Any shop that doesn't make its quota is finished. Any compound that causes trouble will be ended."

He looks around at the orchestra for a moment and then continues. "Everything must run like a clock if they are to keep us. What worries me is getting enough men and scrap to keep things going." He points his finger at me and warns, "Keep the men in line and get that black look off your face! Start pounding away and the orchestra will follow you." His farewell warning is, "Keep that boy in check, and when you get him out of here, if you ever do, then do it quietly."

Verbin is restless and cannot fall asleep. He walks slowly through the aisles, looking grief-stricken as his hand gently touches each of his machines. As he passes, the men slow their cutters so that his fingers can caress the shiny outer cylinders.

The writer comes over to my bench. I continue to work, hoping that he will go away. He gives me a tap on the shoulder. "Karl wants you," he says with a worried look on his face. I peer over at the edge of the woodwinds and see that Karl's bench is empty. The writer points toward the latrine. "He's in there. He's sick. He wants you."

"Everyone's sick in this place," I answer.

The writer's tone is urgent. "He wants you. I don't know why he would want you—but he does. He's in pain. There's something wrong with him that's different."

"Call one of the doctors."

"I wanted to," he says, "but he wants only you."

From the window of the latrine I can see Karl lying on

the muddy floor. Men come and go, but no one bends down to help him.

I lift him up and prop him on a seat. "My back," he screams, "it's my back! I have pains in my back like someone's shoving a knife into me! I'm going to die—I know it!"

I yell back at him, "Calm yourself down! You're not going to die! Everybody has pains with the dysentery!"

"No—no, this is different." He begins to cry, "I want you to promise me something. I know I can't work anymore. Verbin will check me off. I don't want to have to wait in the hut for the guards. Promise me that I won't have to wait for the guards."

I start to tell him that he will be all right, but he doubles over in pain and falls to the floor. The pain does not last long; in fact, it is gone as suddenly as it came. He stares at me with a terrified look.

When I start to walk out, he cries, "Don't leave me!"

"Calm down," I tell him. "I'll see if I can get one of the doctors to look at you."

The conductor waits for me as I enter the shop and wants to know what's wrong with Karl. He seems unimpressed with what I tell him.

"All right," he says, "have one of the doctors go look at him. These fools can diagnose everything, but they can't cure a damn thing." He looks around the orchestra and points to one of the doctors in the second violins. "Ask that one," he says. "He's the one the other doctors bow and scrape before. They call him the 'professor.'"

When I tell the doctor about Karl's pain, his indifferent face begins to light up. "It's not the dysentery or pneumonia," he says. "Yes, I will go see him."

The professor returns after a few minutes and goes over to the bench of another doctor. One by one the doctors leave their places in the orchestra and head for the latrine. When each one returns, he goes directly to the professor's bench. I watch them talking excitedly among themselves. The shift ends without Karl returning.

As we march out of the shop, I see Karl being helped back to the hut. He is surrounded by doctors. They hold his slumped-over body upright. His feet do not touch the ground. I am behind them as Karl is borne into the hut. The doctors can barely hold him up as his body is suddenly wracked with pain. Karl reaches out for his bunk the way a drowning man grasps for a floating piece of debris. He looks drained. The doctors lay him on his back, and each of them takes a turn feeling his scrawny belly.

When one of them sits on my bunk. I tell him to get off. I've never seen any of them show any interest in us. They never looked up as man after man died of all the diseases that thrive in this place. Never did a word of comfort come from their mouths.

"What's wrong with him?" I ask.

The professor does the talking for the group. "He has a kidney stone. We're sure of it." To me this is Karl's death sentence, but there's nothing somber about the doctors. Karl, the idiot, lies there with a look of satisfaction as he basks in the undivided attention of these men.

"There's a chance we can cure him," intones the professor. "Do you realize what this means to us? We finally have the right medicine to cure something—water." He points to the buckets scattered around the hut that catch the leakage from the roof. "Naturally, we have nothing for his pain, but there's a good chance that if he drinks enough water, the stone will pass out with his urine."

Their hands descend on Karl and prop him up. Cup after cup of water is shoved down his unwilling throat. Karl's look of contentment is gone. His only respite from the water is when he doubles over in pain. The doctors become ecstatic when the pain radiates into his groin. They congratulate themselves. "The stone is moving. The stone is moving."

Two of the doctors remain behind when we go out into the night for the food cart. As I pass through the line, I hear Karl scream out in pain. The guards look up from the fire and glance toward the hut. I'm sure they think we are killing each other off; they could care less.

One of the doctors grasps Karl's head while the other holds the cup. The doctors do not let up. The water continues to flow as they take turns drowning him. At regular intervals his blood-tinged urine is checked for the stone. Nothing has passed through yet, and the pain continues. Karl is now totally worn out. He spits the water out faster than it can be poured in.

When the siren blows, it is obvious that the doctors do not want to leave. Karl slumps over, completely spent, and lies on his water-soaked bunk. The doctors file slowly out of the hut.

The professor remains behind and takes me aside. He, too, looks exhausted. Even with the emaciation, there is a certain strength to his face. I can see why the others jump when he speaks. I motion for him to sit on my bunk. He speaks softly. "We want a victory with this man. You can understand this. I know that you want a victory with the little boy. The men die and we can do nothing. We desperately want something out of this place, and that man's stone is probably all we will ever get. The stone is usually the size of a tiny piece of gravel. This little speck means a great deal to us. You know," he says, "in the old days there were bottles and bottles in my office filled with medicine for dysentery. Sometimes I would throw away a bottle even before it was completely empty. Can you believe that I would pour medicine down the drain and open a new bottle? Here we have nothing."

Karl screams out again and writhes about on his bunk. Then the pain stops and he seems to fall asleep.

The professor grimaces as he watches Karl. "We cannot even cure ourselves. We were looked up to by the world because they thought we had the power to heal; sometimes we did and sometimes we didn't. The people didn't know the difference—they always thought we did. If you think you've been brought down to nothing by this place, then just think of us. Here we are nothing."

The cup is again thrust up against Karl's lips. The professor seems satisfied. I warn him about getting out of here before the lights go out. He looks back at Karl going through another spasm of pain and says, "I've heard you talk about needing more time with the boy. Help us get more time with this man. The stone can pass anytime or just suddenly stop causing pain—then he will be well again. Talk to the conductor. Have him ask Verbin for more time. Verbin listens to him. Tell the red cap that we will more than make up for this man's quota. Get us some more time. Please, I beg of you, get the water down him tonight. I know that Avron will help you. Do this and we will make sure you always have bread for your boy."

As he opens the door I tell him, "The best I can get for Karl is to have him live through the first shift. Maybe I can figure out a way to get the second shift. There's no way in the world that I can get more than that. Then it's all over if he's not able to run his machine."

Seconds after the professor is gone, the red cap barges in. He takes one look at Karl who is screaming in pain and warns, "If he's like that in the morning you had better not bring him to the shop, or I'll have your neck. Get the water into him. The way things are now, I don't know where my next man is coming from."

Avron and I take turns with the cup. Karl even talks between the pains. "Can you imagine the attention they're giving me?" he says in wonderment. "Not even a king has this many doctors." He takes a little more, then falls asleep.

Another screaming episode awakens me. I try to bribe him with some bread, just so he will drink a little more. He refuses the bread but does drink a few sips. "It's so good," he says, "to have people pay attention to me." The cup placed against his lips ends his talking.

Moments later he asks, "What if the stone doesn't pass? I asked you this before and I don't want you to be mad, but promise me that I won't have to wait in the hut for the guards. Promise me this. Don't tell me to wait until the morning for an answer like you always do. Promise me now. Please find a way so that I can go quickly without too much pain."

"You will be well," I say as I pass the cup up to his mouth.

He pushes it away and the water spills all over me. His voice rises to a scream. "You know I won't and so do I! I'm not going to get well and I know it! Promise me that I will die quickly! Promise me and swear to it in the name of the boy! Promise me! Promise me!"

I sit there for a moment and then say, "Take the water and I will promise."

"In the name of the boy?"

"Yes, I promise in the name of the boy."

"Thank you," he says in a satisfied tone. He takes the cup from my hand and drinks it down. He is silent for a moment but then says, "I envy what you have with the child. I thank you for letting me collect the bread for him. I know that some of my own bread has gone to keep him alive. When I'm gone, would you have him play something for me? I would like knowing that he played a song for me."

"Yes," I say, "yes, he will."

Avron takes the cup from my hand. I sit back, wondering to myself if Moses had ever become the keeper of a brother afflicted with a kidney stone. Avron whispers to me, "Go to sleep. You need your strength. Everyone knows that something is happening to the shop. I have a feeling that tomorrow will be a day like no other day we have ever seen here."

I lie on my bunk, thinking about Karl. The promise I made to him rages through my mind. I almost find myself praying for the safe passage of his stone.

I begin to worry about tomorrow. Perhaps Avron has learned something in his talks with God. I myself begin to fear that tomorrow will be a day like no other day.

25

The first light of dawn filters through the windows. In the semidarkness, I make out Avron still sitting hunched over on Karl's bunk. All is silence. The eastern sky gradually lightens as I watch for any sign of movement from the bunk. There are no screams from Karl, nor prayers from Avron.

I get up quietly and sit on the edge of the bunk. My bare feet touch the ground and feel the icy chill of the water that litters the floor. Much of the medicine meant for Karl never found his mouth.

From out of the silence a faint groan builds up into an agonizing shriek; Karl is still with me, and I know that nothing has changed. Avron wakes up with a start—rubs his eyes and gropes for the cup. Karl's therapy begins again with a vengeance.

The conductor's face turns almost the same color as his cap when he sees Karl being held up in the line. I support one of his arms, while the cellist from Pavan holds the other. Avron stands behind us to keep him from collapsing.

Karl is so bent over that he can't even look up. Staring down at his pants, he starts crying. "My pants are wet. What will the doctors think when they see that I wet my pants?" Saying no more, he suddenly yanks his arm free to bite down on his sleeve. His teeth almost cut through the cloth, but his scream is muffled.

With half-opened eyes, the soldier goes through his counting routine. He walks right by Karl as if nothing is wrong. It dawns on me that we could have an elephant lined up with us and they would neither notice nor give a damn.

As we march to the shop, I see the doctors carefully working their way through the line toward us. The professor shoves me aside and takes Karl's arm. The doctor from Wiven gathers up the remainder of the body. Karl's feet drag along the ground as he is rushed ahead of the rest of the group and carried toward the latrine. He is quiet for a moment and then doubles over in pain. The doctors lose their grip on him and Karl falls into the mud. His teeth bite through the bill of his cap but not a sound comes out of his mouth. Suddenly he begins writhing on the ground and holds his groin as he suffers through the agonizing pain.

The doctors slowly back away when they see the soldiers converging on Karl. They raise their rifle butts high in the air. I wait for the inevitable. Nothing happens—not a damn thing happens. The soldiers begin giggling. They are doubled over, too, but it is with laughter. I realize that these men with their guns are still little boys. Their young minds find the sight of a man with a hat in his mouth holding his crotch so humorous that they would rather laugh than kill.

Slowly the professor edges toward Karl and lifts him to his feet. The wave of pain has apparently subsided. The two of them rush toward the latrine to the screams of delight from the guards.

The machines have barely started up when I feel a smash across my back. A hand clutches my throat so tightly that I can hardly breathe. The red cap's voice is seething with anger. "I thought I told you not to bring him back. This whole place is going to hell, and you're playing games with those goddamn doctors. Half the camp is to be ended today, and you're frolicking around with a kidney stone."

My loud gagging convinces him that he should ease up

on my throat. He points toward the latrine and yells, "Get the doctors back to their machines. When the noon break comes, you make damn sure that you take that screaming idiot back to your hut." He grabs my neck again for emphasis. "You make damn sure he never leaves your hut again. Now go in there and get the doctors back to their benches—who the hell do they think they are? Do they think they're on the outside where everyone waited in line to kiss their feet?" He curses a few times and then says, "Get in there and tell them that Verbin knows what's going on."

The professor seems annoyed—as if I have disturbed him in the middle of some delicate operation. I grab him and yell, "What are you doing—you can't all be in here. Get some of them back into the shop. The commandant might be coming. The red cap's going wild."

The professor has heard me; he waves everyone out.

I stand beside Karl—he looks more dead than alive. I begin to doubt that I can get him up on Sheleen's table, let alone get the rope around his neck. Bending over, I whisper, "Karl, take the water." He refuses the cup. "Listen to me, Karl, the conductor says I have to take you back to the hut when the noon break comes. He says you can't leave the hut after that. Please, I beg of you, take the water. Maybe the stone will pass and you will be well again."

Karl's look of agony changes to one of terror. He grabs the cup from my hand and takes a large swallow.

I look back at the professor who is busy filling cups from the water barrel. He shakes his head. "I think the stone has moved a little further. We just need a little more time—just a little more time."

"You're not going to get it," I tell him. "The conductor won't allow any more of this. He says that Verbin knows what's going on. You have until the noon break, and that's all. Have mercy on this man; either cure him or kill him."

Karl hears everything. As if in a frenzy, he gorges himself on cup after cup of water.

The professor stares out the window toward the shop. "I wonder," he says as if to himself, "what this man with the foolish-looking red cap did before all this. He was probably a nothing. In times like these, the slime of the earth oozes up through the mud and takes over the world. A man like that could be a somebody only in this hell. The worst of men thrive and the decent ones die."

Karl slowly raises up and motions for me to come nearer. Making sure the professor can't hear him, he says, "You remember your promise, don't you? You haven't forgotten?"

I do not answer him but wonder again if he could be hoisted to the table. If I could only get him to stand still for a minute, that would be enough. There is always Sheleen's assistant to push the table. He can be convinced to do it again. When a man has done something once, he can be made to do it twice.

Taking the cup away from his mouth, I ask, "Karl, can you stand on your own? See if you can get up."

He tries to lift himself but falls back on the ground. Another attack has come. "Karl," I scream, "can you still stand up on a table? It's such a simple thing—anyone can stand on a table. Can you still crawl? Could you crawl to the fence?" He does not speak, and his anguished face gives me no answer.

I realize that the professor is shrieking at me, "Get out of here with that talk! I want water down him—not your words! You just want to see him dead, don't you?"

Karl pleads with me, "Take me away now. I can't take any more of this." He reaches out for me to pick him up. "Take me in and let Verbin check me off."

The professor steps between us and shoves me away. "Get out of here!" he cries. "I'm not going to let you take him out of here!"

I can see that I'm getting nowhere. I grab the professor and wheel him around. His face is impassive as I tell him, "Have it your way—but when the time's up, will you finish him off? No—you won't—none of you will. It'll be on my head to perform the last rites." I point my finger in his face. "You're a damn fool. You're waiting for a stone that will never come. You don't care about this man—it's just the stone, isn't it?"

"Get out of here!" he yells. His voice has lost all traces of its usual dignity. Now he sounds like all the rest of us. "Everyone wants to end it all when they're in pain. Every pregnant woman yells out, 'Never again!' as she goes through labor—but ten or eleven months later she's back in labor yelling, 'Never again.' Now get the hell out of here."

The red cap stands by the shop door, looking at the scrap pile. The expected tirade about Karl does not come. "Look at that goddamn pile," he says. "There've been no deliveries for three whole days. To add to that, the commandant told Verbin that we aren't getting any more new men. Verbin's so damn upset he can't even eat." His face breaks into a sarcastic smirk. "Things are going well—aren't they. This place is crumbling and you're playing around with a kidney stone that is supposed to be the size of the head of a match."

From my bench, I watch Verbin slumped in his chair. His gloomy look leaves little doubt that our world is coming to an end. The red cap helps him up, and together they walk into the office.

The doctors stealthily make their visits to the latrine. Now, at least, these fools are smart enough not to be in there all at the same time.

My machine bangs away. I look at the piece of scrap in my hand and wonder how long this will all last. Everyone here wants more time—just a little more time. I ask myself how much more time I can possibly have with the boy. What will it take to get him to crawl out of here? All I think about is crawling: the boy crawling through the wire; Karl crawling to the line. If I can only get Karl near enough to the rocks, then he can crawl the rest of the way on his own. The tower will go wild at the sight of live game. They will have to shoot. Then I begin to wonder if maybe they won't shoot. Perhaps in their infinite kindness they will just let him rot there forever, screaming at the top of his lungs.

I see Rollin by the window, gazing out at the road. I find myself getting up and walking toward him. As I approach this brooding man, I feel the stares that come from the men. The guards let me pass without even glancing up from their sleep. I stand beside Rollin, but he ignores me. "Can I talk to you?" I ask in a low voice. "Just let me talk to you for a minute." He turns the other way and walks off.

The second I return to my bench, Sheleen's assistant starts in on me. "What's wrong with you—are you mad! No one goes up and talks to them—not even the conductor."

Moments later I see Rollin coming toward me. He does not look at my face, but I feel his tap on my shoulder. His hand motions me toward the dock.

Neither of us says a word as we watch the road. His sad look is always the same. I see him fidgeting and finally I speak. "I am sorry about your daughter." He says nothing. "You once asked me for my help in saving your daughter's life, but I could do nothing for you. If I had had it in my power to help, I would have—I swear it. Now I want your help."

For the first time he looks me in the eye. Angrily he blurts out, "Who are you to be talking about my daughter? Who are you to . . ."

I interrupt him, fearing that he will go into a rage and stomp off. "Please listen to me. Deep down inside, you know I would have helped you. Just listen to me for a moment." He turns away, staring up into the gray sky. The anger has left his face. Slowly I start in again. "We have a man who is very sick. All he asks is that he be allowed to die quickly. He doesn't want the guards to give him a slow death. All I want is your help in ending his life." He turns and gives me a surprised look but does not speak. "All I ask is that you talk to the guards in the tower. Tell them that if a man crawls over the line, they are to use their guns quickly. I don't want them to climb down and spend the rest of the day torturing him. Just ask them to be quick. There's also a chance that he might be left in the hut after the noon break. He will be in hut number four. Tell the guards who go in there to use their rifles. Just a quick bullet to the head, that's all I ask. Just talk to them."

There is a pause. He does not answer. His face takes on a strange look. He turns to me and, in an almost quizzical voice, asks, "Why don't you kill him yourself? Why don't you scum kill him yourself? What do you want from me?"

I look into his questioning face and feel my insides boil over. I scream out as I have never screamed before. "I am like an animal! I slave for you like an animal! I gulp down my stinking food like an animal! I even stink like an animal! When I talk to my own men, I don't even know if I speak the truth! For all I know I am telling them a pack of lies! I have even stolen the food meant for the mouth of a child! I am exactly like an animal except for one thing! I have never killed another human being! I cannot finish off the man I'm telling you about! All I have seen is death— one death after another has piled up around me and smothered me! Each death has drained the humanity out of me! I am now a dried-up old man! I cannot kill this man and still live! Can't you realize that I am holding on to humanity by just a thread?"

I hear my voice cracking. "Talk to the guards. Tell them

to do what they do so well. Just a quick bullet. It's nothing new to them. Is this so much to ask?"

He looks away. There is silence.

A peace comes over me. My voice returns to a whisper. "Please do this one thing for me. Do this for me, and I will give you something that no one else on earth can give you —I can lessen your grief. You know of the boy with the violin. I will have him play for you. The song that comes from his violin is the only thing of human goodness left in this world of ours. Come to the compound tonight when the food cart is here. Listen to him as he plays. Close your eyes, and his song will let you once again hold your daughter in your arms. Let your mind go free, and you will smell the sweetness of her hair. Listen to the violin, and you will be at peace once again."

As I stare at him, I'm not even sure he's heard a word I've said. His face has a faraway look. He turns and walks slowly back into the shop. I stand there for a few moments, alone, shivering in the wind. Then I hear the song of the orchestra, which draws me back inside.

The red cap stands by the window, eyeing the dwindling scrap pile. I don't understand why he doesn't slow the tempo of the orchestra so that we can make what scrap we have last longer. The cutters bang away just like in the old days, but there seems to be a tension in the air. Perhaps everyone now knows that the Golden Age of the shop may be coming to an end.

The siren ends the shift. I look around for Rollin, but he is nowhere to be seen. I hope he is talking to the guards about Karl. I motion to Avron to go over to the artist and help him out of the shop. Without much discussion, Sheleen's assistant agrees to help me carry Karl back to the hut for the last time.

I rush to the latrine, hoping to get this over and done with so that I can have as much time as possible with the boy. Sheleen's assistant waits outside the latrine while I go in. Several of the doctors surround Karl. I find it hard to believe, but he looks worse than before.

As I push the doctors away, the cup of water pours all over Karl's already drenched coat. "Karl, Karl!" I yell. "Can you hear me?" He opens one eye. "Karl, there's no more time. I have to take you back to the hut. Nod to me if you understand."

He not only nods but yells out, "Please get me out of here. I can't take any more of this. Take me away. Do as you promised."

The professor shoves me aside. The place is now filled with all the doctors. "He is staying here," warns the professor. "We will keep on until the guards drag us out of here. We're not letting go of him while there's still a chance." He grasps my arm and pushes me toward the door. Two of the other doctors start shoving me. I brush their hands off my coat.

Turning to the professor, I yell, "If I don't take him now, he's yours. I talked to one of the guards and I think they will finish him off quickly. If I don't take him now, who knows what they'll do to him later when they finally get their hands on him? All you're doing is prolonging his misery—can't you see that?"

"Get him out of here," orders the professor. One of them opens the door and pushes me out. I stand there for a minute and then walk away. I keep hearing Karl scream, "You promised—you promised!"

Sheleen's assistant and I race to catch up with the column heading for the food line. The red cap's iron-hard voice blasts in my ears, "Is he dead yet?"

"No."

"Then what the hell is going on in there with those doctors? I can't have that man floating around this place." I feel his fist smash into my head. "I thought I told you that all this crap had to end. Verbin doesn't like it. He's going to check that man off the minute the second shift begins.

Then he's officially dead whether he's alive or not—do you understand? I don't care if he spends the rest of his life in the latrine, just so he stops that goddamn screaming. If he's still alive tonight, I'll drag him by the neck back to your hut, and by God he had better not come out alive tomorrow." He chooses to say no more, but the bastard's final comment is in the form of another smash to my head.

I take my bread and soup and head for the hut. Karl's screams cut through the air. I sit down on the step, totally beaten. I sense the boy staring at me from his corner of the step. I realize that he is waiting for me to spread Avron's cloth out between us. He picks up the cup and, for the first time, takes some bits of bread from his pocket and on his own drops them into the cup. Still looking at me, he picks up the cup and drinks. He holds the cup out to me and motions for me to drink. I see his head nod in approval as I take a few swallows of the miserable stuff.

Next come the stones that we throw while we eat our bread. "Talk to me," I plead. "Talk to me just this once. Say something." The only sound I hear is one of his pebbles gurgling to the bottom of the pool.

He still stares at me. Perhaps he sees me wince as I hear Karl yell out again. "This is a very bad place," I tell him. "If I were a boy like you, I would run away from here some night when it is very dark. I would crawl through the fence —it would be so easy. After the tower light came by, I would crawl quickly under the wire. Then, if I were a little boy like you, I would keep running until I went over that hill by the road. There you will find the children. They are waiting for you in the park. It's just beyond the hill—on the other side. You will run with them through the grass. It is warm there. You will jump high in the air—you will be free." I hold some bread out to him. "Here, take some of this to share with the children."

He takes the bread and, after looking it over for a second,

stuffs it in his sack. Then he goes back to throwing his rocks.

"You will have plenty of rocks to throw in the park. There are boats there. Do you know what a boat is?" I search the ground and find a small chunk of wood about the size of a pack of cigarettes. I hold it up for him to see. The boat, which was once a piece of a shingle from the roof, is gently launched in the water. With a puzzled look, the boy gazes at the simple piece of wood.

I give the end of the boat a flick with my fingers, and he watches with wide eyes as it bobs across the puddle. He jumps from the step and, kneeling in the mud, propels the boat with his hand back and forth across the pool.

After letting him do this a few times, I grab the boat out of the water and hold it in my hands. He returns to the step with a dejected look on his face. His eyes never leave the boat that I clutch. Holding the boat up to him, I say, "Someday soon you will leave here. When you do, I will give you the boat to take with you. You can use the boat in the park. You and the other children will play with it. The water is too dirty here. The water in the park is clear and clean." His eyes are still fixed on the boat. Now he ignores the stones. "This is a bad place," I tell him again. "Men die here. A child like you should not see such things. Soon you will walk out of here. You will run in the green grass with the other children. You will jump up in the air and try to touch the sky."

He sits there, looking into the pool. After he has passed a few pebbles over to me, we take turns again throwing the stones. I try to move toward him, but he slides further away. "Sit by me, my son. Talk to me—I talk to you. We eat together. Here, look at the boat. Say that you want it and I will give it to you. Talk to me—please talk to me." He says nothing.

Another scream comes from the latrine, telling me that Karl is still with us. The boy pays no heed to the shrieking;

he has been here too long to be surprised by anything so commonplace as a man in pain.

The blast of the siren drowns out Karl's screams. I hold the boat out to the boy. "Come back tonight with the food cart and I will give you the boat. Tonight I want you to play the violin for me. If you play, I will give you a lot of bread. More bread than you've ever had before. All the crust will be taken off. Remember, if you come tonight I will give you the boat."

I place the irregular piece of wood in my pocket and walk toward the men lining up. The boy trudges off, head down, toward the tree.

At first Avron is silent as we stand there in the line. I know that he listens from behind the door to every word that I say to the boy. "Why did you tell him to come tonight?" he asks. Then his one good eye opens with excitement. "Is tonight the night that you're going to lead him to the fence? Do you think he's ready? Perhaps he needs more time. Don't you think he needs more time? Maybe he . . ."

"Damnit, Avron!" I yell. "That child won't even speak to me. This will take months, and perhaps all that we have left is days."

Verbin throws the switch and then walks without hesitation to Karl's empty bench. The black book comes out and then the glasses go on. Somehow Verbin looks puzzled, checking off a man who isn't even there. Karl is now officially dead.

The conductor goes over and talks to the professor. The doctor sits erect, even though several blows land on his head. Then it is my turn. I get ready to grab the red cap's hands the second he tries to choke me. He stands before me with his fists clenched. I raise up a bar of scrap so that he can easily see the gleaming metal. He notes the scrap and, putting his hands in his pockets, says, "That man in the latrine is still alive. Verbin checked him off—he can never set foot in the shop again. I want you to get that through your head. At the end of the shift you will drag him back to your hut and make sure he never leaves there again." He stops for a moment and I think that he is through with me. "By the way," he says, "I don't need a Sheleen anymore. The replacements we will be getting won't need any of your noble words. They're already very well acquainted with this place." He starts to walk away.

"Wait a minute," I yell. "That man in the latrine doesn't belong to me anymore. Tell the doctors to finish him off. He's theirs."

He looks around and a smile comes across his glowering face. "The professor says he's yours!" He doesn't wait for me to say anything.

The orchestra grinds on. All of the doctors are at their benches. None of them gets up to go to the latrine. I rise up and move slowly toward the professor. He pounds away on his machine, even though he knows I'm standing next to him. I pick up a bar of scrap and jam it into his cutter. The machine comes to an abrupt halt. He stares up at me with hatred. The son of a bitch speaks in his professorial tone. "I have discussed this with my colleagues, and we have come to the conclusion that we can do no more for this man. We tried our best, but as you saw he has been checked off. Even if he passes the stone, he's a dead man. Now go away from me and let me work." His machine starts up again.

"He's still alive, isn't he?"

"Yes—but we can do no more for him. He's been checked off—I told you that already."

"And what in your medical opinion will happen to him now?"

"You know what will happen! He will die. Now leave me alone."

"You've given him back to me, haven't you?" He doesn't

answer. I shove the scrap into his cutter again. The blade nicks his finger. He pretends to go on with his work. "Listen to me," I yell as I grab him. "I wanted to take him back to the hut after the first shift, but no, it was a sin against humanity, according to you. Now you've dumped him back on me. Now you can let him scream forever, can't you?" I reach out and grab his head so that he has to look at me. "You've finally risen up through the ooze and reached the surface—haven't you!"

He pushes me away. "We tried. You know we tried. These are difficult times. We are only human. Who are you to be asking any more of us? Now go away. Verbin is looking at us." He starts to screech his machine, and the other doctors follow his lead. I look up and see Verbin giving me the eye. I walk away.

No sooner do I return to my bench when the writer from Anselm comes over. "Karl is still alive," he says. "I was in there. All he does is moan for you. He wants you to come to him. He says it's very important—something about a promise." The writer waits for an answer, but I remain silent. Giving me a disgusted look, he returns to his bench.

I search for Rollin and spot him across the shop by the violin section. I try to catch his eye, but he doesn't look in my direction. I debate whether I should try talking to him again but then think better of the idea.

Again and again I turn over in my mind what the hell I'm going to do with Karl. If I can only get him up on the table. Maybe he will find the strength to stand if he knows the boy will play his eulogy.

Thoughts of Karl fade away as I begin to smell smoke. The sounds of men coughing rise above the noise of the orchestra. The smoke thickens to the point where I can see it gathering beneath the blackened ceiling of the shop.

Several of the guards rush to the windows to stare out into the compound. One of them near me screams, "They're burning down the compounds over in the far corner! Come—look!" The other soldiers run through the aisles and press their faces against the windows. Just like young boys, their eyes light up at the sight of a fire.

Verbin and the red cap also watch from the same windows. Their morose expressions are in stark contrast to the wild excitement on the soldiers' faces. Verbin's eyes redden. He pulls out his grease-stained rag that in happier times caressed his machines and wipes away his tears. The conductor walks slowly away and slumps against the wall. I have never seen such a black look of desperation on his bastardly face.

Over the sounds of the coughing and the erratic pounding of the orchestra, I hear blasts of machine-gun fire in the distance. I wonder if our commandant has put his book down long enough to watch the destruction that he has no doubt ordered. Thoughts of the commandant are forgotten as I begin to worry about the boy. Could he have been caught up and swept away in the flames and bullets? Somehow he must be stopped from roaming around in what is left of the camp.

One by one, the soldiers become bored with the fire. They return to their chairs to sleep off the excitement. Only Verbin remains at the window—a picture of utter grief. The conductor comes over and gently leads the crying man away to his office.

Looking around, I see that everything is covered by a fine layer of ashes. The guards brush each other off to keep their uniforms pure.

Moments later Verbin comes out of his office. He seems to be his old self again. I am always amazed at how quickly this man's mind disposes of tragedy. His eyes search up and down the aisles of the shop. For a moment they fix on Karl's bench. He seems surprised to see it empty. Then he begins his waddling through the orchestra. The black book is drawn from his pocket as he walks through the woodwinds. He stops and taps the architect from Baleni and, with a smiling face, holds out his hand. Warily the architect extends his hand and they shake. Without the warm grin ever leaving his face, Verbin checks him off. The orchestra goes wild.

Another and another and another are penciled out in the same manner. The red cap's fist cannot control the screeching machines. No one, not even the guards, can believe what they are witnessing.

I realize that Verbin is checking off living men; none of them has ever fallen to the floor before. I wonder what the hell he's doing. These are men who can still work—they are the poorest among us, but they can still work. They are half alive, but they are still alive!

I lose track of how many he has checked off while the orchestra thunders away as each handshake is followed by a mark in the book.

Verbin continues on his journey, constantly consulting his book as if following some prearranged plan. No section is completely spared, but the woodwinds are hardest hit. The irregular heart of the shop—this section—is being carved out of the orchestra while it is still beating.

The fat bastard stops and looks puzzled. His puffy eyes search up and down the rows, looking into the faces of the stupefied men. He walks back into the woodwinds, past the writer from Anselm's bench, and stops in front of the artist. My cutter screams out to Verbin, pleading with him to leave this helpless man alone. He extends his hand to the artist, but, after looking into his blank face, withdraws it and makes the fatal mark. The artist bangs away as always with that same peculiar rhythm so characteristic of his detached life. Of all those checked, I'm certain that only the artist is unaware that he will not be alive at this time tomorrow.

Verbin motions for the marked men to get up. The writer from Anselm turns off the artist's machine with tears in his eyes and gets the man to his feet. Like a maître d' ushering patrons to a table, Verbin leads the marked men to the dock. In a daze, they follow him to the rhythm of the deafening roar of the orchestra.

I find myself running to the dock. Verbin looks at the twenty or so men huddled before him. His smile slowly vanishes as he stares into their lifeless eyes. A hurt look then comes over his face. It is as if he is disappointed that he has not received their thanks for all his past kindnesses.

A truck backs up to the dock loaded with men who look like gray ghosts. Their ragged clothes and skull-like faces are covered with ashes. The whole lot of them reek of smoke. The tailgate is lowered, and the replacements are shoved out on the dock and then led into the shop by the guards.

Then the soldiers start pushing our men onto the truck. I grab the artist and bring him over to Verbin. "What are you doing?" I scream into his fat face. "These men have some life left in them. This one is an artist. He is a treasure to the world." Verbin only looks at me with his stupid mouth gaping open.

The guard tugs on the artist, and I feel him being torn from my grasp. I look into his eyes which, as always, are a million miles away. Speaking near his ear, I say, "You have always meant so much to me."

He turns and stares at me. Mechanically he reaches into his pocket; he pulls out a small, smooth stone that I'm sure he somehow dredged up from the bottom of the boy's puddle. I can barely grasp the stone before he is dragged onto the truck. We stare at each other—there is a smile on his face. It is the first look of happiness I've ever seen on him.

The motor starts up and the truck slowly pulls away. The guard on top of the cab yells for the prisoners to sit down. When some of the men do not move fast enough, the soldier smashes away at them with his rifle butt. I see the face of the teacher from Antina turn blood-red after he is struck.

Verbin, also, watches the departure. His eyes seem to be fixed on this man whose head is covered with blood.

I turn to Verbin and scream, "What have you done!"

He does not answer. His round, bulging face turns white. He wheels around and rushes to the edge of the dock and begins retching violently. The rolls of fat on his neck turn red as his vomit spatters everywhere. Even the stacked canisters are hit as the crap from his mouth defiles his beloved spines.

I continue yelling at him as he vomits his guts out. "What did you think happened to all the men you've been checking off? You never saw what went on. You never saw what the guards did to them. You were always hiding in your office. What did you do—hold your hands over your ears so that you wouldn't hear the screams? How could you do this!"

He tries to speak but cannot. Instead, he points toward the door. There stands the red cap.

First, I just stare at this monumental bastard. Then I run over to him and scream into his face, "How could you do this? How can you live off the flesh of your own people? You will burn in hell for this!"

"Get back to your goddamn bench!" he screams. "The guards are looking. Yell all you want, you damn fool, but if it weren't for me you and all the others would have been dead long ago. Now, get back to your bench. Don't do anything foolish. I could have sent Avron out on that truck, but I didn't. Get back to work and get that screaming son of a bitch out of the latrine when the shift is over." He shakes his fist at me. "Listen, you bastard, I had my last chance at some good men and I took it."

There is no way in the world that I can run my machine. I bash the cutter down on the spines and round their edges so that they can cut through no one. Then I smash the cutter down on the scrap and make harmless metal shavings. My machine screams out in anger. A guard looks up at me, and slowly I calm down.

The red cap's new men are obviously veterans from the burned-out part of the camp. I watch one of them a few benches away. He has the look of a man rescued from hell and sent to our heaven. His machine sings in happiness at his resurrection. Except for the replacements, the rest of the shop is still stunned.

Verbin sits sullenly in his chair while the red cap wipes off the vomit that covers the overstuffed body. Tenderly, the rag cleans Verbin's clothes until they are only as filthy as they were when he put them on this morning.

My machine begins creating a long, sharp spine that will slide smoothly in between the ribs of the red cap. Apparently the cutter has second thoughts and turns the dagger into the usual spines.

The screaming of the machines continues even after the shift has ended. Finally a silence overtakes the shop. Warily, the new replacements stand by their machines and then, seeing that the guards are gone, congratulate each other on still being alive. I brush past the men as I race for the door.

The red cap tries to block my way as I start for the latrine. As I dodge past him, he yells out, "Get him back to your hut without making a big production out of it!" I say nothing to him, knowing that I am going to give him a night he will never forget.

I listen carefully as I enter the darkened latrine. The passing light beam coming through the window outlines the body slumped on the floor. I stand over him, trying to hear his breathing. Now I want Karl alive for the red cap. A weak cry comes from him. "I knew you wouldn't leave me. What happened to the doctors?"

Bending down, I ask, "Karl, can you still crawl? Do you have it in you to crawl just a few feet? I'm going to take you to the line. Can you crawl over? The bullets will be quick. It will be all over. You will be free. You'll be finally free."

His hands reach out, and I lift up the soaked body and drag him to the door. As soon as we are outside, I see Avron standing there, waiting for me. "Let me help you," he says. "Come quickly, I think I see the boy standing over there by the tree. Hurry, let me help you get him back to the hut."

Avron reaches out with his one good hand to help lift Karl. I shove him away, saying, "I'm taking him to the line."

"How can you do that? There will be shooting." His voice becomes frantic. "You will be killed. You are the Moses to this boy. The guards will kill you!" Then he pauses. "I know why you're doing this. It's because of the red cap, isn't it? You want your revenge for the artist and the others. Don't be a fool! You know what will happen—you'll be killed. Remember your promise to the boy!"

As I drag Karl toward the line, I yell, "Avron, I am a fool who has made many promises. I made a promise to Karl, and I have made a promise to myself to get even with the red cap. When I am through with these promises, I will return for the boy." In a mocking tone I scream, "Avron, where is your faith in God? If I am Moses, then God will shield me. No harm will come to me from those three machine guns in the tower. Now, go back to your boy."

"Why are you tempting God?" he yells. "Who is man to tempt God!"

When I look around, he is gone. Karl's body is limp as I edge him closer to the line. His back suddenly tenses up, and I know he is about to suffer another pain. I stop and shove my hat into his mouth. His scream does not disturb the night.

The white rocks that make up the line loom ahead. Suddenly the blackness of the night turns to day—the tower light has encircled us. I look up into the blinding light and point first to Karl and then the line. I stop again and point repeatedly to the line and back to Karl. I am sure that Rollin has talked to them when I see the light actually guiding our way to the rocks. Then I see nothing. Karl's face is a black shadow from the after-image of the light. Slowly we go on. I peer out toward the huts, knowing the men are lined up watching me. If only I could see the red cap's face as he goes into a rage.

Closer and closer we come to the rocks that form a perimeter about twenty feet in front of the fence. I have never been so close to this forbidden territory since the day I first arrived. I hear Karl crying. Slowly the features on the blurred face clear. The tears stream out of his sunken eyes. "Can't I have a little more time—just a little more time?"

Crouching low, I drag him till he is just a few feet from the rocks. Another tower light joins in, and everything is a blinding glare of white light. "Karl," I whisper. "The rocks are just a few feet away. Can you see them? I must get out of here. Give me a minute or two to get back to the hut before you start. The tower will make everything quick."

He grabs my hand with an iron grip. His last bit of strength binds me to him. "Have the boy play for me," he pleads.

"Karl, listen to me. Start crawling after I'm gone—the boy will play for you—Avron will say a prayer." In three phrases I've finalized his life, death, and afterlife. I start to crawl away, but he does not release me. As I move, I realize that I'm dragging him away with me. After I bang on his hand, the iron grip slowly opens and at last I am free of him.

Hugging the ground, I back away slowly from the crying man. I point up to the light, which looks as bright as the sun, and motion that I am returning to the huts. Ever so carefully I cross through the circle of light unharmed and lose myself in the darkness. I am relieved when the light does not follow me as I make my way through the mud toward the huts.

Karl's sobbing fills my ears. There is a brief silence, but then the air fills with his screams.

I wait for the chatter of the machine guns, but there is nothing. They can wait awhile. Yes, let them wait—let the red cap tremble awhile more. Let him boil over with rage. Let him drop dead from fright.

I stop for a moment. I am totally out of breath. When I look back at Karl, I see that he hadn't budged an inch. Shielding his eyes with his hand, he looks up at the tower. The lights reflect off his shaven head. I ask myself why the hell he doesn't cross over the line. Enough is enough; why doesn't he move?

The food cart has stopped between the first and second huts. Everyone's eyes are on Karl, sprawled out on the ground. I get up when I reach the first line of men and rush past them, trying to reach my hut. The guards remain in the center of the field, peering at Karl. They do not see me as I make my way quickly from hut to hut. Some of the men turn around and stare at me as I pass by. They give me a blank look; no one says a word. I look across the field and see the red cap gazing at Karl. I wish to hell I was close enough to hear his cursing.

The smoke is still heavy in the air. I find myself holding back a cough. Small fires still burn in the distance where much of the camp once stood. Staring again at the red cap, I try to glimpse his face, hoping that it is white with fear.

One of the guards bellows out a curse, and the food cart starts up again. Suddenly the guards start moving. I try to blend in with the line of men next to my hut. The guards walk by, heading toward Karl. They seem almost in a festive mood, as if they are off to see a sporting match. The soldiers gaze down at Karl as they pass by him. The sight of the dying man sprawled out, clawing at the ground in pain, does not interrupt their banter. Nonchalantly, they walk across the rocks and line up in front of the guard house at the base of the tower. They point to the now motionless body as they laugh and joke among themselves. For them this night promises to be free of the usual boredom.

As I drag myself over to my own lineup, I hear the voice of the writer from Anselm coming from behind me. "Why did you have to do this? You're going to get us killed."

Avron reaches out toward me the minute he sees me enter the line. The side of his face that can still move wears a huge crooked smile. He starts in with something about "Moses," but I interrupt him. "Where's the boy?" I yell. "Where is he?"

Avron turns around and points toward the tree. Through the haze I see what looks like the figure of the child standing alone in the darkness. I hear his high-pitched cough and know that he is there.

My eyes return to Karl. For a moment he is still, but then his screams tell me that he is alive. Why the hell doesn't he move? I know that he can still crawl a foot or two. I can see the three machine guns in the tower trained on him. Why the hell don't they shoot? What does a foot or two of difference on either side of the line matter to these vultures?

When the food cart comes by, I grab two chunks of bread out of the ladler's hand. He doesn't even know what I'm doing—he's too busy gawking at Karl.

I send Avron back into the hut for a blanket, and he returns soon. As each man gets his bread, I point to his chunk. A small piece is dropped onto the blanket. There is no argument—I get a little something from each of them. Only one of the new replacements tells me to Go to hell. He is tough-looking. All of today's replacements look as if they have walked over the weak ones in order to survive. This one has a scar on his face.

I reach out and clutch him by the neck and point to his rye once again. "You came to this compound today on a truck—I can see to it that you leave tomorrow on a truck."

I gesture over to the red cap. "Do you see that man? He decides who lives and who dies. I know him well. Give me some bread, you son of a bitch, or this will be your last meal!" He peels the crust off the rye and drops half his ration on the blanket.

I look across the field and see the men still standing in their lines, even though they have been fed. Hardly anyone has moved. Karl has them mesmerized. Then I notice the red cap shoving his men back inside their hut. The force of the red cap's look is enough to thin out the ranks of the other lines of men, even the ones on our side of the field.

Avron taps me on the shoulder. I look around and see the boy standing a few yards away, eyeing the mound of bread.

I wrap the bread up in the blanket and hold it out to him. He stands there with the bow in one hand and his violin held under his chin. I shove the bundle under his arm.

Just then I hear Karl scream out, "The song! The song!" It dawns on me that the fool isn't going to cross the line until after he hears the violin play his own eulogy. The poor son of a bitch has never had any part of his life on his own terms. Now, after all these years, he's decided that his death will be when he chooses. This weak little man has me dancing. I have to be the one to arrange all the details of his death.

The boy points with his bow toward my pocket. For a second I don't know what he wants. I pull out the wooden boat and hand it to him. Swiftly, he grabs it and hides it under his coat—but not for long. He pulls the irregular little piece of wood out again and stares intently at his prize. Each side of the boat is carefully examined.

Kneeling down beside him, I say, "Come, my son. I want you to come with me. We will go together, and you will play a song for that man who is lying in the mud. He is in pain. Your violin will make him happy. Do you know what 'happy' means? It is how you will feel when you leave this place."

As I talk, the boy gazes off in the direction of Karl. The child's face becomes somber and his blank stare returns. I notice that he is shivering again.

Gently, I whisper to him, "Come, I will go with you. Your violin will play him a song." I start walking away, but he does not follow. His sad eyes never leave Karl. "Come, my son, we will go together."

Head down, he begins walking with me. I quicken the pace. He is at my side, the bread tucked tightly under his arm. Faster and faster we walk—his step is now alive. Looking at him, I can even imagine some excitement running through his once lifeless body. He runs alongside me to keep up, just like a child rushing to go on a long-awaited holiday. A little smile crosses his face as he steals a glance up at me. In his hurry, the bread nearly falls out from under his arm.

A warmth passes through me as I watch him racing along at my side. As I gaze at him, I start to feel that he finally must trust me.

I hear Karl scream. Suddenly I ask myself, *What the hell am I doing to this little boy?* All the warmth leaves me. I am about to reward this child, who has lived on nothing but horror, with the sight of another death. The whole world is mad, and here I am creating more madness.

Karl screams out again for his song. I realize he must be silenced. He must be. We continue our frantic dash toward him. I hear the conductor screaming curses at me as we pass his hut. Strangely, I no longer have the need to enjoy his misery. Now I have enough of my own.

Seeing the lights on in the huts, I know that there's still time to keep going. We come closer and closer to Karl.

Avron is just behind us. I hear him panting, out of breath. He says nothing, and I wonder if any of his heaven-sent threats could stop what is taking place. Perhaps all his energy is devoted just to breathing.

I stop well before the rocks. Karl is about thirty feet

away. The guards look up from the man mired in the mud and point to us. Their rifles remain slung on their shoulders. They must be savoring each moment of this most unusual night.

Karl raises his head from the mud and, shielding his eyes, peers in our direction. I doubt if he can see a thing under the brightness of the lights.

The boy looks at me, his protector. "Walk only a few steps in front of me," I warn him, "and play something for the man. I'll be right behind you. Don't go near him."

After hesitating a moment, the boy walks slowly toward Karl. The child doesn't take his eyes off this strange-looking man whose face is blackened by the mud.

"Play for him, already!" I yell. "Hurry up and play."

The boy's podium is a dry spot between two mud puddles. Carefully he lowers his bundle of bread and places it before him on the ground. Then he turns around and stares at me with a frightened look. The bow shakes in his hand.

"Play for him—just a little song—play for him!"

One of the tower lights dashes along the ground, away from Karl, and picks the boy out of the darkness. Instinctively, Avron and I back a few feet away into the shadows. When I hear Avron praying for the boy's safety, I curse myself for what I have done.

The joking of the soldiers suddenly ceases. They come to attention as the commandant rushes out of the guard hut and pushes his way to the front of their group. He stares coldly at Karl and without hesitation raises one hand toward the tower and with the other points toward Karl. I hear the clicks of the tower's machine guns being put into the firing position. The guns wait for his order. It does not come. He surveys the scene once more, first gazing at Karl and then for a moment at the boy. A faint smile crosses his face and his hands return to his hips. He and the soldiers relax to await the rest of this night's entertainment.

Under my breath I yell to the boy, "Play something, already!"

The first few notes linger softly and then suddenly rise upward. The song darts back and forth in flight through the night sky. The sweet tones climb higher and higher through the layers of unseen smoke and unfallen ashes that litter the darkness. The song soars upward as a bird in flight. The music becomes like a dream. I hear the song again. I have no idea how long he has played—I never do. The flowing tones of the violin are slowly descending. Now and then a note rises up into the darkness, but it is drawn inexorably back to earth. Then the song is over.

Beside me, I listen to Avron's choked-up voice murmur his thanks to God. Clearly I hear his final word—"Amen." The commandant is slouched over. Perhaps even a man such as this was lost in the music. He looks around and quickly throws his shoulders back into their usual posture.

The light drifts away from the boy. The violin and bow are held limply in his hands. Rubbing his eyes, Karl strains through the glare of the light to catch a glimpse of the child. The boy does not move. The bread that lies before him has never been so well earned. Not wanting him to see any more of what is about to take place, I whisper, "Turn around and come back to me." The child does not move—he keeps staring at Karl.

Karl turns from the child and, with both hands, reaches out for the white rocks. Ever so slowly he pulls his leaden body over the barrier. The lights illuminate every move of his tortured journey across the line. Finally he places his feet against the rocks and, with all the strength left in him, propels himself into the death zone.

The few men remaining in front of their huts race inside for the safety of their bunks. No one knows how wild the machine guns will be once the explosion begins.

We wait, but there is only the quiet of the night. Nothing happens—nothing—not a goddamn thing. Karl lies there on his back, completely worn out by his long march. The pain comes again, and he does nothing to muffle his screams. They pierce through the night so loudly that I'm sure the whole world can hear his cry.

I reach out to the boy, hoping to get his eyes off what he is about to see. He shrugs my hand off his shoulder. I plead with him, "Take your bread, my son, and go to sleep. Go wherever you go at night and sleep. You will come tomorrow and we will play with your boat." He does not move.

Minutes pass—the tower is silent. The commandant and the soldiers watch intently as Karl sinks deeper into the mud with each spasm of pain. Karl's head rises up and he stares toward the commandant. Pointing up at the tower, he pleads for the order that will pull the triggers. "Even one bullet," he yells, "just one little bullet." His hands beat the mud in desperation.

I look at the commandant, who once again wears the same imperious face. I know now that the bastards are going to let Karl scream forever while the stone slowly slices through his insides.

Karl's blackened face turns toward us. Shielding his eyes from the light, he seeks me out. His trembling finger points directly at me. Everyone looks at me now: the commandant, the soldiers, Avron, even the boy.

Karl begins screaming at me for all the world to hear. Over and over again my ears are bombarded with, "You promised—you promised!" The boy keeps staring at me. Avron has the decency to turn his head away and look up into the heavens.

Smiles cross the faces of some of the guards as they, too, peer at me. On this night they have not been bored—I have created a memorable night for them. Now I am the one expected to perform. The guards wait for me to do what the tower will not do.

I expect the light to be trained on me, but I am spared this. The agonized yelling continues. Karl screams out to let everyone know that he has relegated my black soul to the deepest layer of hell. Where does he think I've been living all this time?

I look out at this screaming man who never stops with his chant: "You promised—you promised." I wonder why I didn't slit his goddamn throat long ago. Now this sinking ship is going to carry me to the bottom with it. He calls out to me, "Kill me—you promised that this wouldn't happen —kill me." The soldiers begin clapping their hands in time with Karl's chanting. Perhaps the thought of us killing each other intrigues them.

Why the hell can't the tower finish him? They thrive on killing. Why can't Karl just crawl to the fence? Yes, if he can only crawl to the fence, they'd have to stop him. He doesn't move. I hear his call over the clapping of the guards. A faint look of amusement comes to the commandant's face. Now I wonder if the red cap also wears a smile.

My heart is racing as it smashes against my chest. The nausea creeps up into my throat. My lice are quiet— they're too terrified to bite.

Avron puts his hand on my shoulder and, in a grave manner, says, "Go to him and do what you have to do. Moses killed a man, and now you must do the same."

I stare into the face of this fool of God and scream, "Moses killed a man, but the man was an enemy—Karl is one of ours!"

"You are right, but you never treated Karl as if he were a friend—you always regarded him as if he were an enemy. Now, go do what you are destined to do. It is a sin to let him suffer like this. You are Moses, and God has led you to this point. Do what you have to do."

I kneel down before the boy and whisper to him, "That man is in pain. I must end his pain. Always remember that your song gave him happiness. Always remember that you gave me happiness. When I crawl over to him, I want you to walk away. Go to wherever you sleep. I will be gone after tonight. Avron will sit with you on the step tomorrow. He will take care of you. He knows about the pebbles and the boat. You will listen to him and do what he tells you."

I look into the boy's face. Even in the shadows I can see that he is crying. His mouth opens. For the first time his lips move. "Don't leave me alone," he cries. He has finally spoken. I have finally heard words come from his soul, which is now alive.

"I have to go to that man."

Then Avron kneels beside the boy and, in a voice sounding like a prophet, says, "Listen, my son, God will let no harm come to this man. God will return him to you. God will see that he is not killed."

I look first at the three machine guns in the tower and then at the commandant's pistol holstered in his belt. I put my arm around the boy and hug him. He does not draw away. Holding him, I say, "I must go now. Stay with Avron. There is no one else on this earth to leave you with." The sounds of the boy's sobbing fill my ears. I get up and take a few steps toward Karl. I scream back at Avron, "Get the boy out of here!"

Slowly I begin walking toward Karl, who leads the way with his curses. I can no longer hear what he says. His screams sound like the same cries that came from my children as they were torn from my arms. I begin to race toward him to silence finally these cries that have reverberated through my brain for so long. I will never have to hear them again.

As I cross the line, I pick up one of the white stones. It fits snugly in my hand. Standing over Karl, I know that my face must show as much compassion as the devil's. His curses have ceased. My eyes are dazzled by the blinding glare. I can barely see his face. I speak to him softly. "I'm here as I promised. If you only knew what I just left behind." Sitting beside him, I give the tower the chance to finish us both off. I hear the click of the guns again being made ready to fire, but I wait in vain for the bullets. I hold my arms out and point to Karl and then myself. The tower does not accept my offer.

Slowly I raise the rock high above my head. Karl's tortured face watches my every move. "I'm sorry," he says. "Please forgive me." He utters nothing more. There is silence for a second, but then he lets out a thunderous scream as I bash the rock down on his head. My hand feels the impact crush his skull and break it to pieces. His whole body writhes in pain as his hands cradle his broken head. Screaming out in agony, he rolls back and forth in the mud. He is still alive. My blow has only compounded his misery. Now the jagged chips of bone stab into his brain while the kidney stone tears out his guts.

I sit immobilized in the mud, watching the havoc that I have created. Looking at my hand, I see that it is covered with blood. All I can think of are Sheleen's words—"the noble life"—"the exalted life." Karl's screams blast through me. His life and mine are about to end in this filth. Other men die after a long life filled with strength. Other men die with the comforting knowledge that their lives have been full. I sit here sinking deeper into the mud.

I can barely pick up the rock for another final bash to his skull. I am whipped, I am worn out, I am an animal. The poet crosses my mind. I wonder again where he is at this moment. I wonder where I would be now if only I had followed him into his Promised Land. As I pick up the rock, I look over toward the boy. I can make him out still standing next to Avron. I have brought out the spark in him. He has finally spoken, but it has taken my death to do so.

The rock is held high over my head once again. My hand moves back and forth to get a fix on his writhing, crushed head. The rock comes down hard. I feel the bones give way under the force of the blow. He is quiet. A small blood vessel in his head spurts like a fountain and then dribbles off to nothing. Karl is at peace. My hands are drenched in blood. Slumped over, I wait for the end.

I look up into the glare and see a uniform right in front of me. There is wild yelling from the soldiers by the guard hut. Perhaps they are screaming their appreciation to me for a performance well done. Through the glare I see the pistol pointed in my face. I wait for the pain of the bullet. No one ever hears the sound of the shot that kills him. I will have the highest-ranking executioner—the commandant. For once in my life I will have the finest.

He speaks, "Get up, damn you." I look up through the glare. It is not the commandant, but Rollin. "Get out of here. They're going to kill you." He lifts me off the ground and shoves me behind him. Slowly he pushes me across the line away from the soldiers. The guards are screaming at him as we back away.

I yell at him, "You animal, why did you make me kill that man? You could have done it so easily. One shot from you and no one would have given a damn."

With wild rage in his eyes he looks at me and screams, "I talked to the tower, but you can see they didn't listen to me. I have never killed a man. How can you ask me to do what you yourself didn't want to do? So you think I am an animal. I, too, have held on to being human by a thread. Who are you to want me to become an animal? Get back to your hut. They will kill you. Never talk to me again! Never even look at me again!"

I dash away into the darkness. The tower light does not follow me. Looking back at Rollin, I see him standing just where I left him. His eyes are fixed on the boy. They stare at each other for a moment, then Rollin turns and walks toward the guard hut. The commandant curses him loudly as he passes. "Why did you do that? Why did you have to step in the way? I thought you were going to shoot him, but no, you just let him walk away. He belonged to the gunners in the tower!" Then looking at the other soldiers, he screams, "Goddamnit, you know that if they go over the line they belong to the tower." The officer points toward Karl's body and yells up at the tower, "There's not much there but he's yours if you want the practice."

The commandant's voice is drowned out as the guns from the tower open up on Karl. Each machine gun explodes in full fury. Fire bursts from the barrels as the bullets tear through the dead body. The guns continue long after the body has been cut to bits. There will be little left for them to pick up. The blood will be consumed by the mud, and all trace of Karl will be lost forever.

Finally the shooting stops. The lights no longer mark the spot where Karl once lay. The commandant and the guards are gone.

Just as if this had been any ordinary night, the tower lights begin their aimless rounds of the compound. In the darkness I see the boy. He seems to be staring at the spot where Karl had been. The child looks up at me as I rush toward him.

I reach out and put my arms around him. I pick him up and hold him tightly against me. He lays his head on my shoulder as I sway him back and forth, humming the song he played this night. I hear his sobbing voice, "You came back. You came back." As I hold him, he pleads, "Tell me the story. Tell me about the park and the children."

His head still rests on my shoulder. I feel the hand that clutches the violin draped around my neck. I whisper to him, "Someday you will leave here. There is a park just over the hill. It is warm there. You will be with children. You will run and jump with them. There are no fences there. It is . . . "

I hear someone behind us. "Put the child down and get back to your hut," yells a guard. "Can't you see the lights are out?"

Lowering the boy to the ground, I beg him, "Come with me. Stay in my hut." He does not listen but walks away slowly into the night. Moments later I see him by the east gate. Outlined in the dim light, he plays a few notes on the violin. The soldiers open the gate and he disappears into the next compound.

I make my way toward the darkened hut. With each step I take, my feet sink into the mud. I have killed a man. I walk through an unseen puddle of water and feel the cold wetness pour in through a hole in my shoe. It is so good to feel the earth and still be able to walk upon it. I am somehow still alive, just as Avron said. I know that I have reached the boy, just as Avron said. I don't understand anything besides this.

The night is clear—the smoke has blown away. The stars are in the same positions in the sky as they were when I was a child. The peaceful stars never change. I continue onward, savoring each touch of the wind. Now I even rejoice at the bites of my lice, for I know they pay no heed to a dead man.

The door opens the minute I start climbing the steps to the hut. I know it is Avron who welcomes me. As I walk into the hut, he kneels down and reaches for my blood-stained hand and kisses it. "You are truly Moses," he says. "God answered my prayers and you were allowed to live. God has made the boy a human being once again, and now he will follow you and enter the Promised Land. God has given all men a purpose—some more noble than others—but we all have meaning . . . "

The word "noble" grates through my head. "Avron," I cry, "I killed a man tonight. After five thousand years of civilization, I picked up a rock and bashed in the skull of a man."

"Yes. Yes," he answers, "but in your despair at killing a man, you picked up the boy and finally rekindled the life that was buried within him. I saw how the boy then cried like a child. I heard how he finally talked to you. Everything has its purpose. We are in the hands of God. Had there never been an artist or a red cap or a Karl, you would still be dropping pebbles into the water with a child who would not speak to you. The boy is everything and we are nothing. You will lead him to the fence so that he can enter the Promised Land."

"Avron, I intend to keep that child for my own. I am not going to deliver him to the outside and then drop dead as soon as he's safely out of here."

"Wish all you wish, want all you want, but God decides. Think about tonight. I know you felt you were a dead man the minute you crossed over the line to kill Karl. The hand of God intervened to save you for your higher purpose. You are truly Moses. God did not let Moses enter the Promised Land with the children of Israel because he, too, killed a man. You are Moses—God will not let you enter.

"Tomorrow night, when it is dark, you will lead the boy to the fence. He will walk out unscathed into the Promised Land. The guards will never notice him. If you try to cross over with him, I know there will be shooting."

Avron's voice weakens. I lead this worn-out man back to his bunk. I have been here long enough to know that he, too, is about one day away from being free of this place. I cover him with his blankets. "Avron, tomorrow I will give you what you want." He says no more.

Karl's old bunk and that of the artist are now the property of two of the replacements. Their snoring and coughing have a strange, foreign sound. I go to my window and watch the light beam. It sweeps past the line where Karl had once lain and passes over the spot where the boy had once stood. The beam stops and outlines a small lump in the mud. It is the boy's bread, still wrapped in the blanket. For a moment the light scrutinizes the little mound and then dances off through the night.

26

There is the sudden roar of the machine guns. Carefully I edge toward my window and watch flames shooting up into the semidarkness of the morning sky. The fires are only three or four compounds away. Each day the destruction is closing in on us. The devastation edges ever closer, like a plague of locusts devouring everything in their path. Even with all this, I seem to know that Avron has arranged for us to survive at least another day so that the boy can be delivered into the Promised Land.

I try very hard, but I cannot rid Karl from my mind. A jagged shudder goes through me when I think of last night.

The guns have awakened everyone. Karl's replacement sits on the edge of his bunk, busily scratching his unshaven head in the vain hope of stilling his lice. He looks up at me and says, "You don't know what you have here, do you? No one ever shaved our heads. No one gave a damn about anything. Everyone in the whole camp dreamed of being in this compound. When I was a child I gave a beggar some money. He told me that someday I would have good luck. Well, he was finally right—I was sent here yesterday instead of being trucked off and shot. This compound is a heaven compared to what we had. It was a madhouse—the guards preyed on us and we preyed on each other. Everything is different here."

The artist's replacement gets up and walks over to us. There is a long scar on his cheek and an animallike gruffness to this man that already I don't like. "What my friend is trying to tell you," he blurts out, "is that we are lucky to be alive. We intend to stay alive, even if it means walking over your dead body. Don't pull anything again like you did last night. Where we came from, that wasn't tolerated.

234

The war's coming to an end, and maybe we can outlast the war. Don't you meddle in anymore. That boy is bad luck. I always kicked him out whenever he came into our compound."

"Touch the boy," I warn him, "and I'll use a rock on your head. The next time it will only take one smash rather than two." The morning siren silences us.

As I walk through the hut, I see the faces of the men turn away from me. Only Avron greets me with his half-smile. He takes my arm as we walk outside. Over and over again he tells me what I must say to the boy to convince him to leave this place. Every other word is about God. Only one or two of his utterances stick in my mind as he rambles on: "How can anyone explain why the strings of the violin haven't broken? How could a child live in this place without the help of God?"

I do not let him finish. "Avron, tell me again that I am Moses. I killed a poor, helpless human being. If I am just an ordinary man, then what I did has made me an animal. If I am Moses, then it was destined to be, and I'm still a human. Avron, tell me that I am Moses."

Taking my hand, he whispers, "You are Moses."

What he says is still not enough to calm me. He continues on about God while we stand in line, but I no longer listen. My eyes are drawn across the field to the red cap. He stares morosely at the scrap pile, which dwindles each day. He does not look at me; I know that this will come later.

As we march to the shop, Avron suddenly stumbles and collapses in the mud. "It is nothing," he says as we get him to his feet. He has that same distant look in his eyes that I have seen so many times before on the faces of men who are about to leave us.

Even before going to my bench, I scan the room, searching for Rollin, but he is not in the shop. I count the guards —he is the only one missing. None of them pays any atten-

235

tion to me. Once again I am thankful that I look like all the rest of the living corpses.

For the first time I'm almost desperate, waiting for Verbin to throw the switch. My mind is filled with visions of being taken out and shot for what happened last night. Verbin, too, does not look in my direction. His hand grasps the lever, but then he stops. I hear the sound of planes high overhead. The guards rush to the windows, looking upward. There is doubt in their faces as they try to figure out if the planes are "theirs" or "ours." Verbin does not wait to find out. He always looks uncomfortable when the machines are idle. The switch is thrown, and the fat man relaxes as the roar of the machines drowns out the rest of the world. The tension leaves me as I watch the guards warm their hands over the stoves. No one has yet singled me out for revenge.

I know that I will have to deal with the red cap, but for now his only interest is the window. Within minutes he signals the coming of the commandant. I slouch down in the chair, trying to hide myself behind the machine. Nothing seems out of the ordinary as the man of the book walks in. Hurriedly, Verbin peers down at a piece of paper listing the needs of his machines that only the commandant can fulfill. The officer marches right by Verbin without even glancing at him and goes directly into the office. Verbin follows dutifully, a respectful two paces behind. When they are inside, the red cap edges toward the office door.

The orchestra plays on quietly until I hear a stirring coming from the woodwinds. Some of the new replacements are bold enough to desecrate the sanctity of the officer's visit by getting up. They use the time to shove our men aside, hoping to get benches closer to the stoves. The guards, frozen at attention, do not rush in to smash away at these bastards. These new men with their long, straggly hair are like a pack of barbarians who have invaded us.

The red cap dashes through the aisles. With a long bar

of scrap he flails away at the barbarians until they are all driven back to their original benches. The bar comes down hard on each of them as they learn firsthand the rules that govern this place. Just so they do not forget, the red cap grabs two of them by the hair and smashes their heads together. Then, after bowing and putting a smile on his face for the guards, he slinks off to station himself again by the office door. Once more the orchestra runs smoothly.

Minutes later, the commandant walks out alone. Judging by this man's face, no one would ever know what was happening in the world. He is always erect, the picture of strength. I know that if the end finally comes and the commandant must surrender, it will be he who demands that the victorious enemy officer kneel down and give up his sword.

The red cap bows low as he holds the door open for the commandant. When the officer is gone, he ups the tempo of the orchestra and returns to Verbin's office.

They are together for several minutes when, with obvious difficulty, the conductor helps Verbin out of the office and deposits him in his chair. Verbin sits there with a hopeless expression that makes us fear that our world has just come to an end. The machines become nervous and run off-key. The conductor's look is just as bleak as he constantly adjusts his cap while pacing back and forth in front of the orchestra. Then he walks out on the dock and stares at the canisters that cover almost every bit of space. I try to think back to when the last truck came for our spines—it has been days. A chill goes through me as I realize that our spines now mean nothing to anyone but us.

For the first time the red cap looks in my direction. I tense up as he starts toward me, and then I slow my machine down. Instinctively, my hand reaches down for a bar of scrap. He stops a few paces from me and, with surprisingly little venom on his face, reaches into his pocket. A long cigarette butt is thrown on the top of my bench. With just the right amount of sarcasm he says, "Take it, it's my way of thanking you for last night." Then his tone changes to its usual roughness. "Let's have a smoke in the latrine."

I sit there clutching the cigarette for a moment. I do not have a match. I know he does. I get up and follow him. On his way out, and without even breaking his stride, he knees one of the barbarians in the back. With one piercing stare he empties the latrine of its sole inhabitant—some wretch in the midst of vomiting.

Without even looking at him, I ask, "Well, what the hell do you want?"

He slumps down on the bench. He sounds exhausted. "Goddammit, sit down already." He lights his cigarette and holds the match out to me. I sit down a few feet away and take a puff or two.

I stare at him and I'm almost ready to laugh. "I'm becoming just like you, you bastard. It's almost a joke. I go from being a disciple of that Sheleen to following in your footsteps. Perhaps I'm even worse than you. I killed a man with my own hands. At least you just pull the strings and someone else does the killing."

A derisive look comes over his face. "I suppose you could come to be like me, but I doubt it very much. For one thing, there isn't time. It takes a long time to get to be like me. I have had to age slowly—just like fine wine," he laughs. "I've been here a long time."

He rests his head against the wall and gazes up at the ceiling. "This place is like an overloaded lifeboat that's always being tossed about in a storm. Anyone who can't row has to go overboard, or we all drown. Someone has to pitch the worn-out ones over the side, and that has been my job. It's better to be the one who throws."

I look at him and ask, "What do you want from me? I know you want something."

He gets up and paces in front of me. "When I first came, I looked around the shop, and everywhere I saw men dying

238

of starvation or being kicked to death by the guards. In those days, to live for even two weeks was a major achievement. Things were very different before Verbin. I looked around at all the death and decided that no matter what, I was going to survive in this jungle. Well, I did. I am the ultimate that this place can produce."

"Why didn't you ever try to escape?"

"I thought about it, but I saw what happened to those who tried. There was always a bullet waiting. Becoming a slave was the only way to continue living. At first I was foolish enough to think that if I worked harder than anyone else, they would keep me. My machine produced more than any ten men, but no one ever noticed. In those days the guards shot men just to make the time go faster. The commandant didn't give a damn what went on, just so he got his canisters filled with spines and had time to read his books. It never dawned on him that dead men cannot run machines. Our shop never made its quota in those days. None of them did.

"Then Verbin arrived on the scene. The man he replaced was an out-and-out sadist. The minute I laid my eyes on Verbin, I knew that there was my only chance for living. It took no great genius to see that he could never run the shop. At best, he would last a week and then be fired. There was something about him, though—a rare combination of stupidity, decency, and, above all, desire. He wanted to succeed at something for once in his useless life. I decided that I would become the finest slave any master ever had. He would finally keep a job and I would keep my life. He was like a child. I had to handle him delicately, or he'd go off in a corner and sulk. Everything had to be presented to him so that he thought it was his own idea. I gave him the success he wanted and I kept my life. Now he can't do a thing without me—he even asks me when to take a leak. He thrived and so did I. I ate the fat that he trimmed off his meat when it fell on the office floor. When the fact that I was starving got through his fog-covered brain, he had the decency to shove the fat and other scraps to the edge of the table so I wouldn't have to lick them off the floor. Never once has he ever thanked me. The extra scraps, my red cap, and maybe the long cigarette butts are his thanks.

"At first he was tongue-tied when he had to talk to the commandant. I worked with him until he could at last stammer out what I wanted. Now the idiot doesn't know when to stop talking.

"The commandant looks upon him as some kind of dumb animal that learned to speak and walk on its hind legs. Once, the commandant even brought some officers in here just to gape at Verbin. It was like a visit to the zoo for the commandant's friends. They went away laughing, and Verbin was ecstatic. The idiot thought they had come to show their appreciation for the shop going over its quota.

"The guards were harder to deal with. They had to learn that all hell would come down on their heads if they bothered a man who was still able to work. I taught Verbin to put fear of the commandant into their heads. I even taught the idiot how to stare at the guards to get them back to their corners. Together, in his office, we practiced giving the evil eye over and over again. At first, all he could do was cross his goddamn eyes when he tried to stare at the soldiers. They laughed as they beat the hell out of the men. It was not hard to convince him that he would lose his job if he couldn't control the soldiers. Dutifully he practiced the art of scrunching up his fat face at home, until now he can make even a sergeant shake in his boots.

"I've even had a great deal of help. Your Sheleen, while he was with us, made you fools think you were living in a utopia. His influence still lingers—at least our men don't slit each other's throat over a piece of bread. Avron could always be counted on to convince the few still religious ones that all of this is God's will. I have lived and I intend to live on, no matter what it takes. While I live, the rest of you have a chance of living. Without me, you'll be dead, and without all of you working, I am dead."

Grabbing me by the arm, he says, "Listen, we need each other. I know you are trying to get the boy out. You need more time, and I'll need your help to get more time. Everything has changed. The commandant just told Verbin that all the compounds will be ended the minute their scrap piles are gone. Verbin has totally fallen apart. The stupid son of a bitch doesn't even know who's winning the war. I know that the guards have orders to start shooting the minute the machines are out of scrap. The commandant must be playing games with Verbin because he told him that we still had to keep up our quota of spines. Fortunately, I don't think anyone's keeping track of the canisters."

"How much scrap do we have left?" I ask.

"Even with slowing the machines down to almost nothing, we will run out before the second shift ends tonight."

"I've got to have another night. Just one more night."

His face lights up for the first time. "Good, that's just what I thought. Then you are with me. I need you. This afternoon we will take the scrap that is left in the other compounds. Our machines will keep running, and with luck maybe everyone will forget about us. The war will pass us by, and I will walk out of here. Do as I say, and you will walk out with me."

He gets up and heads toward the door. "Wait a minute," I yell, "how are you going to get the scrap?"

"Don't worry about that," he says. "Verbin's getting a truck. This afternoon you and I and some of the others will get the scrap. We'll take some of the new replacements with us. Those animals will do anything to stay alive. Our own men are useless."

"What about the guards?" I ask. "What makes you think they'll sleep through all of this?"

"Whiskey!" he says. "We'll get the scrap just like we got the new replacements. Verbin will be passing out bottles again. The soldiers will line up for their bottles just as if he was giving out gold. Their discipline is falling apart. They have to be losing the war."

"Where the hell is Verbin going to get that much whiskey?"

"How the hell do I know? His job means everything to him. I told him to do it, and he will do it. Let him worry his fat head about it. I told him to steal if he has to. For all I know, he has." He laughs. "If things get bad, we'll bottle our soup and give it to the guards. They'll drink anything."

I stare at him as we begin to walk out. It is strange—I almost find myself saying, "thanks." I am about to thank this bastard for all he has done for us. "Wait!" I yell, "I know you had to adapt to this place but why in hell did you have to adapt so well? Why in hell did you have to go beyond what you had to!"

He turns around and grabs me by the collar. In a low seething voice he says, "How would you know all that I had to do? How would you know if I went beyond what I had to?" He turns and walks away. His voice is now fatigued and just above a whisper, "Hurry up, we've got to get back. For all I know, the shop is sinking and it's now under ten feet of water."

Leaving the red cap to stand by the remains of the scrap pile, I walk into the shop. The men bang away on their machines and do not look up at me. Perhaps anyone who bashes in a skull is banished from the noble society.

The conductor enters the shop and immediately slows the orchestra. Verbin sits sullenly in his chair, smoking one cigarette after another. Looking at him, I can see that the idiot is busy talking to himself. The red cap walks over to him, and for the first time I see a certain brusqueness to the way Verbin is lifted out of his chair. Then the two men enter the office.

Everything is different now. The guards seem nervous. They ignore us as they gather in small groups to talk among themselves. No attention is paid to one of the men as he falls to the floor.

The orchestra starts to return to its usual rhythm. Now, no one follows the lead of my machine as I try to slow the tempo. The red cap's fist, however, has lost none of its power. He calms the orchestra until the cutters have barely enough power to carve out a spine. The guards return to their chairs, but they cannot fall asleep. Perhaps they have become accustomed to the loud, pounding clatter of the machines to dull their minds. Again I look for Rollin, but he is nowhere.

The red cap is out on the dock counting canisters when the shift finally ends. I make my way over to Avron's bench and help him to his feet. His is still the only friendly face in the entire shop. "The boy must go tonight," he says as I lead him through the aisles. "He must be out of here as soon as it's dark. I have the feeling that you have no more time."

Avron looks up when he hears shots coming from the compound to the north. He grabs my arm even more tightly. "You must get him out tonight. There will be no more nights." His one eye scans the area around the tree, looking for the boy. When he finally spots him, he nearly shakes my arm out of its socket. "Talk to him. Make him understand that he must leave here. This is your last chance. Last night God preserved your life for one reason. You are working hand in hand with God."

The bread is dry and stale. My cup is filled with what looks like boiled water with a chunk of carrot floating on top. Avron stuffs his entire piece of bread into my pocket.

I dig the crumbling chunk back out and hand it to the cellist. "Take Avron back to the hut," I tell him, "and shove some food down him."

The boy has a shy look on his face as he approaches. First he stares down at the ground and then up at me. Then I see the most beautiful, magnificent smile. Only a child could have such an expression in the midst of all the misery of this place. For the first time, he sits right beside me as we eat. The bread he offers me is fresher than what I give to him. Hesitantly he asks, "Do I have to drink the soup?"

"No, my son, you don't have to. Today is a special day." I hug him. He seems oblivious to the smoke and smoldering fires in the distance as he flings his stones into the puddle.

"Tell me the story," he says. He nods as he hears the same tale that he has heard so many times before. I am about to tell him to return tonight, when he darts off the step and launches the boat on the water. His little hand guides the boat from one corner of the pool to the other.

Leaving the step, I kneel beside him. "Tomorrow, my son, your boat will be sailing through the clean water in the park. This is your last day in this place. This is a very bad place. It is not for a child. You don't see any children here, do you? All the children are in the park."

The boat drifts aimlessly on the water as he stares blankly into the dark pool. I hold his hand and say, "Tonight you will come with the food cart, and then I will show you the way out of here. Come tonight; this time there won't be any shooting. Tonight you must leave here to join the children in the park. They are waiting for you."

I guess I did not expect a look of elation to cross his face, and there is none. I try to smile at him, but I cannot. He reaches down and plucks his boat out of the water and then just stands there, gazing off toward the hills. The long, ragged coat hangs well below his knees. The brim of his cap hides his eyes; the drops of water drip off the boat clutched in his hands.

"My son, do you understand what I'm telling you? You must come tonight. I will give you bread. There will be no more killing. You must come back tonight. You will come back, won't you?"

"Yes."

"This is a bad place, isn't it?"

"Yes," he says, "this is a bad place."

I pick him up, and this time his body is limp. He rests his head on my shoulder. The siren blows, but I don't want to put him down. "Stay here until tonight. Hide under one of the huts. I'm afraid of all the fires."

When I put him down, he walks away from me without looking back. He is oblivious to the pools of water that up until now had been sought out for his stones. The violin plays and the east gate opens; then I lose him in the smoke that hovers over the entire camp.

Avron stands beside me and says, "He can never be yours. No one can possess what belongs to the entire world. Did you make the boy understand?"

"I think so," I tell him. "He will be here tonight."

The cellist leads Avron to the shop. From the looks of the old man, this will be his final day. I have the feeling that Avron and the boy will be given their freedom at the same moment.

This time, the conductor is the one to throw the switch. He lowers the tempo until the orchestra beats out a song as slow as a death march. The red cap points toward the woodwinds, and, as if by some prearranged signal, six of the barbarians get up from their benches and head for the dock. The soldiers pay no attention to them. Next, he motions to me, and I join the group.

We stand there among the canisters that are now piled

so high that they tower above us. The conductor nervously searches the road and curses under his breath. "Where the hell is that fat bastard? He should have been here by now."

I look around and see that the artist's replacement is standing next to me. He pokes the red cap and demands to know, "When will we get our heads shaved like everybody else here? The lice are killing me."

The red cap turns and gives him a seething look. "Shut up, you goddamn animal," he says, "or I'll send you back to where I found you."

After that, we wait in silence. A guard appears at the doorway, and the first sight of his uniform brings a mechanical smile to the red cap's face. "Where's Verbin?" asks the guard.

With an almost angelic voice the conductor answers, "He will be back very soon. I think he's getting something for all of you."

The guard leaves with a contented look.

The conductor checks the orchestra to make sure that the dirge continues. When he returns to the dock, I ask him, "What about the commandant?"

"What about him? I can't worry about everything. Who knows, he might even enjoy seeing us steal from each other. He certainly doesn't mind us killing each other. You ought to know that. Who knows, all this might strike his cultivated taste for drama." He looks at the road again and fumes, "Where the hell is Verbin?"

Seconds later, the red cap takes his hand and smashes it against a canister. "That stupid son of a bitch!" he screams. "I ask for a truck and he gives me a horse."

Craning my head around the red cap, I see Verbin leading a pathetic-looking white horse hitched to a huge wagon. They reach the main gate, where Verbin is greeted by a chorus of laughter from the soldiers in the tower. Verbin's face is all smiles as he waves to the guards like a returning Caesar.

The closer the horse comes to us, the greater the kinship I feel toward the emaciated beast. Each of its ribs sticks out in high relief. Verbin's joy fades when he sees the red cap. Apologetically, he squeals in his singsong manner, "This is all I could get. Don't be mad at me. The army has taken over every truck for miles around. This is all I could find. I was lucky to get him."

Some of the soldiers start to jump onto the wagon, thinking they will find more of Verbin's liquor, but stop when they see that the inside is empty. A half-dozen of them congregate around the horse and start to joke about how the damn thing has seen better days. They are in a jovial mood, and I begin to think they've been into their bottles already. The red cap orders us onto the wagon, which obviously has served a long career in a barnyard. I sit down on the floor with the others.

Verbin stands next to me, holding the reins, and still apologizes to the conductor for the lack of a truck. "I tried. Believe me, I was lucky to get this."

"Goddammit, get going already," yells the red cap. Slowly the wagon lumbers around the shop and heads down the field between the huts toward the east gate. We lunge forward each time the soldiers fling a rock at the horse's rear end.

The soldiers open the east gate and we pass into the next compound. The conductor starts swearing the minute he sees how little scrap remains in the stack next to their shop. He tells Verbin to stop beside the pile. We climb off the wagon and warily make our way toward the scrap. "Quickly, you bastards," whispers the red cap, "get that stuff on the wagon."

Our guards talk and drink with the soldiers stationed in the compound. All of them seem totally unconcerned as we pick the ground clean of the metal. Within minutes there is nothing left.

The horse does not respond to Verbin's gentle demand

that he move on. After the red cap gives the horse a smash in the ribs, the wagon starts up again. We are almost to the next gate when a prisoner comes running out of the shop screaming, "What are you doing—that is ours! Bring it back!" The man races toward the slow-moving wagon. The guards look on, seemingly amused as the red cap hits the man across the face with a bar of scrap. He is still lying on the ground as we enter the next compound.

What little scrap we find is thrown on the wagon. Two skeletal-looking prisoners watch silently as we rob them of their lives. The wheels start sinking in the mud, and it takes all our strength to get the wagon going again. Verbin pulls out another bottle from under his coat and gives it to the soldiers of the compound. I am amazed to see them open it and each take a gulp without even looking over their shoulders to see if an officer is watching.

The red cap peers into the next compound, looking among the smoldering remains for any sign of scrap. He shakes his head and yells at Verbin, "There's nothing there. We'll head on." He points toward the group of northern compounds that are still inhabited. Before we leave this compound, I check the distant guard towers. They are manned, but still I think the boy can crawl out of here.

Our entourage passes through a burned-out compound where ashes and charred boards mark what once had been huts and a shop. Verbin finds some of their spines littering the ground and yells triumphantly to all, "Look, you see, no one makes spines like my machines."

We move on to the next compound. I keep expecting to find the boy sitting by a pool, either dropping rocks or playing with his boat, but I don't see him anywhere.

As we come closer, I notice that the scrap pile in this compound is relatively large. I tense up when I see that it is guarded by two prisoners. The red cap runs over to me and yells, "All right, now I need you. Take a bar of scrap and hide it under your coat and follow me."

We walk toward the two men, who have long pieces of scrap raised in their hands to use as weapons. The red cap puts on his smile and waves at them. "Come on over. We're delivering you some more scrap. Help us unload it." The two men drop their bars and start running over to the wagon.

The red cap whispers to me, "When they reach the wagon, you bash the one without the teeth and I'll get the other one." The two men pass us by and peer excitedly into the wagon. In an instant, with one blow, the red cap has brought down his man. "Get the other one!" he screams.

I stand there frozen in my tracks, watching the man without the teeth wheel around and go for the red cap. The bar of iron falls from my hand. My fist will no longer rise up and strike down another man. The red cap smashes away and, with the help of our barbarians, finishes off the one without the teeth.

I do nothing. The pile is loaded on the wagon. The red cap brushes the mud from his hat, which had fallen to the ground during the melee. He looks at me, more dumb-founded than angry. Out of breath, he screams, "What do you think I brought you along for? What's wrong with you? Sometimes I wonder why I keep you."

He walks away, shaking his head. Then he waves an-grily to Verbin, motioning that we should head for the next compound.

I stand there for a moment but then slowly follow be-hind the others. After a guard gives me a rifle butt to the back, I rush to catch up with the wagon. I feel numb.

With little difficulty, the red cap and the barbarians loot two or three more compounds—I lose track of the number. The wagon lumbers on. The bottle is passed around. No one offers resistance; the prisoners just watch in stunned silence.

"Get behind the wagon and push!" yells the red cap.

I can see the wheels sinking deeper into the mud as we

go on. I wonder how much more the wagon can carry.

Finally we reach the compound just to the north of ours. Even before the soldiers open the gate, I can see a bunch of men standing around their scrap pile. Without a doubt they've probably seen everything that has gone on. The sharp ends on their bars of iron are pointed toward us like swords. The red cap waves the wagon into the compound. Verbin, seeing the defenders, pleads, "We have enough. I've got to get the wagon back by four o'clock. We have enough."

The red cap answers impatiently, "Shut up and keep on going."

We draw ever closer to the men with the swords. Suddenly some of the soldiers stationed in the compound run out and shout at the defenders to get back in the shop and return to work. The prisoners do not move. One of our guards yells to the soldiers to come over. The order to return to the shop is forgotten. All together, the soldiers go off in a corner to laugh and drink among themselves.

I look at our barbarians and see that now they have second thoughts about this whole trip. The red cap stands by the wagon and silently studies the defenders.

Again Verbin begs the red cap to return to our compound. "We have enough," he whines. "They'll kill you. You told me we'd work together forever. You said the shop could only run with both of us. We have enough scrap. Please, let's go back. We have . . . "

The conductor shakes a fist at him, saying, "Shut your goddamn mouth. Can't you see I'm trying to think?" Next, the red cap turns to me but then looks away in disgust.

The artist's replacement runs over to Verbin. "Get us out of here!" he screams as he points to the defenders. "Get us back to the shop!" The rest of the barbarians crowd around the fat man, who just stands there petting the winded horse.

Dropping his bar on the ground, the conductor walks

slowly toward the armed prisoners stationed in front of the pile. They follow his every step with the sharp points of their bars. With a smile on his face, the red cap holds his open hands out in front of him. He begins talking. I can't hear what he is saying, but slowly the swords are lowered. I count eight of them surrounding the red cap. Verbin wrings his hands. His terror-struck eyes never leave the conductor.

They continue talking on and on. I can see that the guards are becoming bored; their bottle is empty.

Then suddenly the red cap turns and motions for Verbin to bring the wagon toward the pile. The defenders throw down their swords. They actually join us in loading their pile onto the wagon. We work side by side until the ground is bare.

I stare at the red cap in amazement. He stands by Verbin and takes a quick drag from the fat man's cigarette. I know that if Avron were here, he would be thanking God for this miracle.

The horse strains, but it is our combined sweat that finally pushes the wagon to the east gate. The minute the wagon passes into our compound, the red cap calls a halt. He walks over to Verbin, who is still clapping his hands with delight as he gazes at the huge pile of scrap in the wagon. The red cap and Verbin begin talking, and the longer they are huddled together, the more I start questioning the miracle. All I can hear is the red cap asking Verbin, "Do you understand? Do you understand?"

Apparently Verbin does, for he walks over to our guards. Their rifles are then unslung and aimed at us. With his good-natured smile, Verbin asks the eight men who allowed us to take their scrap to step forward. They do so without ever taking their anxious eyes off the red cap. Verbin directs one of the guards to lead the eight toward our shop. A look of total relief comes over their faces as they march away.

The other guards keep their guns trained on the rest of us. A bayonet hovers just inches from my stomach. Perhaps all at once it dawns on me why the scrap was given up without a fight. The red cap has traded our lives for those of the defenders' so that his scrap pile will grow in size and last forever. There were once so many lifeboats foundering in this place; now only his will remain afloat.

The artist's replacement starts to make a run for our shop, but he gets only a few paces before the guards smash him to the ground. He crawls back to our group and then gets another rifle butt to his head. We stand there, waiting. The man next to me asks why the red cap has done this to us. I do not answer him. My knees begin to weaken as I see the guards open the small gate that leads into the north compound.

With what might even be called a courtly manner, Verbin says to us, "I want to thank you for all your help while you were here." I can't believe it, but this moron actually seems sincere. "You were with us only a short time," he says, "but I appreciate your good work. We are sending you to the next compound. It is a good shop. Yes, it is a good shop. I know the man who runs it. He lives just a few blocks from me. You will like it. Yes, you will like it. Yes, I know . . . "

"Goddammit, shut up!" screams the red cap. "Get them out of here already!"

I look at the red cap and he looks at me. He has finally won. Neither of us speaks. I start thinking of the boy. Will Avron take him out of the camp? Will he even listen to Avron?

Verbin stares first at the conductor and then comes over to me. "You've always been a good worker and taken good care of your machine. We want you to stay with us. Come back to the shop." I can't believe he is talking to me.

I stand there dumbfounded as the guards lead the other men away into the north compound. One of them resists and is shot down on the spot. After that they go quietly, except for the artist's replacement. He screams out at the red cap, "May you rot in hell, you dirty son of a bitch!"

The red cap does not reply. Verbin, however, has a hurt look on his face, like a man hearing his best friend's honor besmirched.

We watch the last of the barbarians disappear into the north shop. The artist's replacement is still screaming out his curses.

With a fatigued, downcast look on his face, the red cap turns to me and says, "It's hard to make a living in this world, isn't it?"

"Why did you keep me?" I ask.

At first he says nothing, but then he answers. I wonder if even he's perplexed. "I don't know. I really don't know why anyone would want to keep you."

"What is it you want of me? What in hell could I possibly do for you?"

"For the time being, you can shut your damn mouth and start unloading the scrap. Verbin will send our new men out to help you. While you work, you can tell them pretty little stories of Sheleen and the noble life we have in this place." He gives the old horse a disgusted look and walks off toward the shop. I watch him disappear through the door and wonder why on earth he didn't trade me with the others.

The wagon is deeply mired in the mud. There's no way we can get it to move. We make trip after trip to the pile, which grows steadily in size. All the while Verbin hurries us along. "You see," he pleads, "I gave my word to the man that I would have the horse and wagon back by four o'-clock. Please hurry. You see, if the man doesn't have his wagon, he can't . . ." I drown his squeals out of my head.

Working alongside me is one of the men who came to us in the trade for the scrap. He looks older than any living man I have ever seen. In a euphoric manner, he tells me repeatedly how lucky he is to be in our compound. I have my choice of listening to him or to Verbin. I choose to listen to this man. Without my asking, he tells me that he was once a farmer. My arms ache from lugging the scrap, and I slump against the wagon to rest. The horse searches the bare ground in vain for a blade of grass to eat. The farmer stops and rests beside me.

Pointing to his old compound, he says rather proudly, "I've been here longer than anyone, even longer than the boy. I've been here two summers and three winters. Somehow I lasted where all the others . . ."

"What do you know of the boy?"

"It's very sad, isn't it? Such a small child."

"I know all that already. When did he come here?"

"I don't remember. I lose track of time. It's easy to do here, isn't it? One day he was just here. I think it was that first summer. Yes, it was that first summer. I walked out of the shop to get my food and he was just standing there. He went from man to man, playing his violin. Even then it was that very same song—something like a lullaby. At first everyone was afraid to be near him, but when the guards didn't seem to mind, we fed him a little. In fact, at first the guards even seemed to be amused by him, but the child always ignored them. He was only interested in us. He would look up into the face of every man and play his violin. The child would talk to each of us. My friend took a special liking to the boy. This man had been the mayor of Mullen. Can you imagine such an important man? He was the mayor of a city of over two hundred thousand people. Can you imagine . . ."

"What the hell did the boy say to the men?"

"Now that I remember back, it was very sad. He would ask every man if he was his father. He asked me that on the very first day I saw him, and when I told him no, he never played for me again. Only when he was really hungry would he take my bread. The mayor gave him too much food, and naturally he didn't last long. A lot of men gave him all their food. I guess it was an easy way out of here. The boy came back almost every day, checking the faces of the new men. In those days there were many new men. It was very sad. After a time the boy stopped talking. No one could get near him. His face became sadder and sadder."

"Where did the boy come from?"

"I don't know. The mayor once told me that the boy said something about him and his mother and father being taken to one of the big camps. The father must have then been sent to a work camp. Who knows? As near as the mayor could figure out, the mother must have told the boy to find his father. Who knows? Probably the boy just walked out of the main camp, playing his violin. He must have walked a long way looking for a work camp. I remember it very well, the very first thing the child asked me was, 'Is this a work camp?' But that was a long time ago. I think he's forgotten how to talk. The child's become a bitter little creature, just like the rest of us. Who knows, maybe he's even forgotten who he's looking for. It was very sad; some of the men were meaner to him than the guards. At least, a few of the guards would feed him sometimes. The men knew that to feed him would mean that they would starve to death even sooner." He looks toward the shop and says, "I must finish up here and get a good machine. Let's go."

I grab him. "Wait a minute. Why do they let him roam around here?"

"Who knows? Even the mayor didn't know. Now, let me go back to work. Remember one thing, don't get involved with the boy. A lot of men did, and they starved to death. Several of them even got shot because of him. Most of the time I just wished that the boy would drop dead and be put out of his misery. It got so that I finally ignored him. I just want to live. We would have killed you if you had tried to take our scrap. Even if it meant the guards shooting us, we weren't going to let you take what was ours. Tell me, can we trust that man with the red hat?"

"I don't know; I really don't know."

Verbin interrupts. "Gentlemen, gentlemen, please finish off the wagon. You see, I must return the horse and wagon by four o'clock. This man I borrowed the horse from . . ."

As soon as I enter the shop, I can see that the conductor has changed the rules. Bars of scrap lie by each bench, but they are not being used. The machines are busy reworking spines that came from the canisters on the dock. I watch Sheleen's assistant split each spine in two. At this rate the sacred pile will remain untouched, and we will last forever. According to the gospel of the conductor, we will last as long as the pile. It is not comforting to have one's life hinging on the size of a stack of garbage.

The red cap walks through the aisles. "Only use the scrap when the gaurds are looking," he says. At this moment all the soldiers are lined up in front of Verbin's office, waiting for the shift to end.

As the red cap walks by, I screech my machine to get his attention. After I point toward the guards, he says, "Oh, them, they're waiting for more bottles."

"Why did you keep me? Was it because of the boy?"

"I'm impressed that you give me such human motives." Then he just walks away.

I go through the motions with my cutter, but it is difficult to maintain the slow tempo. All I can think of is the boy; I wish I could have seen him when he first came here. Gazing out the window, I try to picture him, long ago, walking down the road and stopping people to ask, "Where is the work camp?" I can see him playing his violin to immobilize a passerby for directions or even something to eat. But why do they allow him to stay here?

Sheleen's assistant pokes me. "What's wrong with you? You're racing your machine again."

At the sound of the siren ending the shift, the guards barge into Verbin's office. The red cap looks pleased as he stands before his scrap pile. He grabs me as I walk by. "It's not hard to get things out of Avron. The man's not smart enough to lie. He tells me that tonight you're taking the boy to the wire. It's difficult to understand all his ramblings about God, but he mumbled something about you returning the boy to God. I don't give a damn about how you choose to deal with God, but I don't want any shooting. The whole place is ready to go up in flames. All the compounds around us are out of scrap, and the guards know it. They're finished. They'll be ended tonight or tomorrow. Verbin himself will be guarding our pile all night. The idiot can barely tie his own shoes, but he does know what will happen to his shop if he doesn't have a scrap pile. If Verbin can understand all this, then surely you can, too. I know you're going to try to get the child out, but don't make another one of your grand productions like last night. Just tell the boy to walk out of here by himself. They don't give a damn about him. The war is ending for us. Maybe it will just pass on by. With luck, they will forget about us. When the fighting starts, the soldiers will suddenly get homesick and just drift away and leave us alone. Don't do anything to sink the ship when we are so near the sight of land."

"The boy will leave on his own. It is not meant for me to go with him."

The red cap walks away, looking satisfied.

The bread ration is only half the usual amount. I ask the ladler for a little something for the boy, but he shoves me aside. A guard watches nearby, and I can do nothing more than swear at the ladler under my breath.

The cellist leads Avron over to me, and the old man stuffs his bread into my pocket. When I try to press the piece back into his hands, he refuses, saying, "After tonight, I will have no need for such things."

"Where is the boy?" I ask.

Avron turns and points toward the tree.

I wait on the step, but the child does not join me. The sound of his coughing comes from the side of the hut. I get up and find him leaning against the building. The chunk of bread I hand him is quickly gobbled up. I have never seen him so hungry, but then I realize that, with virtually all of the camp destroyed, most of his hunting ground is gone.

I take him by the hand and whisper, "Come sit with me on the step." Neither of us says a word. The night is quiet; the winter chill is no longer in the air. I put my arm around him, knowing that this is the last time we will sit together. Perhaps I'm waiting for him to ask to hear the story. I hear him start to sob.

"Why do I have to go away from here?"

"You've been here a long time. It is time that you go. This place will be burned to the ground. You see what's happened to most of the camp. There will be nothing left but the mud. Tonight you will crawl under the fence and join the children."

The door opens and I see Avron standing behind us, supported by the cellist. In a hoarse voice Avron says, "Bring the boy in. He must be made ready for his journey."

I feel the child tense up as I lead him into the hut. He looks around at all the men staring at him. Even with his plugged-up nose, I can tell that he doesn't like the stench of the place. Half dragging the child, I bring him over to Avron. The boy's eyes avoid the old man's battered face. With obvious difficulty, Avron kneels down before the child and reaches out for his hand.

"Let him take your hand," I whisper. "This is a good man." Slowly the arm is extended and the little hand is grasped by Avron. The old man kisses the child's hand and begins praying as he has never prayed before. The child stares in wonder at this bent-over, ancient man whose blind left eye never blinks or closes.

Even under the dim light, I am appalled at the sight of the child. He is so filthy and ragged-looking that I know he could never blend into the outside world.

Even while Avron prays, I take off the boy's hat and begin washing his face with the little tablecloth. It does no good; I can only get through a year's worth of dirt before the boy's irritated expression tells me that he has had enough. He loosens his hand from Avron's grip and backs away, but the prayers go on unabated.

Looking around at the men in the hut, I spot only one coat that might be close in size to the ragged monstrosity that the boy is wearing. I go over to the man in the blue coat and tell him that I want it for the boy.

The man bursts into tears. "My wife gave me this coat —it's the only thing I have left."

I point to the coat again. "I want that coat. Either give it to me, or I'll take it." Still crying, he slowly unbuttons the coat and hands it to me. When I turn around, I hear him call me "a bastard, just like the red cap."

The boy heads for the door when I try to take off his long bedraggled overcoat. Trying to calm him, I say, "You must have a new coat if you are to play with the children in the park." He allows me to empty his pockets of their contents —a few bits of bread and a handful of small round stones. His old coat almost rips apart at the seams as I take it off him. The only part that is intact is the glistening right sleeve. When I remove it, the sleeve is like a rigid tube that stands by itself on the floor.

He clutches at his equally worn and filthy undercoat. I know that there is no way in the world that I can rid him of this frayed long jacket. The outline of the violin protrudes through the coat. I open the collar and see the irregular scars on his chest that form his numbers.

The minute I put the blue coat on him, I realize that it

259

is too big. The damn thing reaches to his shoe tops. He starts to raise his sleeve, but my rag gets to his nose first. My gesture seems to amuse him; a smile crosses his face. I return his bread and stones to the pocket of his new coat.

One by one, most of the men walk over to him. Some put bits of bread into his sack that lies open at his feet. Others just touch him. Even the crying man, who minutes before owned the coat, comes over and touches the boy's hand.

With his arms upraised, Avron continues his chanting. The boy still seems befuddled by the strange rantings of the old man. Then the light bulb flickers out.

I guide the boy toward the door and reach out toward Avron. He removes the boy's cap and kisses him on the head. Gently, Avron pushes the boy over to me. "He is in your hands. The spirit of God is in your hands. Lead him to the Promised Land."

After waiting for the searchlight to pass, I fling open the door, and, guiding the boy along, we run down the steps. I push him ahead of me as we race alongside the hut. "Quickly, crawl under the hut with me and try not to get your new coat dirty." The crawl space is so damn narrow that I have to lie on my stomach. He at least can sit up by leaning his head forward. I feel the ground and, fortunately, it is dry. His breathing is quite rapid and he begins to cough.

I hold his hand. There is so much I want to tell him. "Take this for the children," I say as I fill his sack with the rest of my bread. "The children are just over the hill. You will go through the gates just as you always have. Play your violin, and the soldiers will let you through. In the darkness you can crawl under the wire at the far end of the camp. Stay away from the tower lights. When they pass, get out of this place and hide in the bushes along the road. Keep walking, even though it's dark. Go beyond the hill until you find the children. You must go very far from this place. Keep walking, but don't tell anyone where you came from. If anyone asks who you are, just tell them that your parents were killed in the bombing. If you are hungry, look for a woman. Yes, look for a woman with a child and she will help you. A woman will always help you. If you are hungry, just play your violin and someone will give you food. Just keep walking farther and farther away from here. Keep looking for the children in the park. This place is going to be burned to the ground, and you must be far away from here before this happens. You are a child and you belong in the park. Do you understand what I'm telling you?"

He says nothing. He doesn't even nod.

"When the light passes we will crawl out, and you will head for the gate. Go out the same gate over by the tree."

I start to move, but he grabs at my coat. "Why can't you come with me? Why can't I stay with you? I don't want to go away."

"I cannot go with you. There will be shooting if they see me. The guards will let you pass, they always do."

In the darkness I hear him start to cry. Raising my voice, I say, "Listen to me. Your father's not here in this camp. You must go. There's no reason for you to stay anymore. Your father's not here. There will be no more new men coming. You've seen every man who's ever been here. Your father's not coming here!"

He is silent.

The light passes. I give him a nudge, and he follows me out from under the hut. Hurriedly, I brush off his coat and shove his long hair under his cap. I hug him again for the last time. "Run away, my little one, and never stop running. Someday there will be a smile on your face; you will jump up and reach for the sky. Run away; go now, and may Avron's God be with you."

He doesn't move. I grab him and push him around the side of the hut as the light passes by. "Go already. There is nothing for you here anymore. This is a place of death, and you must live. Get out of here already!"

Finally, after I shove him again, he slowly walks away toward the east gate He stops for a moment and looks back. Amidst his sobbing I hear him yell, "I put my hands in the mud and wiped them on my coat!" Then he fades into the night.

I stand by the corner of the hut, dodging the lights. Moments later, from out of the darkness, he appears before the east gate and plays his song. A lone soldier opens the gate, and the boy walks slowly off into the blackness. My eyes follow him long after he has disappeared.

My hand finds the artist's smooth stone in my pocket. I pull it out and clutch it with all my strength. My arms reach up toward the black, starlit sky and I strike my fists up at the heavens. I scream out, "Goddammit, God, why must life be so hard?"

The night remains quiet. Now and then, waves of planes fly unseen high overhead. The camp and its machine guns are silent.

I stand by my window, watching the passing lights. Avron's chanting never ceases as his prayers guide the boy's every step on his journey into the Promised Land. I am so alone. One should never have children; it is too difficult to lose them.

The hours pass without the sound of bullets. Watching from the window, I keep wondering where he is at this very moment.

I make my way over to Avron. He reaches out and takes my hand. His voice is weak. "This is the happiest day of my life," he says. "The spirit of God is once again abroad in the land. Soon this darkness will come to an end." He squeezes my hand. "You are Moses, and you have been blessed by God."

I walk away and let him lose himself in his prayers. Later, I hear him humming. Once again, even with his crippled hand, he is playing his lost violin.

I stay awake all night by the window. The dawn gives a golden color to a narrow strip on the black horizon. I lean against the window, totally fatigued. A new day is about to come, and with it my child will be free to run abroad in the land.

27

For the first time, I barely hear the wailing of the morning siren as it cuts through the darkness of the hut. I lie there, my body feeling like a lead weight tied to the bunk. I don't give a damn any more. The boy is gone. There is no reason to get up. My thoughts are no longer in the camp; they are with the child, wherever he is.

The men shuffle by men on their way to the door. No one stops to plead with me to get up. No one even takes the time to see if I'm alive or dead. Now I know what it must be like to die alone, and I don't like it. I am the one who delivered the boy, but what was done last night counts for little to anyone now. For a moment I think of escaping, but I don't have the strength even to flee my bunk.

Most of the men have gone out to line up. Slowly I sit up and peer over at Avron. He, too, has not left his bunk. The cellist stands over him, begging him to go outside. I know how Avron feels; we've both served our purpose, and there's nothing left.

The cellist runs over to me. "Talk to him," he pleads. "He won't get out of his bunk. He's saying the prayer for the dead over himself. Talk to him. Don't leave him for the guards."

I tell the cellist to get the hell out of here. When he is gone, I walk over to Avron and slump down on the side of his bunk. "Old man, are you getting up?" He doesn't answer. His head is buried under the blankets. I try to recall some biblical prohibition against staying in bed when you're supposed to be making spines, but I can think of nothing.

He peeks his head out from under the covers. The battered face is so withered. In a thick voice he says, "There is nothing left for us, is there? The boy kept us alive, and now he's gone. Leave me alone. I can't work anymore. I've served my time. I've done what I was placed on this earth to do. God understands this; why don't you? Now, go out and line up."

"You're right, Avron. I'll wait with you for the guards."

"They'll kill you!"

"Avron, what makes you think that? They're all religious, God-fearing men. They must know that Moses died peacefully."

He sees the smile on my face. I help him up and we head for the door.

Our men stand silently in their lines. Everyone stares at the surrounding compounds. Beyond the fences, we can see the men being loaded onto trucks. The only sounds are of their guards screaming at them to hurry up. The prisoners push and shove and even climb over each other to find a place on the trucks. When there is no more room, the guns mow down the excess men. Their bodies are thrown atop the trucks and rest on the living. A few make a run for the fences, but they do not get very far. I close my eyes so that I will not have to witness any more. Avron's voice drones in my ears. "Perhaps it would have been better if we'd stayed in the hut and waited for them. Thank God the boy is gone."

Finally the sound of the guns dies down, replaced by the racing of the truck motors. From out of all the chaos comes order. In each of the compounds, the trucks line up in orderly rows and patiently wait their turn to drive out of the camp. Then in single file, like precision marchers, they carry their silent cargoes out of the camp and head toward the south.

We remain in front of our huts, watching the trucks. Ours is the last compound still alive in the entire camp. Everyone's eyes now turn to our scrap pile. Not to have scrap is not to live. If it were not for the guards, most of the men would probably run over and bow down before the twisted pieces of metal and give thanks.

The red cap stands at the head of his line, still watching the last of the trucks. His face is somber. I agree with him about how hard it is to make a living.

For the first time, the guards walk around with their rifles drawn. We wait, but no one yells out the order to march. Spontaneously, we ourselves begin to rush to the shop like frightened children racing into the arms of our mothers.

As I run up the steps of the shop, I take one last brief look at the road, and my eyes follow it up over the hill. Somewhere, over on the other side, the boy is moving ever further away from here.

I take Avron to his bench. His eyes are drawn up to heaven as he cries out, "God, God, you're through with me. Take me away from here." Then he stares at me as I place him in his chair and cries out again, "God, you're through with this man. He has served you well. Free this noble man from bondage."

I still cannot live with the word "noble," and I walk away as Avron's cries echo through the shop.

The red cap runs over to me and says, "Shut that damn fool up, or I'll see to it that he goes to heaven right now."

Avron becomes silent on his own. As I head for the bench, I see that the men look at me now. One of the doctors reaches out and touches my hand as I pass by. "You led the boy out," he says. "You are a decent man." Perhaps by freeing the boy, I have atoned in their eyes for freeing Karl.

The orchestra has barely started up when the red cap orders me and a few others out to the pile. Verbin and his tired horse have brought us more food for the machines. This time the wagon is loaded with canisters filled with spines from the compounds that were just ended. I look at their spines and all I can think of is the old phrase, "A man's good works live after him."

As we unload the canisters, the writer from Anselm sidles up to the horse and, reaching into his feed bag, steals a handful of oats. He knows that I have seen him and whispers, "I used to refuse a dinner if it was served a little cold; now I'm less particular."

The red cap sends us throughout the orchestra, dumping the spines next to each bench. When I return to the wagon, Verbin is standing there, holding the foreign spines up to the light. He pulls the red cap over and, with a pained expression on his face, says, "Look at these. You see, they never learned to make good material. If you can't make a spine right, then you don't deserve to have a shop. Haven't I said that before?" The red cap nods, and his irritated look tells me he has heard all this many times before. Verbin continues, "You see, they are not the same size. None of them have barbs. No wonder they closed their shops down."

Verbin belches, and the red cap uses the pause to interrupt his babbling. He motions toward the horse and says in a loud voice, "Get that damn horse out of here and get back quickly."

Verbin, looking like a man without a care in the world, leads the puffing horse toward the main gate. On his way, I hear him thanking the horse for all his help, just as he thanked the men he checked off.

The red cap watches him waddle off toward the gate where some man—probably the owner of the horse—patiently waits. Turning to me, the red cap sneers, "That horse has more brains in his butt than Verbin has in his head." Then, in a slightly kinder tone, he says, "Well, I hear you finally talked the boy into leaving. You always were good with your mouth. You'll need more than your mouth to survive this day. If the commandant will only leave us alone for a day or two, we'll be fine. If everyone will only forget we're here."

We follow him inside. Verbin returns, and the red cap

267

takes up his position by the window, waiting for the officer. I try to go through the motions of chipping away at the irregular spines. Fortunately for my fingers, they are all dull.

The soldiers do not sleep, nor do they pay attention to us. I can smell alcohol on some of them. They gather in small groups and talk about the war. Women are not mentioned anymore. Their faces, once so invincible, now look worried. Everyone in this place has the same anguished expression. Verbin alone lives in his dream world. He hums as he oils and cleans his machines and gives each of them a warm smile as he passes. His eyes are oblivious to the metal shavings that pour into our canisters. The man's simple mind is lost in the songs of his cutters.

My simple mind is also lost as my eyes blur into the up-and-down pounding of the cutter. In place of making spines, I manufacture visions of the boy in some far-off Garden of Eden. In my dreams, the boy has become a man. His long, matted hair is cut, but try as I might I cannot stop his nose from running. The face is also the same. He still plays the little violin, and wherever he goes, his song brings peace to all who hear him.

My machine races on, and so does my mind. I place myself in the audience of a symphony hall where he is the guest soloist. He plays magnificently, and after the performance I go backstage to see him. At first he does not know me, but then, after I hum his lullaby, he embraces me and tears come to his eyes. His wife and children are there. She has the same face that graced the artist's window. I hold their son and daughter in my arms, and he tells them how I brought out the spark of life that lay hidden within him.

My dreams come to an abrupt end as all the machines start pounding at once. Looking around, I see everyone feeding real scrap into their cutters just as in the old days.

The guards stand at attention as the commandant enters the shop. He takes only a few steps inside, looks around, and then hurriedly walks out.

The smile slowly fades from Verbin's face as he holds up his hands in desperation. Angrily the red cap races over, screaming at the fat man, then shoves him out the door to chase after the commandant.

Minutes later the door opens and Verbin slinks in. He holds his hands over his ears so that he won't have to hear the curses of the red cap that follow him to his chair. Then Verbin gets up and runs to his office and slams the door. Nothing stops the red cap, who barges into the office. The machines go wild when the two of them do not come out. Finally the conductor emerges from the office, and his strange smile is enough to calm the orchestra.

He walks to the dock and closes the sliding door. Trying to avoid the looks of the soldiers, he goes from bench to bench, passing out more spines for us to turn into dust. Dumping a handful of spines at my feet, he says, "I think our commandant has decided to discharge himself from the army. No one knows where he is. He just drove off to fade away into the confusion that is all around us. Listen, you can hear the artillery in the distance." I hear nothing but the machines. "Soon this will all be over. The guards will drift away. There will be no one to give them orders. Finally, they'll just go home. They'll forget us. We'll become invisible. The war will pass us by, and we'll walk out of here."

Then he grabs me by the neck. He always grabs me by the neck. "You're not going to try to escape, are you? You got the boy out—that was enough for you, wasn't it? You'll stay here, damnit. You'll remain invisible with the rest of us."

Then he becomes almost ecstatic. "Do you realize that by tomorrow at this time we might be free? The guards will drift away. Just think, had I been a saint, you'd all be dead now. Your boy would still be here, robbing you of your bread crumbs."

Verbin reappears from his office looking distraught, but then, seeing the red cap's smile, he, too, suddenly takes on a festive look. His ruddy face beams as he busies himself replacing a bearing on the professor's machine. Now Verbin has all the parts he needs. The silent machines in the empty shops around us provide him with a rich treasure.

He stands beside me, listening to make certain my machine is in good health. "You will have new bearings," he says. "You see, I've made a mark in my book to give you new bearings." Then, in an earnest voice, he confides in me. "The red cap says that all of you want to work for me, no matter who wins the war. The red cap says the shop will last forever. You see, to make war every army needs spines. The red cap says that even the enemy will keep a shop that produces good work." He wipes my machine with his rag and, humming some simple song, shuffles off to the next bench.

The red cap stands in the corner, eyeing one of the guards who is edging ever closer to the door. The soldier silently slips out and disappears. The tempo of the orchestra picks up, and the red cap, in his happiness, does nothing to slow us down. I look at the men and see the first rays of hope etched in their skulls. Perhaps all of this will end in life, rather than death.

The soldiers never leave the window. I hear the constant rumble of the trucks and tanks on the road, but I cannot tell by the guards' faces if their comrades are moving up or retreating. Now I hear the beautiful thunder of the artillery in the distance.

Now and then, one of our men falls to the floor. It is so tragic that they could not have waited just a little longer to know the outcome of this play. Avron looks around and stares at the fallen men. I have little doubt that he envies them and that he prays to God for weakness so that he, too, can fall over and be set free. He makes no pretense at running his machine. This old man of God just sits hunched over his bench. Verbin comes to him and begins talking incessantly. Perhaps he thinks Avron has forgotten how to run his cutter. Verbin's mouth never stops. Fortunately for Avron, the fat man is talking in his deaf ear.

I start to worry about the child. What if he gets caught up in all the fighting? I try to put all this out of my head by reliving the dream of the boy playing in the concert hall. Looking at the window, I plead with my mind to form the face of the artist's woman.

My view of the window is suddenly blocked by the writer standing in front of me. Minutes before, his face was filled with hope, but now all that has vanished. He looks sick. "I'm sorry," he says. "I don't want you to tell this to Avron and I don't want you to get mad, but I must tell you something."

"Goddammit, what is it already!"

He hesitates a moment and backs slowly away. "The boy has returned. Don't get mad now. See for yourself. He's sitting on the step of your hut. I'm sorry to be the one to tell . . ."

I shove the bastard aside and race for the window. A passing guard gives me a smack, but I do not move away. In the distance, the boy sits there on the step, head down, dropping stones into the puddle. I want to scream out so loud that heaven can hear me. The guard orders me to get back to my bench and gives me a nudge with his club. I feel the trifling blow and finally cry out in agony as if I've been pierced by a white-hot poker. With an amazed look on his face the guard walks away, staring incredulously at his club.

The red cap runs over to me and looks out the window. "Goddammit," he says under his breath, "that little bastard has nine lives." Then he looks at me. "You goddamn fool, what ever made you think that little animal would walk away from the first person who ever petted him? What ever made you think a child that age would run away from home? This stinking hole is all he knows."

The son of a bitch grabs me. "Well, what are you going to do now?"

Shoving his hand away, I scream out, "I'm going to take him out of here myself and no one's going to stop me!"

"Don't give me any of your mouth. We'll walk out of here together. Soon this will all be over. I will walk out of the gate first, and then you will lead that little bastard out with you." He stares at me, waiting for an answer. "Well, say something already! Just ask Avron, and he will tell you it's God's will that the boy came back."

Looking out at the boy, I say, "From now on I can trust only in myself. You can trust in luck and that idiot, Verbin. Avron can trust in God. I will trust in myself and the darkness tonight."

"You stupid son of a bitch," he yells, "you're going nowhere tonight! You're not going to ruin everything!"

"I'll kill you if you do anything to stop me."

Just then the guards start for the door. There is no siren. Their leaving means the shift is over. The men get up and begin to file out.

The red cap plasters a smile on his face and says, "Let's forget this for now. Tonight is a long way off. We will talk later." He walks toward Verbin, who busies himself picking up the crushed cigarette butts that the guards have left on the floor.

The cellist remains behind, standing watch over Avron. The old man sits slumped at his bench, staring glassy-eyed at his maimed hand.

I look up at the cellist and whisper, "Does he know yet?"

Shaking his head, he says, "No."

After waving the cellist out, I kneel down next to Avron.

Without even looking at me, he says, "Something's happened to the boy, hasn't it? He's dead, isn't he?"

"No, Avron, he is still alive. He never went away. He's sitting on the step."

The old man begins to sob. With all the energy left in his body, he picks himself up out of the chair. He stands in sorrow by the window, looking out at the boy. Then he begins to cry. His eyes turn upward and are lost in the gray, overcast sky. "Why, God?" he sobs. "Why didn't You take him? We kept him alive for You. He was our offering to You. What did I do wrong, God? Where did I fail You? The boy is worthy, God. Why, God, why?"

I take his arm and slowly lead him out of the shop. A guard watches as we walk toward the hut. He does not strike out at us.

The men are lined up, but there is no food cart. The red cap shoves and curses his men back into their hut. He raises his arm, and the sight of his fist is enough to send the men in the rest of the lines running back to their shacks.

The boy does not look up as we approach. Avron continues wailing up to heaven and then gazes down at the child. The old man tries to speak, but he is too choked up. I hand the weeping man to the cellist, who helps him up the stairs into the hut.

I sit down beside the boy and watch as his eyes never leave the muddy pool. Almost whispering, I ask, "Do you have any bread? I'm very hungry." Without looking at me, he reaches into his sack and pulls out a little piece of rye and holds it up to me. I take it and break off a small bit and pass the remainder to him. "Take it and eat, my little one. You must be very hungry."

I put my arm around him and he bursts into tears. Between cries, he says, "I didn't put my hands in the mud and get my coat dirty." Then he holds his right sleeve up so that I can see that it never touched his nose.

A slight smile comes to his face when I wipe his nose on my sleeve. I hug him again. "Everything will be all right now," I tell him. "Tonight, when it is dark, I will take you out of there. This time we will go together and find the park. You and I will be together. I won't let you go alone this time. Do you understand me?"

He nods and for the first time looks at me.

I pick him up and point him toward the tree. "Go over to the last hut, and when the guards aren't looking, crawl under it. Make sure they don't see you. Crawl under and hide until I come for you. It will be dark. Don't come out even if there's shooting. Now, don't cry anymore. Tonight I will come for you and take you to the children."

I watch as he walks away. His step is like that of a little old man. My eyes do not leave him until he disappears around the side of the last hut.

The men sit on their bunks, staring into their empty cups. They seem lost in their hunger and in the uncertainty of this day. As I head for Avron's bunk, one of the men asks me why there's no food cart today. I pass him by and let him stand there wondering.

Avron lies buried in his bunk, still asking God, "What did I do wrong? I was faithful to You." His voice is weak and his words come with difficulty.

I kneel down beside him. "Avron, Avron, we made a child out of him. He was an animal before. A child would be afraid to run away. Don't you understand?" He stares up at the ceiling, and I begin to wonder if he's still alive. Whispering into his good ear, I say, "Avron, it is all so clear to me now. Listen to me. I'm telling you the truth. I swear to you I am, in the name of the boy. You said I was Moses. I'm not. Sometimes I think I'm little better than the red cap. Avron, you are the Moses. You are the only one decent enough to be God's Moses. You never lost your faith—the rest of us did. Listen to me, please. Without you, the boy would have died long ago. You kept him alive long before

I came here. Without you I, too, would have ignored the boy, just like all the others. You, Avron, you are the Moses. You brought us through all of this alive, and now the boy and I will go into the Promised Land tonight. Know that you are the Moses and that God has not abandoned you. You have done all that God has asked. Burn what I am telling you into your mind. Please tell me that you've heard me. Blink your good eye; let me know that you've heard me." I take his hand. "Avron, clutch my hand if you've heard me. Squeeze my hand so that I know you believe what I say is true."

Perhaps his hand grasped mine—I don't really know. Moments later the hand goes limp, and quietly, I place it by his side. I know he is dead.

The cellist walks over and covers the old man's face with a coat. He looks at me and, with tears in his eyes, asks, "Did you really believe what you said to him?"

"Yes, I spoke the truth. How could I do otherwise to such a man? He was the best of all of us. It was easier to become an animal like the red cap or to give up completely like a Sheleen—or to wander aimlessly like myself. He alone lived like a man in this cesspool."

We stand there for a few moments and then walk out. Gently, I close the door behind me.

No one is lined up. The men stream into the shop with the taunts of the red cap in their ears. "Get in already," he yells. "No one is to see us anymore. Stay off the dock and don't go near the latrine." Before the shop door closes behind me, I get one last quick look at the hut that hides the boy. Everything is quiet there.

The guards are clustered again around the window, watching the road. Perhaps the red cap is right: There are fewer of them. I count only twelve.

After switching on the power, the red cap turns and seems to search through the shop. I see Verbin's empty chair. The red cap runs into the office and comes out immediately. Then he slowly opens the door to the dock and peers out for a second. Moments later he stands by my machine. "Where is that fat bastard?"

"How the hell would I know? Maybe he's run off with the commandant."

"You're crazy," he scoffs. "This place is Verbin's life. There's no way in the world he'd ever leave here." He looks over at Avron's bench and then at me. He says nothing. The expression on my face tells him everything.

The door opens and Verbin bursts in with the broadest smile. He rushes over and, out of breath, starts blurting out to the red cap, "Come outside, quick. I got some more machines. There are three good ones on the wagon. They're the best in the whole camp. Come outside and look. You'll be happy with me. They're almost new, you'll be . . ."

The red cap slaps him across the face. "Goddammit, we don't need any more. Can't you get that through your thick head? We have a scrap pile and that's enough." The red cap hesitates for a moment and then very gently puts his arm around the man he has just struck. Verbin stands there, holding his face. In a soft voice the red cap says, "You're right, we might need those machines. Let's unload them quickly so that they won't be out in the weather."

Verbin's smile returns as he rounds up several of us to unload the wagon. We look at the red cap, and he nods for us to go out with Verbin.

One by one, we lug the machines in and set them down in back of the shop. I see two of the soldiers eyeing the horse and wagon, and so does the conductor. He calls Verbin over and says, "Let the soldiers take the horse back. We need you to stay here and run the shop. You know how the soldiers beat the men when you're not around. This can ruin the machines. Tell the soldiers where to go. With all the tanks on the road, they'll be able to cross over to the city more easily than you." Verbin nods and runs over to the two soldiers.

The red cap stands beside me. "That's the last we'll see of those two. The minute they get onto that wagon, they'll become farm boys again and disappear." He looks around the deserted compound for a moment and asks, "Where's the boy?"

"I don't know."

"Don't give me that. You've got him stashed away somewhere. If you think you're going to sneak out of here with him when it's dark, then you're wrong. You're dead wrong. We're all going to wait this thing out quietly. Look up at the tower. There's only two of them—there should be three. Can't you get it through your head that they're going to disappear into the woods the minute the fighting gets near here? Listen to the artillery—it's getting closer. If it's a question of my life or yours, you know which one I'll choose. Now, get back inside. No one's leaving this shop until this is all over!"

I walk back in and start counting the minutes until nightfall. I have learned that ten beats of the machine equal about a minute. The time passes slowly. The cutters smash away at the spines, making little metal shavings that at best could maim only an army of pygmies.

Verbin works painstakingly over the new machines, getting them into working order. He aligns the cutters so that they will be balanced as they smash downward into a spine. Suddenly there is the roar of an explosion and the entire building trembles. The orchestra misses a few beats but goes on playing. Verbin looks up for a moment and gazes out the window. I know he can see that his city has been hit by the shellfire. His face is somber but then comes alive as the new machines begin to shine under his tender care.

Slowly the soldiers drift away from the window. I hear the word "retreat" from their lips. With a quick glance out the window, I can see the trucks making a headlong dash down the road toward the south. Even if I hadn't looked at the road, the faces of the guards would have told me everything: The end is coming. They sit slumped in their chairs. They look as exhausted as if they themselves had been fighting in the trenches.

The conductor, sensing victory, ups the tempo of the orchestra. We are now beating out a triumphal march. I see faint smiles come to the faces of our men. I watch the red cap marching through the aisles and know that this bastard is a genius.He is going to bring this sinking ship into port. The red cap will open the gate, and the boy and I will walk out of here together. I keep thinking about Avron. If only he could have waited a little longer—he could have seen with his own eyes the boy step into the Promised Land.

The orchestra answers each exploding shell with a chorus of song. Verbin continues his frantic polishing, and the guards fall into a deeper despair.

One of the soldiers stands hesitantly by the door, as if he is agonizing over running away or remaining at his meaningless post. I give him silent encouragement to turn the knob and get the hell out of here. Finally his turmoil is over; he opens the door and starts to walk out. Suddenly the door is slammed shut and the guard runs back into the shop, yelling to his comrades. They rouse themselves—douse their cigarettes and come to attention.

The conductor dashes for the window and takes a quick look outside. He commandeers the nearest machine and screeches the cutter. The grating sound blasts into everyone's terrified ears. Lifting a bar of scrap off the floor, he motions for us to begin making real spines. Next, he backs Verbin into a corner, but the idiot still polishes his machines. The red cap grabs the rag from his hand and throws it to the floor. Verbin has a bewildered look as his simple mind receives the conductor's hurried instructions. His huge head nods methodically as he tries to indicate that he understands all that I'm sure he cannot possibly comprehend. Over the sound of the machines, I hear the red cap scream, "Now, repeat to me what you're going to say!" Verbin's mouth moves as if by rote. The red cap angrily shakes his head and shoves Verbin toward the door. The fat man stands there, trying his best to tuck his shirt in, but it is all to no avail.

Everyone in the shop stares at the door. Perfect spines pour out of the cutters in regular cadence. Verbin goes through the motions of giving his speech, but periodically he looks over at the red cap for reassurance.

The door is smashed open and two soldiers rush in with drawn guns. Moments later a captain stomps in. He looks shocked at finding an inhabited island in the otherwise deserted camp. His uniform is sloppy, and I find myself amazed to see an officer unshaven. He is probably a tank commander—his face is dirty except for the white rings around his eyes where his goggles must have rested.

Verbin bows before the officer and his mouth starts blurting out his entire lesson. The captain gives Verbin a disdainful look, which shuts him up in midsentence. After a few words from the officer, Verbin signals to the red cap to turn off the power. The machines grind to a halt.

The place is silent as the officer walks through the aisles, gazing contemptuously at us and our machines.

Verbin runs up to him and digs into a canister to pull out a handful of our gems. Shoving the spines into the officer's face, he squeals, "This shop makes the finest shrapnel in all the world."

The captain brushes him away. "I don't give a damn what you do. Who's in charge of this place? Why haven't these prisoners been shipped out?" He seems outraged as his eyes scan our guards, looking for their badge of rank. All he sees are a bunch of young privates. Turning to Verbin, he yells, "What's going on here? Where's the officer in charge?"

With a quick glance at the red cap, Verbin bows and

answers humbly, "You see, our commandant left for just a little while. He's a colonel. Yes, he's a colonel and you are a captain. He will be back very soon. Our colonel knows we have a scrap pile, and he says that we are to keep working as long as we have a scrap pile. We always follow his orders. He is a very smart man. He always reads. Let me show you the scrap pile. It's just outside the door. You must have seen it when you came in. Our commandant says we are to work. You see, he's a colonel. Let me show you the pile."

The red cap stands in the corner, burying his head in his hands. Verbin continues rambling on. "We make the finest shrapnel. You must have the spines that we make to keep on with the war. Our colonel will be right back. You are a captain. Our colonel . . ."

"Shut up, you fool!" screams the officer. He's had enough. Yelling to one of his men, he asks, "Do we have any empty trucks?"

A sergeant answers, "No, sir."

The officer looks at Verbin and says, "I don't know what the hell is going on in this place, but this area is going to be overrun. We have orders to pull out of this whole sector. Then, yelling at his sergeant again, he says, "Get some more men in here to guard this place and see if you can round up some trucks."

Verbin starts squealing, but the officer shoves him aside and hurries out of the shop.

Within minutes we have five more soldiers assigned to the shop. The first thing they do is run over to our guards and ask for cigarettes. In hushed tones I hear them talking about how badly the war is going. These new soldiers are filthy—never before have I seen uniforms covered with mud. They pay little attention to us. Two of them, looking totally exhausted, go over to a corner and curl up on the floor and fall asleep. The rest of the guards rush to the window to watch the vehicles pull out of the camp and join the retreat down the main road.

Verbin still stands staring at the door, mouthing some nonsense. He looks lost, and so do the rest of us. The conductor stands by the window, holding his cap in his hand. He is slumped over, and I think that I can even see tears in his eyes. We have been discovered, and all his best-laid plans have gone to hell.

Perhaps by habit—perhaps to find some measure of peace—Verbin walks slowly over to the switch and turns on the power. Some men work their machines; others just sit there in a daze. Then, one by one, the cutters start striking down on the spines. Each man plays his own song, but the orchestra is as lifeless as its players.

I hear a scream above the pounding clatter. The conductor has smashed his fist through a window. He stands there, leaning against the wall with the blood dripping from his hand. His face is a picture of twisted sorrow. He reaches into his pocket and pulls out a cigarette butt. For the first time he smokes openly in front of everyone.

I keep looking at the door, waiting for the captain to return with his trucks. If only I could get the hell out of here, but there's too much daylight.

Verbin comes alive and begins walking through the aisles, oiling his machines. From time to time he bends over and picks up a wayward spine that has fallen to the floor. The ship is sinking, but the idiot still keeps the deck clean.

The orchestra beats away at its own pace. Sitting on the floor in a corner, the red cap blows a smoke ring into the air. The man who had a solution for all occasions has been beaten.

The time passes. A few more men topple to the floor. They lie there dead, never knowing the final details of the last act of this tragedy. They are fortunate, and so was Avron. God spared him and let him die in peace. Still, the trucks do not come.

A shot rings out, and the lawyer from Eren drops to the floor. He crawls a few more feet toward the door, but the second shot stops him forever. The soldier reloads his rifle, then leans it against the wall—and goes back to sleep.

I keep thinking that if I can only get to the latrine, I could slip away and reach the boy. If only the goddamn darkness would come.

The writer steals his way over to the red cap, and they exchange a few words. The writer is directed into Verbin's office. A steady stream of men files into the office, which has now become our latrine. Verbin doesn't seem to mind. He's found his rag on the floor and, with a peaceful smile, walks the aisles, cleaning his machines.

The soldiers pace back and forth between the windows and their chairs. Two of them walk out on the dock and slide the door closed behind them. I start counting the minutes. The longer they're gone, the less chance they'll return. The conductor peeks out the door, and I can tell by his expression that they are gone forever. The life gradually returns to his face and his bastardly look is with us again. His bloody fist swings through the air, and the orchestra beats once more to his command. His step quickens as he goes through the aisles, passing out more spines for us to beat into dust. When he is gone, I take a piece of scrap and make myself a dagger. This time it winds up in my pocket, rather than in the bottom of the canister.

The darkness comes slowly, and with it the shelling slackens. Verbin turns on the overhead lights, only to have them switched off immediately by the red cap. The fat man makes a weak protest, shrugs his shoulders, and for the first time today collapses in his easy chair. Moments later he is asleep.

The tension begins to wear on us. A man in the cello section gets up and starts screaming. The red cap's fists beat him back into his chair. The man no longer yells.

Now it is too dark in the shop to chance actually running the machines. The cutters could just as easily make a spine out of a finger as a piece of scrap. We pound on our machines in the semidarkness as the cutting blades smash down at nothing.

As if they've heard the nonexistent siren, the guards decide the shift is over. They get up and head for the door. I can't believe it as I watch them walk out just as if this were any ordinary day.

The machines idle down and the men begin to get up from their benches. "No one's leaving this shop," orders the conductor. "No one goes out on the dock and no one goes out the door. From now on we don't exist. The captain's gone and his trucks haven't come. The world is going to pass us by. You will all listen to me and do as I say. I'll kill anyone who makes a sound." With that, even the coughing becomes muted. "I'll kill anyone who goes near a door. Listen to me." A burst of shelling drowns him out for a moment. "Listen to me. The trucks have not come—we still have a chance. The guards will run away and tomorrow will be ours."

No one answers. The men walk around with nowhere to go. Finally, most of them just lie down on the floor. The coughing becomes louder again.

The sky turns black, except in the north where occasional shell bursts light up the horizon. Guided by lanterns, the trucks inch their way down the road toward the south. A truck stalls, and I hear the distant voices of the soldiers cursing. After a tank shoves the truck off the road, the retreat continues.

Perhaps the red cap is right. Maybe all trace of us has been wiped clean from the face of the earth. I look out at the dark outlines of the huts and wonder if the boy will still be waiting for me in the morning or will run off if I don't come for him tonight. I'm so goddamn tired and tense that I can't think straight anymore.

Sheleen's assistant leans over and asks, "What do you think?"

"I don't know. I don't know anything anymore."

"Well, I think he's done it. The red cap's done it. Tomorrow it will all be over." He goes into a fit of coughing, and I begin to wonder if he will last through the night.

In a hoarse voice he asks, "Where's the boy?"

"He's here. I've got to decide what to do with him. I've . . ."

A wild scream reverberates through the shop—it's the red cap swearing. "The bastards," he cries, "the goddamn bastards! They've turned on the lights!" I run to the window and see that he's right. The towers around the camp train their beams up and back along the fences. The lights poke through the windows of the shop, and the men dart for the safety of the shadows. I slump back into my chair, knowing that the towers and their guns are still alive.

Looking out again, I see that the entire camp is lit up— even the towers in the distance shine their beams amidst the ashes of the burned-out huts.

Interspersed between the coughing are the sounds of crying. I hear Verbin's voice asking, "Can I turn on the lights now? It's so dark in here. Why can't I go home?"

"Shut up," answers the red cap, "or I'll put your fat head under a cutter."

I try to sit still, but I can't anymore. The goddamn cold tension runs through me like electric shocks. I get up and start crawling toward the door, passing some of the men lying in the aisles. Even before I reach the door, I know he's there. The glow of the red cap's cigarette alternately brightens and dims as he puffs in and out.

Reaching into my pocket, I take out the knife and clutch it in my hand. Slowly I get up and go for the door.

Startling me, he says, "You won't need the knife."

"Move away from the door. I'm leaving, with or without your blessing."

He waits for the light to pass—then opens the door and says, "I have one last cigarette; I'll share it with you."

"I'm leaving, and you're not going to talk me out of it."

"You fool! I'm not going to talk you out of it. This may be our last day on earth. I don't know. Now, I want you to go, but first let's have one last cigarette together."

He walks out into the night and motions for me to follow him. I hang back, but he grabs me, and together we make a dash for the latrine. The knife never leaves my hand.

We sit together in the darkness while he fumbles through his pockets for a match. From the light of the match I can see that his hand is still oozing blood from all the cuts. He takes a puff and hands the butt to me. We say nothing as each of us exhausts every bit of life from the cigarette.

"You know," he says, "the only one who will come out of all this will be the commandant. We'll probably all be killed. The guards will die on the last day of the war. Verbin will get killed trying to keep his shop from being burned to the ground. The commandant is another story. That bastard has faded away with all his goddamn books. The war won't even touch him. He'll live a long and prosperous life. Our bones will have turned to dust, and that son of a bitch will still be living. Then, on his deathbed at the age of ninety-five, he'll be surrounded by his adoring children, grandchildren, and great-grandchildren. All of the bastards will look alike—each of them will have a strong chin. Each of them will have a book under their arm as they pay their last respects to their dearly beloved patriarch. Only we, the long-since dead, will know what a goddamn bastard he really was."

We crouch down as the light shines through the latrine window. "I can't understand these idiots," he says. "The goddamn lights will draw the artillery down on them, but still they keep them on."

"All right," I say, "enough of this. What the hell do you want from me? I want you to know that if you're thinking of killing me, I've got a knife in my hand and I'll get to you first. Nothing will stop me!"

He laughs out loud. "You goddamn fool, you're starting to sound like me. Can't you understand that if I had wanted you dead, you would be dead? I've always wanted you alive. I didn't always know why, but now I do."

"Why would you want me alive?"

"We were once so much alike."

I wonder why the hell he's telling me this. "Goddammit, I know we are alike. But never forget, I killed just one man. Who knows how many you put away? Who knows . . ."

"No, no. It's not that. It's before all this. In the old days. I was once a decent man. I was a teacher, can you believe that? I was a teacher. I was a good one. I was . . ."

"Why is this so important? I must get to the boy."

"Just give me a minute more." He fumbles in his pockets, looking for a cigarette. All he finds is a match. "I have to talk to you. I had a wife and son once. When all this began, we went into hiding. A friend let us stay in his cellar. This friend had one great failing—he was a saint. Within a few days the cellar was filled with six more refugees from the outside. I was the one who asked these people to hide with us. I had a son—he was a beautiful child—only four months old. His name was Michael. He cried constantly. I tried everything to quiet him down. One day the house was surrounded and searched. My Michael wouldn't stop crying. We heard the soldiers upstairs. The others in the cellar started looking at my baby. The crying continued—then they started looking at me. I could see the terror in their eyes. I had to do it, There was a chest of drawers. I put him in a drawer. I had to. I left the drawer open a crack. He went to sleep and the crying stopped. The

286

search finally ended and I quickly opened the drawer, but I saw that my Michael would never cry again. The screams of my wife replaced those of my son. The soldiers heard her crying and came back. They killed my friend, the saint, right there on the spot. We were all taken away. I am all that's left." He is silent for a moment. "From the moment my son stopped crying, I knew I was dead. I had also smothered out my own life. I was made for a place like this. After what I did, it was very easy to adapt. But you were different. You remained human throughout all this. Even with killing that Karl, you remained human. I was once like you. Do you understand now? To let you die would have been like killing what I once was. I committed suicide once—I couldn't do it again. Do you understand?"

All I can do is nod that I understand.

"You must know," he says, "that I did what I had to, to stay alive. I had to live so that I could have another Michael. I want another son to take the place of the one who wouldn't cry anymore. When I have my new Michael, perhaps I will become again what I once was."

After what I have heard, all I can do is wonder where I would be now if this man had not adapted so well. I clutch at his arm. "Why don't you try the wire with me? Maybe we'll all make it."

He thinks for a moment and says, "Maybe you will and maybe you won't. Perhaps it will be me who walks out tomorrow. Who knows, I might find your body lying by the fence. I can't leave here. Every man ties himself to something and can't break away. For me it has always been the shop. The shop would survive and so would I. You have tied yourself to that child. The chains we make for ourselves let us run in only one direction. I don't know what tomorrow holds for either of us. Who knows, probably neither of us will see another day. I must get back to my shop, and you must try the wire with your boy."

I take his hand. "If I could still pray, I would pray that

you would have another Michael." He does not respond. I start to open my mouth, but nothing comes out.

"Good-bye," he says. When the light passes, we run off in our different directions.

As I dive under the first hut, I see the outline of the red cap as he enters the shop. I keep going and then rest for a moment under the second hut. Light pours out of the windows of the guard hut at the base of the tower. No one has given the order to the idiots in the towers to shut off the damn lights. Who knows, maybe the order to shut off the lights would have included the order to shut off the lives of those in the shop.

A sudden artillery barrage brightens the sky. With each thunderclap from the guns, the tower lights momentarily stop their wanderings around the camp. When quiet returns, the beacons continue looking into the empty huts and along the glistening barbed wires.

Finally, I make a dash to my own hut and crawl under. I know that Avron is asleep just above me. I make a vow to myself that if we get out, I will come back when this is all over and bury the man. After the light passes, I make a run along the back side of the next two huts and then plunge myself under the boy's hut. Crawling through the darkness, I hear his snoring interspersed with coughs. The light sweeps by and dimly outlines his sleeping body. I reach out and try gently to awaken him. Touching him, I feel the little boat that he holds in his hand. It was always difficult for me to awaken a sleeping child. Carefully I shake his arm while humming his song.

He sits bolt upright, just missing striking his head on the floorboards. Rubbing his eyes, he stares around in the darkness. I hug him and whisper, "Wake up, my little one, I've come to take you away."

"You will come with me this time?" he asks. "You will take me to the children?"

"Yes, this time I will take you all the way to the park to

be with the children. But we must go carefully or there will be shooting." I take the boat out of his hand, saying, "I'll give it back to you if you promise to do everything I tell you." Pointing toward the fence that runs behind the hut, I whisper, "When the light passes, I'll run for the fence and spread the bottom wires apart. When I yell for you, you'll come running as fast as you've ever run in your life. You'll keep running after you squeeze through the wires and never stop until you've reached the trees up on the hill. I'll be right behind you. Do you understand me? I'll be right behind you."

I wait, but he says nothing. "Now, listen to me. If the light gets me when I'm at the fence and there's shooting, you're to stay right here. Do you understand? You're not to run to me. You're to hide under this hut. In a day or two there'll be new soldiers here. They'll have different-colored uniforms. They will be good to you. Do you understand? Now, keep listening to me. I know you'll get to the trees. When you do, you'll stay there even if the guns get me; you'll still hide there. Stay hidden in the bushes and wait for the new soldiers. Never come back to this place. Do you understand me?"

He says nothing. "Do you know what I'm telling you? Damnit, say yes or no!"

He begins to sob, and I realize that I've probably been screaming at him. I hug him again. He reaches out, and I feel a piece of bread being placed in my hand. Who knows, he probably thinks I'm mad at him. I break the peace offering in two and return half the bread to him. The sobbing stops.

"Why can't we go together?" he asks. "If I go first, then maybe you won't come. You will come with me, won't you?"

"You have my word that I will go with you. Do you know what it means when I give my word?" He doesn't answer. I dig into my pocket for the stone the artist gave me.

"Here's a stone for you. It's a very special stone to me. It means a great deal to me. I'm giving it to you to keep forever. It means that I will come with you, but I must know that you are out of here first. Do you understand me now?"

"Yes," he replies, and then, pointing to the fence, he says, "This is not a good place. There's a better place over there."

He tugs on my coat and motions toward the huge south tower at the edge of the compound to the east. I realize he knows this place much better than I do. Perhaps he's right. I think for a minute. "Now, listen to me. Go through the gate by the tree like you always do. Then hide under the first hut. I'll come for you in a few minutes."

"Why can't we go together?"

"We will, but first you must go through the gate like you always do. Play the violin, and the guard will open the gate for you. Then I'll meet you later. You know I will; you have my special stone."

I give him a shove, and then, after a moment's hesitation, he scampers out from under the hut. For about a minute I lose him in darkness until finally I see him outlined under the light of the east gate. As always, the violin opens the gate. The soldier watches the boy drift off into the darkness, and then he enters the guard hut and closes the door. All is quiet.

After timing the lights, I crawl out and race for the old tree. The light sweeps through its withered upper branches as I hug the ground. The fence is just a stone's throw away. With the knife in my hand, I crawl through the mud toward the fence. My hands grip the stones that make up the death line and I crawl over. A chill runs through my body as I think of Karl. With my hat covering my hand, I grasp the lowest wire. It is taut.

The door of the guard hut suddenly opens and I bury myself into the mud. The glow of the soldier's spent cigarette arcs through the air. I'm close enough to hear the hiss of the cigarette as it drowns in a puddle of water. When the door closes, I smash my knife against the wire, but it does not break. The strand finally snaps under the weight of my shoe. Quickly I rip off my bulky outer coat and submerge it into the nearest pool. Squeezing under the wire, I feel the barbs rip into my back, but surprisingly there is no pain. Being a skeleton has only one advantage in this world: You can crawl through fences that bar ordinary men.

As I race for the first hut, I realize that the boy is running by my side. He tugs at my arm as he leads me past one deserted hut after another. The south tower looms closer and closer. Its searchlight does not move but points down, illuminating the huge gate that leads to the outside world.

As we near the tower, I shove the boy under the hut closest to the gate. I crawl beneath and catch my breath. From under the hut I look up at the tower and see no sign of life.

"He's asleep," says the boy.

Taking his hand, I say, "Now, listen to me. You go first. Can you get through the fence? I don't care if he is asleep. You must be quiet. Take off your new coat and leave it here. You can squeeze through more easily. Look over there in the corner where it's darker. There's a place in the fence where the bottom wire is just hanging loose. You can crawl through right there. Don't stop even if there's shooting. Just keep running up the hill until you reach the trees. Do you understand me?"

"Yes, yes. I told you I would." He takes my hand. "The guard will fall asleep," he whispers. "He always does."

I reach over to unbutton his coat, but he lunges away from me and darts out from under the hut.

When he is in the open, he gets up and starts walking toward the fence. He's walking so goddamn slowly it will take him a year to get to the corner.

"Run toward the corner," I half whisper. "Damn it, run

already." He doesn't listen to me. I know he can hear me. He still keeps walking. Instead of heading for the corner, he goes straight to the main gate. I can't believe what he's doing.

"Come back here!" I yell. "Get back here!"

He stands at the foot of the tower, looking up at the machine gun which points directly down at him. As I start to crawl out to bring him back, I see him bend down. He's going to crawl under the gate.

I scoot back under the hut, and when I look around again, the boy hasn't moved a damn inch. He just stands there with the same goddamn blank look on his face, staring up at the tower. He bends down again and reaches for the end of the chain that locks the gate. An ungodly clanging noise breaks through the night as the boy pounds the chain against the iron bars of the gate.

The clanging finally stops, and I hear a roar of laughter coming from the top of the tower. I see a soldier poke his head out the window and, with a laugh-filled voice, yell, "Ah, it is you. I've been waiting all night for you."

As the guard climbs down the ladder, the violin begins to play bits and pieces of what sound like peasant folk tunes. I look at the soldier's face and I am amazed to see that he looks delighted. Between songs, the boy points his bow impatiently at the lock. The soldier stands beside him as if he is enthralled by the songs.

Finally, I see that irritated look on the boy's face. He has had enough of this. The violin stops and is hidden under his coat. The child points again to the lock.

Still laughing, the soldier reaches into his pocket and hands the boy an apple, which is grabbed up and immediately dropped in the sack.

The laughter booms out again. "You're in a hurry tonight, aren't you?" says the guard. "Well, maybe that's good. You mustn't come here anymore. There will be fighting all over this place soon. I won't be here anymore after tonight. You tell your parents that you can't come here anymore. What kind of parents do you have to let you keep coming to this filthy place? A little boy like you shouldn't have to feed his family. You should be out playing. Why do your parents let you stay out so late? My parents were poor, too—we had nothing—but my father never made me beg for food. Even in the worst of times, I never had to beg. My father would never let me be around prisoners like they have here. What will become of you with parents like you have? Why doesn't your father work? With the war, everyone can find a job."

The boy keeps pointing to the lock. He edges away when the soldier pats him on the head. Producing the key from his pocket, the guard starts laughing and says, "Good-bye, little boy—you are a strange one. You never talk, do you?"

The lock is opened and the gate swings out enough for the boy to squeeze through. As he walks away, the soldier calls after him, "I'll miss you. Be a good boy now, and don't let your parents make you beg for food anymore. Run home—the night air is bad for you. That's why you're always coughing." The soldier's laughter dies down as he peers out after the child, who is lost to the darkness.

After locking the gate, the soldier climbs slowly up the ladder. With each step I hear him humming the songs of the violin. When he gets to the top, there is silence.

I remain under the hut, mired in the mud. I want to scream out to Avron, but I know that his ears hear nothing. Over and over, I say to myself, "Avron, Avron, we gave our lives to free a child who all along could come and go as he pleased. I was not his Moses and neither were you; he never needed one. He has parents—he must, or how else could he have lived? Who knows how many men starved to death so that our bits of bread could feed him and his family? Avron, we played a monumental joke on ourselves. Day after day we saw him let out at the east gate. Never once did it occur to us that for a song they would let him in or out of any gate."

I lie there for a while, feeling utterly drained. My coughing wracks my body. Then I think of all that has passed; I want to spend what time I have left away from here.

Gathering my strength, I pull myself up out of the mud and rise up from under the hut. The far ends of the fence are in the shadows. As I race alongside the huts, I look up at the tower. All is quiet; the light still does not move. I stop and lean against the hut opposite the portion of the fence I have chosen. I stand there as if my feet are frozen to the ground. It is just as if I were a child again, standing at the deep end of the swimming pool. I couldn't jump then, and I can't jump now. When I was a child, someone finally had to push me in—now there's no one. I remain there, thinking what an ordinary son of a bitch I am. One day I can even make myself Moses, and now I find that I am a nothing. The lice start sucking out what life remains in me, and I begin running. The only way to quiet the bastards is to run. I head for the fence, and with each step I take, I feel the mud grasping at my feet to keep me tied to this place. Falling to the ground by the fence, I spread the wires with my hands. They are loose—no doubt they've been used before by men who had the guts of a poet. The price of admission to the outside is cheap—I squeeze through with only a few barbs cutting into my skin. Their stings are little more than the bites of my lice.

I jump to my feet and start running for the trees. The ground is firm and nothing holds me back. Roaring through my mind are the words, "It was so easy. It was so goddamn easy. Even long ago it would have been so easy to get out."

The tall outlines of the trees come closer and closer. The stench of the camp slowly leaves my nostrils, and I breathe in deeply to smell the freshness of the air. I stop running and walk the rest of the way through the darkness. The night is calm; the harshness of the winter is over.

I reach the bushes and my hands grasp the foliage. Sitting down, I look back at the camp. The lights still make their grand tours of the entire hellhole. For a few seconds the shop is lit up, then the scrap pile. The twisted metal reflects the light like a thousand little mirrors.

I sit there waiting for some feeling of elation to flow through what is left of me, but nothing happens. I came here with nothing, and I leave with nothing. Everything seems to fall into place. The boy had to have had parents to survive all this time. I laugh to myself and think that the more desperate the man, the greater are his fantasies. I look down again at the camp and spit into the wind at this playground of the weak.

The light hits the shop again. I can picture the red cap spending the night in terror, watching the road and hoping that none of the trucks turn off and head for the shop. I worry that all his hopes will probably burst like bubbles in the morning. I keep thinking of Avron. If he were still alive, he would have dropped dead the minute he learned how the boy walked in and out of here whenever he wanted to. The poet was right. The whole goddamn world is mad, and man himself is the author of this insanity.

A wave of planes flies overhead and drowns out my thoughts. As their droning sound fades off in the distance, I hear the violin. First comes the lullaby, but then there is the song he played the night Karl died. The notes fly upward into the darkness, and as they rise, I get up and start climbing the hill through the trees. The song climbs ever higher into the heavens. I find myself running and stumbling toward the song that darts back and forth through the night.

The violin ceases, and I know that he must be listening for me. I hum the same song back to him, and the violin begins soaring upward again into the black sky. I know that he is somewhere just ahead of me. As I rush forward, all I can think of is the first time I ever saw him—that forlorn, grotesque little creature standing there in the darkness of that freezing night.

I hum his song again and race for him. The bushes part and there he stands. I pick him up and sway him back and forth in my arms. He rests his head once again on my shoulder. I whisper to him, "Hello, my little one. All this is over. There will be no more of this for you. You will live like a child from now on."

His voice sounds as if he has been crying. "When will you take me to the children?"

"This will all be over by tomorrow. We must hide here until then." I put him down and ask, "Where do you live? Where do you sleep? Where are your parents?"

He doesn't answer. I ask him again, "Where are your mother and father?"

"It was a long time ago," he says. "The soldiers killed my mother—I saw them do it. It wasn't these soldiers, but some other soldiers. They shot many people. I don't know where my father is. I could never find him. I think he's dead, too. The soldiers who shot my mother didn't tell the soldiers here about it. The soldiers here think I have a mother and father. I don't know why they think that. I don't like the killing. I want to go away from here. Take me to the park. Tell me the story again."

"Where do you live?"

"I live here. It is very cold when it snows."

Looking around in the darkness, I see nothing. I clear a space on the ground and sit down. Holding him in my arms, I begin, "Someday you will leave here. There is a park just beyond the hill. There are children . . ." I look down at him. He is asleep.

28

I am jarred out of my sleep by another artillery barrage. Even before my eyes open fully, I know he is gone. My hands hold nothing. In the darkness, I search the ground. My fingers feel only the damp earth. I call out to him, but all I hear is my own voice and the pounding of the guns.

My first thought is of the goddamn camp. Could he have gone back there again just as he had each day for years? I jump up and stare off in the distance at the south tower. The camp is quiet. Now and then I can make out the dimmed headlights of the trucks still fleeing down the road. I keep telling myself again and again that he couldn't have returned to the camp. I hum his song, but the violin does not answer.

I hug the earth as the ground shakes under the impact of the guns. Looking up, I see that the northern part of the camp has been hit and is in flames. I scream out again for the boy, but the explosions drown out my cries. He is gone, and the world around me is being ground into nothing.

The sun rises slowly in the east. For a moment its rays are as brilliant as the fires that burn in the camp. The morning light comes quickly and the flames die down. The dawn filters through the trees. I look around and see that I am in a little clearing. Between the sounds of the exploding shells, I hear his unmistakable snoring. My magnificent child who has kept the human spirit alive within his little body has but one flaw: He has never learned to breathe through his plugged-up nose.

I walk toward the sound of the snoring and stand beside what I know is his home. Peeking out between some broken, twisted boards is the very top of his head. The rest of his body is hidden from view, sandwiched between what were once the walls of a lean-to that has collapsed on its side. The fallen roof with its rotting shingles covers the sleeping child like an umbrella. Surrounding him are layers of coats and blankets. It is as if he has protected himself from the elements by a cocoon made up of our cast-off clothing.

I kneel down and watch him. His head jerks back and forth whenever he coughs. I keep wondering to myself how he could have survived all the cold and endless nights of bitter loneliness. Each night he must have dreamed that the very next day he would find his father. At least we had the miserable company of each other; he had only the numbing cold. My mind goes back to the time the guard smashed him. He must have lain here in pain day after day, night after night.

Bending down, I touch one of the decayed boards that juts out over his head. The wood crumbles in my hand. Off to the side, in front of the broken-down hovel, is a little pile of the smooth, round stones. He has them stacked up neatly in anticipation of our daily visits on the step.

He begins coughing again, and slowly his head appears from between the coats. After rubbing his eyes, he looks up at me and smiles. I reach down, grasp him by the shoulders, and deliver him from his cocoon.

I pick him up and hold him in my arms. "My son, this is the first day of your life." After hearing what I say, he gives me a sleepy-eyed, puzzled look. I laugh to myself and say, "Someday you will understand, but perhaps today is not the day."

When I put him down, he walks back to his fallen shack and reaches between two other boards. Covered in a blanket are his violin and bow. They are unwrapped and then hidden under his coat.

"When do we go to the children?" he asks.

"We must stay here until all the soldiers are gone. When the good soldiers come, we will go away from here forever." Pointing down the road, I explain, "When the new soldiers come, I will take you up that road, and together we will see what's on the other side of the hill."

He sits down and takes the apple out of his sack. The apple is smashed to pieces on a broad, flat rock. He indicates that I should join him. Together, we eat; both of us use the sides of our mouths.

Daylight has come. I look down and for the first time get some idea of how vast the camp once was. The city, which stood for hundreds of years, has become a mass of rubbish in less than a day. Now both the camp and the city look as if they were created by the same architect.

The road is still filled with retreating soldiers. As they flee, they completely ignore the camp. In my mind, I can see the smile on the red cap's face, and I in turn also smile.

My smile fades as, moments later, I see the death of the shop coming into view. I know that from where I sit, I am able to see the trucks even before the red cap. Hope must still be ingrained in his face. Four empty trucks buck the tide of the retreat and make their way up the road. By now he must have seen them, for they are turning off the road and driving into the camp.

The guns from the tower fire a few bursts. One of the men running from the shop falls to the ground dead. He does not wear a red cap. There has been so much killing, but even on this final day there has to be more.

The boy begins to cry. He has been watching. Taking him in my arms, I hold his head down on my shoulder so that his eyes will see nothing more of what is about to be. I can do nothing to close off his ears. The guns blast away again and his crying continues.

The trucks line up in front of the shop. Soon they are filled to overflowing. Some men run. The guns stop them. They litter the ground. Who they are I cannot tell—nor do I want to know. I do not hear their screams; the boy's crying fills my ears.

The guards converge on the overloaded trucks. Perhaps

they do not wish to retreat on foot. Only one truck is emptied of its prisoners. They are quickly lined up in an orderly row to make it easy for the bastards to shoot them down. For the first time since I came here, the sky is absolutely clear and the sun shines warmly on this spring day. But the black winter is not over yet.

After the guards climb out of their towers, the trucks speed out of the camp to join the cortege heading south. The road is now like a raging flood—men and their machines overflow its banks. Finally, the trucks filled with my brethren pass from view.

Gradually the road empties, except for a few tired and wounded stragglers. They weave back and forth, trying to get away. Some drop and never get up. I see how the mighty have fallen; they have taken so many down into the depths with them.

The camp is silent. The only sign of life remaining is the pile of scrap that gleams in the sun.

I put the boy down. "It's all over," I tell him. "The killing is all over. You won't have to see any more. The soldiers are running away. Now try to forget all the things you've seen and heard. From now on it's a new day."

He looks around and we watch the road slowly empty of the soldiers. Then the civilians come; first there are only a few, then there are hundreds. They move even more slowly than the soldiers. Some head north; others wander toward the south; some do not move at all.

The people on the road suddenly stop and then rush off into the ditches. From over the top of the hill a tank column comes into view. The refugees crouch motionless as the tanks and armored cars filled with soldiers race by.

Pointing down at the road, I tell the boy, "Those, my son, those are the new soldiers."

"They look like our soldiers," he says. "How do you know these soldiers will be better to us than our soldiers?"

"They will be. They have to be."

The vehicles disappear as they rush after their fleeing enemy. In a way, I am surprised. In my mind, I always imagined the final battle would be of epic proportions. On this day, however, the only deaths I have actually seen have been ours.

He tugs at my coat. "When will you take me to the children?"

"Now, my son. Now we will leave this place and go on the road." I stare at my child and feast my eyes on his excited, happy face.

As we start to walk away, he takes one last fleeting look at the broken-down hut that had been his home. Then he reaches for my hand and together we walk down the hill.

When I head toward the camp, he pulls on my arm and leads me in the direction of the road. We walk through the forest. The sun filters through the branches and casts its rays around us. The rest of the world seems a million miles away. For the first time in a long, long time, the cold tension has left me. I am warm now.

We come out of the trees and head for the road. I lift the boy across the ditch and we begin walking on the pavement. The beginning of the camp is just ahead of us. I see the first of the bodies lying in the ditch. One is a soldier. The other is from the shop. He has to be, for no one else on earth could look like that.

As I peruse the dead, the boy's eyes study the living. The human remnants of the war pass by us as if in a trance. They walk aimlessly, clutching their scant possessions. No one seems to pay attention to us—they are oblivious to everything but their own suffering. If only they had always been oblivious to us. Now only in the depths of their downfall are we considered fit enough to be left alone to walk among them.

The boy's eyes never leave the sleeping face of a baby

cradled in its mother's arms. At first the woman looks horrified when she sees the boy, but then slowly a smile comes over her face.

A few soldiers mix in with the long line of refugees. The once sharp creases of their uniforms have long since been rubbed smooth. They are now as bent over and exhausted as all the lesser mortals of this earth.

Of all the hundreds of cast-offs of the war, only the boy seems excited by the sights and sounds around him. We begin to pass the camp, but he turns his eyes away from this monstrosity to gaze at the people. His step is lively as his eyes flash up and back along the road.

There is a sudden hush and the people race for the ditches. I grab the boy by the arm. Of all the people, he and I alone stand by the roadside.

Several armored cars race by and then come the tanks, followed by truckloads of soldiers. Intently the boy studies the faces of the men as they stream by. "They look just like our soldiers," he says.

The boy is still filled with doubts even after I tell him, "They're good soldiers. You don't see them killing anyone, do you?"

We begin walking again after the convoy passes. It is difficult to keep up with the child. I almost lose him in the crowd.

I stop when we come upon the turn-off to the camp. Looking down the narrow road, I see a line of trucks in front of the main gate. The victors have come to liberate the camp. Their trucks have come to this place empty, and they will leave empty.

The boy sees me staring at the camp. His face grows sullen. "You said we wouldn't go back there," he cries. "You said you would take me to the park with the children. I don't want to go back—it is a bad place. You said it was a bad place."

Gently, I take his hand and try to calm him. "I just want

to go back for a little bit—just a little while—then I'll take you away. I promise I'll take you away. Please come with me. You don't have to walk into the camp. Wait for me by the gate. I want to see if any of the men are still alive. Maybe some are just hurt. I want to make sure the dead are buried."

Even with my reassurances, he still looks worried. I start toward the camp and, with quick glances behind me, make sure that he is following. Several of their soldiers are leaning up against a truck. They look bored. All soldiers look bored. Their talking stops when they see us. I don't need to look into a mirror. Their strange, shocked faces give me some idea of what I look like. One of them cannot take his eyes off the boy. Finally this soldier screams out in pain as the smoldering cigarette hanging from his mouth burns his lip.

They are as young as our soldiers, but they have none of the military bearing that I expected to see in conquerors. The more I look at them milling around the place, the more I wonder how the hell they won the war.

We are barely on the camp road when suddenly I hear that voice. A wave of nausea passes through me. It is that same goddamn high-pitched squeal. "Ask him, ask him. He will tell you that I can run a shop." Verbin comes rushing toward me as if I were the messiah. Right behind him comes an officer and three soldiers. "Tell them, please tell them that I run the best shop in all the camp. They won't listen to me. You see, they don't seem to know what I can do for them. Tell them. Please tell them . . . "

He tries to take me by the arm, but I smash his hand away. Then, screaming at him, I ask, "Is anyone alive? What happened to the red cap?"

The fat ass doesn't even hear me. He goes on with his pleading. "Tell them, I beg of you. They're going to burn down the shop. They say the place is filled with disease. You can still work here. I need you. You can help me run the shop. Tell them how I ran the shop. They need the spines for the war. Tell them how I always went over the quota. Tell them . . . "

The officer gives Verbin a look and the fat mouth stops. Then his face reddens as he bursts into tears.

This officer seems nothing like a soldier. He wears glasses and looks as if he spent his life in a library. "I'm supposed to be an interpreter," he says, pointing to Verbin, "but I don't think I understand this man. If I do, then he's an idiot. I can't believe him. Why would anyone admit to having any part in this place? Can you believe that he wants to work for us! The man is utterly stupid. We know what went on in these camps, and here he is bragging about it. My men want to take him behind a building and shoot him."

I look at all the soldiers with their guns. Some of them point at Verbin. A bayonet is held just millimeters away from his huge gut, and its tip moves back and forth in time with Verbin's breathing. The young soldier is laughing. Verbin is trembling. He trembles just as I did when the guns were aimed at me and I thought I was being traded away with the barbarians.

I look at the officer. "Please, let him go home. If you shoot him, you might as well kill off half the people on this earth. He caused none of this. Let him go home and be what he was before the war."

The officer shrugs and then waves the rifles away.

Turning to Verbin, I ask, "What the hell happened to the red cap?"

"I don't know. You see, the trucks came. There was shooting. I've looked all over. I can't find him. I did find his red hat. You know, the one he always wore. I put it on the scrap pile. We have enough scrap. You could wear his red hat. The shop could run again. We . . . "

I grab him by the arm and shove him toward his smoldering city. "Go home and don't come back here again."

"Why couldn't you tell them how I ran the shop? You know I never hit a man." Slowly he walks away, crying. I watch as he stumbles down the road, all the while gesturing with his hands as his mouth pleads with the wind. Finally, he is lost in the mass of people.

I see the officer staring at me. Looking at his unlined face, I have the feeling that he and I were once about the same age but that I have lived so much longer.

"You were lucky," he says. "You're the only one we've found alive in the entire place." From a list, he starts rattling off name after name of men, asking me if I know any of them. He looks anxiously into my face for any sign of recognition. Finally, seeing none, he stops. His voice is filled with emotion. "Did you know that some of the greatest musicians died in these camps? For some reason they sent violinists to this camp. No one seems to know why."

I tell him that I never knew why they did anything. My mind drifts back to the poet and his answer to this very same question: "Our captors are cultured men, so why shouldn't they love musicians?"

"I saw a child with you," he says. "I didn't know they did this to children. Why did they do this to children? How could they . . . "

He goes on talking. I look for the boy. I become terrified that something has happened to him. He is nowhere to be found among the trucks and the soldiers in front of the camp. Then I see him. He is eyeing a soldier. The soldier has just bitten into a piece of bread. As if entranced, he stares down at the boy and hands him a piece of bread, which is taken and placed in the sack.

Quickly the violin comes out. The bow reaches for the strings. The song begins. The hardened faces of the soldiers turn toward the child. The music soars ever upward, even higher than the now empty guard towers. It reaches out toward the road. The people on the road stop. Their eyes search out the source of the song that is the only thing of beauty amidst the surrounding desolation. No one moves. There is silence, except for the song of the violin. The officer stands beside me; his eyes close.

The brilliant sun of this first spring day glistens off the surface of the violin and reflects like a beacon up toward the heavens. As always, I am soon lost in the music. My mind becomes flooded with sunlit images. I see myself walking with the boy through the greenery of the Promised Land. I see the face of the woman that the artist used to etch on the frozen window. Now her eyes are warm and real. In the park, I see the poet surrounded by his wife and children. He reaches out to welcome us. Then the pictures are slowly lost from my view. The music begins to descend. The song returns back into the violin. The bow comes to rest.

The boy stares up again at the soldier. The man has that faraway look. Slowly he hands the remaining bread to the boy, for the symphony he has just been given.

The soldiers no longer look bored. Perhaps their thoughts are of home. Slowly the refugees take up their journey. There is a strange silence. The officer seems dumbfounded.

We walk toward the child who stands with his gaze fixed on the nearby road. The piece of bread that he just won remains uneaten in his hand. When he sees me, the chunk of bread is held out. I take it and put it in his sack.

The officer seems ecstatic as he kneels in front of the boy. The face of the child, however, becomes forlorn.

The man doesn't seem to know what to say. Then, finally, he speaks. "Finding a child like you alive in this place is a miracle. Where did you learn to play the violin like this?" Then he is silent for a moment. Excitedly, he says, "You learned from all the violinists who were sent here, didn't you? My God, all that is left of them is you, isn't it? I want you to come with me." Pointing toward me, he says, "This man can come with you, too. You must be fed.

You are sick. You can't be lost to the world. Finding you alive has been the only good thing to come out of this war. You must . . . "

The child turns from the man and stares again at the road.

All the life empties from the officer's face. Looking at me, he asks, "Doesn't he understand me? Help me make him understand. What is his name?"

"Michael." The name just blurts out of my mouth.

Turning to the boy, he says, "Michael is such a nice name, my son." Then, pleading once again, "Michael, I want you to study the violin with some of the great teachers. I know some of them. They will be kind to you. They will be nice to you. Do you understand me, Michael? So many violinists died here. I don't want you to be lost."

The child's eyes slowly drift again toward the road.

"Michael, come with me. You will have all the bread you want. You will be clean and have fine clothes. You will be warm."

Throwing his hands up in the air, the officer asks me, "Why won't he understand? This child is a gift of God. Never before have I heard what he just played. Talk to him. Make him understand. You have to. There's the hand of God in the way he plays."

It is as if Avron were still alive and giving me commands emanating directly from heaven.

I start toward the boy. Before I can even reach him, his face suddenly comes alive. Pointing toward the road, he screams out, "The children! The children!" Filled with elation, he looks up at me. "You always told me I would see the children! You always told me I would be with them!"

I turn and see a truck filled with children slowly making its way up the road toward the hill. It is obvious that they are more of those left homeless by the war.

He begins running toward the road faster than I have ever seen him move before. Then he stops and turns to me.

Our eyes meet. I try, but I can say nothing. I cannot find words. Perhaps the look on my face diminishes his joy— I don't know. Maybe there is a tinge of uncertainty in the tone of his voice. "Those are the children you always told me about. You told me to go and be with them."

Perhaps he waits for me to say something. Perhaps not, but then he is gone—running toward the crowded road and the truck.

Seconds later, he is swallowed up and lost in all the humanity.

The officer's voice thunders into my head. "He's getting away. How could you let him go?"

Without taking my eyes off the road, slowly I begin to speak. I don't even know if he hears me. "It was meant to be. He was lent to me for just a little while. The human spirit was locked up within him for safekeeping. Now it is being returned to the earth. The child was meant to run abroad in the land."

In an instant I spot the boy again. He dashes alongside the truck, and a man lifts him up and places him on the back. The truck continues plodding its way through the masses of people.

Now my eyes never leave him. Through my tears I see my Michael jumping up and down; with his upraised arms he reaches for the sky. He looks back, and, with a broad smile on his face, he waves to me. I make my hand rise to wave good-bye to him. The other children begin jumping, and I see their dead expressions come to life. Then, as the truck reaches the crest of the hill, the boy becomes strangely quiet. I see him push against the back of the truck and hold his arms out to me. I can see his face in the distance. It is filled with the total desolation that I, too, feel.

The officer takes my arm. "You saw the look on him just then. My God, man, that was the face of a frightened child. He's only a child. He needs someone. He is a gift of God, and why shouldn't you have all that God is willing to give?"

He reaches into his pack and hurriedly stuffs some small packages of food into my pockets. Then, pushing me toward the road, he says, "Go, my friend. There's nothing more for you here. On the other side of that hill there's a parklike place—really a beautiful place. We passed it on the way here. They've set up a processing center. I'm sure that's where the children are being taken."

We say good-bye. I begin to walk on the road. The sudden roar of explosions makes me turn and look back at the camp. I see the soldiers racing through the compounds, pouring gasoline on the huts. The whole place is ablaze. My eyes are lost in the fires. The hut that was mine crumbles before the flames. The black smoke billows up into the cloudless sky and momentarily blocks out the sun.

Within minutes, everything is a smoldering ruin. Only the red cap's gleaming pile of scrap remains as it was. His cap lies on the very top. I turn away from the dead camp and find myself running up the road to reach the life that lies just beyond the hill.